FINANCIAL MANAGEMENT WITH LOTUS 1-2-3®

FINANCIAL MANAGEMENT WITH LOTUS 1-2-3®

Paul D. Cretien
Baylor University

Susan E. Ball
University of Florida

Eugene F. Brigham
University of Florida

The Dryden Press
Chicago   New York   Philadelphia   San Francisco
Montreal   Toronto   London   Sydney
Tokyo   Mexico City   Rio de Janeiro   Madrid

Acquisitions Editor: Ann Heath
Developmental Editor: Judy Sarwark
Project Editor: Cate Rzasa
Design Director: Alan Wendt
Production Supervisor: Diane Tenzi
Director of Editing, Design, and Production: Jane Perkins

Copy Editor: Nancy Maybloom

Library of Congress Cataloging-in-Publication Data

Cretien, Paul D.
  Financial management with Lotus 1-2-3.

  Includes index.
  1. Lotus 1-2-3 (Computer program)   2. Business—
  Data processing.   I. Ball, Susan E.   II. Brigham,
  Eugene F., 1930–   .   III. Title.
  HF5548.4.L67C74   1986   658.1'5'02855369   86-6267

  ISBN 0-03-003104-4

Printed in the United States of America
789-018-987654321

Address orders:
383 Madison Avenue
New York, NY 10017

Address editorial correspondence:
One Salt Creek Lane
Hinsdale, IL 60521

CBS COLLEGE PUBLISHING
The Dryden Press
Holt, Rinehart and Winston
Saunders College Publishing

Lotus is a registered trademark of Lotus Development Corporation.

*To Sarah, Steve, and Sue
for their love and dedication*

The Dryden Press Series in Finance

Brigham
Financial Management: Theory and Practice,
Fourth Edition

Brigham
Fundamentals of Financial Management,
Fourth Edition

Brigham and Gapenski
Intermediate Financial Management,
Second Edition

Campsey and Brigham
Introduction to Financial Management

Clayton and Spivey
The Time Value of Money

Cretien, Ball, and Brigham
Financial Management with Lotus 1-2-3®

Crum and Brigham
Cases in Managerial Finance, Sixth Edition

Fama and Miller
The Theory of Finance

Gitman and Joehnk
Personal Financial Planning, Fourth Edition

Harrington
Case Studies in Financial Decision Making

Johnson
Issues and Readings in Managerial Finance,
Third Edition

Johnson and Johnson
Commercial Bank Management

Kidwell and Peterson
Financial Institutions, Markets, and Money,
Third Edition

Lorie and Brealey
**Modern Developments in Investment
Management,** Second Edition

Mayo
Finance: An Introduction, Second Edition

Mayo
Investments: An Introduction

Myers
**Modern Developments in Financial
Management**

Pettijohn
PROFIT

Reilly
**Investment Analysis and Portfolio
Management,** Second Edition

Reilly
Investments, Second Edition

Tallman and Neal
Financial Analysis and Planning Package

Weston and Brigham
Essentials of Managerial Finance,
Eighth Edition

Weston and Copeland
Managerial Finance, Eighth Edition

Preface

Prior to the 1970s, most financial calculations were done using mechanical calculators or slide rules. Electronic calculators took over in the 1970s, with mainframe computers used for large-scale computations. In the 1980s, personal computers have assumed a dominant role, and today, a business that does not use computers is about as competitive as a finance student who takes an exam without a calculator. Indeed, a single financial analyst with a $1,500 personal computer can get more work done than four analysts working with calculators.

Because of these economic realities, it is crucial that students with a serious interest in financial management develop a minimal level of "computer literacy." A few years ago, one needed to be a programmer to use a computer. Today, however, highly efficient software packages enable one to perform useful work with just a few hours of training--and to become quite proficient in a few weeks.

For financial analysts, the best of the new software products is Lotus 1-2-3®, a spreadsheet program that can do all types of analyses that would otherwise require a skilled programmer and a mainframe computer. Furthermore, since 1-2-3 is by far the most widely used spreadsheet program, its users can exchange programs readily. Finally, most published applications programs (such as solutions to cases) are written in 1-2-3. The goals of this book are (1) to teach you how to use 1-2-3 and (2) to provide you with a set of template models that you can use to analyze a wide variety of financial problems.

Intended Market

The book was written with several types of people in mind:

1. <u>Finance Students</u>. People who are currently taking a course in financial management, or who have had such a course and now want to learn how to perform financial analyses more efficiently, can benefit from the book. We assume some knowledge of the essentials of accounting and finance, but we have structured the book so that one can learn 1-2-3 concurrently with a course in financial management.

2. <u>Business Students in General</u>. Although our focus is on finance, the book will also be of interest to general business students, both because Lotus 1-2-3 models can be used in all areas of business operations and because all business students need (and are required to gain) some knowledge of finance. At the University of Florida, our MBA students cover the first part of the book in their first semester (while they are taking accounting) and then work through the later chapters in conjunction with the introductory finance course during the following term.

3. <u>Corporate Analysts and Financial Executives</u>. Many corporate analysts and financial executives can perform their jobs more efficiently using 1-2-3. Both the basics of 1-2-3 and our specific models dealing with such topics as cash budgeting, capital budgeting, capital structure, and lease analysis are useful to such readers.

4. <u>Small Business Owners/Managers</u>. Lotus 1-2-3 is especially useful for the owners/managers of small businesses who do not have ready access to mainframe computers.

Relationship with the 1-2-3 Manual

Lotus Development Corporation provides a 344-page Reference Manual with 1-2-3, Release 2. Although this Manual is very thorough, it would take most people quite a while to learn enough to do anything useful. The Manual is designed as a <u>reference</u> book, not as a textbook, so trying to learn 1-2-3 from it is a bit like trying to learn English from a dictionary. Also, the 1-2-3 system was developed for a wide variety of purposes, and going through the Manual requires one to learn some functions that a financial analyst would use only rarely. Our book speeds up the learning process by concentrating on the elements necessary for financial analyses and by explaining the most critical things first.

Note, though, that we do not cover all the refinements in the 1-2-3 system. As you develop your skills and begin to tackle more complex jobs, you will need to refer to the Lotus Manual. Throughout this book, we provide frequent references to the Manual, both to help you learn how to use it and also to refer you to its more detailed explanations for some of the things you may want to do on your own.

Although it would be useful to have a 1-2-3 Manual handy when you work through our book, it is not essential. We anticipate that many of our readers will be students working in a university computer lab, and in such an environment it is often difficult to get a copy of the Manual. Therefore, we have made the book relatively self-contained, at least for the types of problems the typical finance student will encounter.

Release 2 of Lotus 1-2-3

Three versions of 1-2-3 have been published--Release 1 (the original), Release 1A, and Release 2 (which came out in October 1985). Our book was ready to go into production when Release 2 came out, so our first thought was to delay it for a few weeks while we added an appendix to cover differences between Releases 1A and 2. It soon became apparent, however, that the two versions were too different to make our plan feasible. It also became apparent that Release 2 is a vastly superior product--it is better in many small, subtle ways, and it also has some major new features, including the ability to handle multiple regression analysis and to do programming tasks that formerly had to be done outside of Lotus in Basic or some other programming language. This convinced us that we should rewrite the book to include a full discussion of the Release 2 features.

Anyone who purchased 1-2-3 after October 1985 automatically received Release 2. However, an embedded base of Releases 1 and 1A in the millions still exists. If you are still using an earlier release, we urge you to take advantage of Lotus' upgrade plan, which permits you to purchase Release 2 at a 70 percent discount. It is well worth the additional money, no matter how satisfied you are with Release 1A. (Release 2 will accept all models written in 1 or 1A. However, the reverse is not true--a Release 2 model will not run on a Release 1 or 1A system. Release 2 does have a translation feature that permits a version 2 model to be converted to one that will run on 1 or 1A, but translation difficulties occur if the Release 2 model uses features not contained in the earlier versions.)

Organization of the Book

To help you become operational in 1-2-3 as rapidly as possible, we have structured the book so that the most critical material is covered first. Thus, when you finish Chapter 2, you will be able to do useful work, and subsequent chapters build upon that base and expand your abilities. By the time you complete Chapter 7, you will have covered virtually all of the commands that 95 percent of 1-2-3's users ever employ, and you will be able to solve most types of financial problems. Of course, your initial programs may not be the most efficient and your output may not be as pretty as you would like, but you will be able to do some useful work that would have been virtually impossible without the computer. In addition, you will have a firm base upon which to build better models and to modify models developed by others for your own needs.

In Part II we provide a series of models for various types of financial analysis. These models will be useful for financial analysts in their businesses and by business students in case courses.

Model Diskette

As we were writing the book, we saved all the models we developed--both the illustrative ones used in the early chapters and the larger ones given in the later chapters. These models are provided on the diskette that accompanies the text. In Part I we often show several versions of the same model to illustrate the effects of different commands on the model or to show the model at various stages of its development; in these instances, all of the versions of the model were saved as separate files.

Our diskette is write-protected, meaning that it can be copied onto another diskette, but not changed. You should copy our diskette and then use the copy as your work diskette. Put the original away and use it only to recopy lost models back onto your work diskette.

Our diskette was developed using Release 2. Consequently, if your system has Release 1, the diskette will not be helpful. That is not a serious problem with Chapters 1 through 7, as most readers would want to make their own models, but it would be a major problem for Chapters 8 through 15, where we present template models. Therefore, we developed a Release 1 diskette, using Release 2's "Translate" feature. This diskette can be obtained <u>by adopting instructors only</u> by writing or calling:

Ms. Betsy Webster
The Dryden Press
1 Salt Creek Lane
Hinsdale, IL 60521
1-800-323-7437
(312)920-2450 (in Illinois)

These instructors can then make the Release 1 diskette available to their students to copy. Logistical problems prevent us from offering the Release 1 diskette to individual users.

Acknowledgments

Many people aided us in this endeavor, including Dana Aberwald, Katherine Brigham, Laura Brigham, Barbara Bruening, Lou Gapenski, Richard Kish, and Kay Mangan, who provided considerable assistance in testing the models and clarifying confusing sections of the text. Fred Yeager used a draft of the manuscript in his classes at St. Louis University and helped us develop the exercises which follow each chapter. Both his and his students' comments helped us immensely. In addition, Rudyard Goode, Roger Miller, Thomas Hindelang, and Robert Porter reviewed the manuscript and models and offered many helpful and insightful suggestions. Melissa Davis, Jean Gilbert, and Terry Sicherman typed and helped proof the various manuscripts, and The Dryden Press staff, especially Ann Heath, Nancy Maybloom, Cate Rzasa, Judy Sarwark, Diane Tenzi, and Alan Wendt, helped greatly in all stages of the developmental and production process. Finally, we owe a great debt to the Lotus Development Corporation for creating 1-2-3, and to Caroline Camougis of Lotus, who assisted our project by providing diagrams for inclusion in the book.

Conclusion

No other event has had as much impact on financial management as the almost simultaneous introduction of the IBM PC (and its compatibles) and Lotus 1-2-3. As we stated earlier, one analyst using a Lotus-equipped PC can do more work than a roomful of people with calculators. This has serious negative implications for the number of people who can get jobs as financial analysts, but it has equally positive implications for their productivity. These are indeed the best of times and the worst of times--the best for those who can use the new technology, but the worst for those who cannot. If this book helps put you in the first category, we will have achieved our goal.

Paul D. Cretien, Waco, Texas
Susan E. Ball, Gainesville, Florida
Eugene F. Brigham, Gainesville, Florida

June 1986

Contents

Part I **Introduction to Lotus 1-2-3** **1**

Chapter 1 **The Basics of Lotus 1-2-3** **3**

Computer Components 4 Getting Started 9
Using the 1-2-3 Worksheet 22 Summary 42

Chapter 2 **A Sample Worksheet** **47**

Constructing a Spreadsheet Model 48
Saving and Retrieving Files 58 Printing 61
Sensitivity and Other Topics 68 Summary 79
Summary of Commands 80

Chapter 3 **DCF Analysis** **87**

Relative and Absolute Values: An Example 88
Using the Spreadsheet for DCF Analysis 96
More on DCF Analysis and Financial Functions 104
Summary 117 Summary of Commands 118

Chapter 4 **Graphing Techniques** **123**

Creating Graphs 123 Saving the Graph for Later Viewing 132
Naming the Graph and Using Named Graphs 132
Printing Graphs 135 Another Illustrative Graph 139
Summary 143 Summary of Commands 144

Chapter 5 **Statistical Functions, IF Statements, and Data Base Operations** **150**

Statistical Functions 150 Lookup Function 155
IF Statements 159 Move Command 164
Data Commands 166 File Commands 179 Summary 184
Summary of Commands 186

Chapter 6   **Regression Analysis and Other Topics**   **191**

Regression Analysis 191   Word Processing with 1-2-3 197
Small (Compressed) Print Option 201
Solving Complex Equations 204
Alternative Recalculation Procedures 209
Protection Features 211   Summary 214
Summary of Commands 215

Chapter 7   **Macros**   **221**

Basic Macros 222   Rules for Creating and Using Macros 223
An Illustrative Macro 227   Summary 231

Part II   **Financial Analysis Models**   **235**

Chapter 8   **Analysis of Financial Statements**   **237**

Chapter 9   **Financial Forecasting**   **265**

Chapter 10   **A Cash Budgeting Spreadsheet**   **285**

Chapter 11   **Lease versus Borrow Analysis**   **297**

Chapter 12   **Capital Structure**   **317**

Chapter 13   **Capital Budgeting**   **339**

Chapter 14   **Bond Refunding**   **357**

Chapter 15   **Option Pricing and Bond Duration**   **371**

Appendix A   **DOS Commands for Lotus 1-2-3**   **385**

Appendix B   **Command Tree Diagrams**   **409**

Index   **418**

Part I
Introduction to Lotus 1-2-3

Part I consists of seven chapters; they cover the basics of
1-2-3, and when you finish them, you will know how to develop and use 1-2-3 models. Part II provides some "template" models which perform selected types of analyses
commonly used in financial management.

   We begin, in Chapter 1, with essential information
about the Lotus system, including how to get started.
Chapter 2 then covers the basics of creating, saving, and
printing spreadsheets; Chapter 3 deals with 1-2-3's built-in
financial functions; and Chapter 4 discusses graphing.
Building on this base, Chapter 5 moves on to some of 1-2-3's
most advanced commands and functions, while Chapter 6 covers
regression analysis and other features. Finally, Chapter 7
covers macros, which are special 1-2-3 programs which enable
one to do within the 1-2-3 system much of what can be done
with "regular" computer languages such as Basic or Fortran.

   If you are a new user of 1-2-3, you should read and
study the first five chapters carefully, making sure you can
follow all the steps and create spreadsheets as instructed.
Be sure you understand this material thoroughly before going
on to Chapters 6 and 7, and to the financial models in Part
II. If you are an experienced 1-2-3 user, on the other
hand, you can skim the table of contents of Part I and then
read only those sections containing material that is new to
you or required to refresh your memory before going on to
the model chapters. In any event, all readers should be
comfortable with the material in Part I before using the
models in Part II, because a knowledge of the basics of 1-2-3
is necessary to understand the logic of the models.

   The chapters in Part I are designed to teach 1-2-3 in a
systematic, step-by-step manner. While this approach facilitates learning, it is not the optimal layout for reference
purposes. To improve the book's usefulness as a reference
manual, we have ended each chapter with a summary of the
commands discussed in it. In addition, all 1-2-3 commands
are listed in Appendix B, and we provide a detailed index at
the end of the book.

Chapter 1
The Basics of Lotus 1-2-3

Table of Contents

Computer Components   4
Getting Started   9
      The Lotus 1-2-3 Package   10
      Using 1-2-3 on the IBM PC   11
      Using 1-2-3 on the IBM XT   18
Using the 1-2-3 Worksheet   22
      1-2-3 Commands   24
      Moving Around the Worksheet   32
      Entering Data   34
      Correcting Errors   39
Summary   42

- -

Computers can perform arithmetic calculations, make compar-
isons among values, sort data files, and construct both
graphs and tables designed to help the user interpret
results. However, the user must <u>program</u> the computer to
tell it how to process the input data and lay out the
output. Lotus 1-2-3 is a <u>partially completed</u> program--it
has already done most of the work, so the analyst needs
merely to complete the 1-2-3 program rather than to write a
program from scratch.
      We should note at the outset that two versions of 1-2-3
exist--Release 1 and Release 2. Anyone who purchased a new
copy of 1-2-3 after October 1985 automatically received
Release 2, and anyone who owns Release 1 can upgrade to
Release 2 at a cost of $150. Since Release 2 is
vastly superior to Release 1, we have written this book
focusing primarily on the new version. However, the book
can be used with Release 1, and we have noted places where a
Release 2 command is not available on Release 1.

Some readers will be familiar with computers, but not with 1-2-3, while others will be unfamiliar with either. This first chapter is, we hope, simple enough for a total novice. That means that people with some computer background will find much of the chapter boring. Bear with us through the first part of the chapter, though, and we guarantee that you will soon get over your boredom. It is hard not to get excited when you see what 1-2-3 can do!

Computer Components

The computer components necessary for using Lotus 1-2-3 include (1) an input device (keyboard) for entering data and instructions, (2) a central processing unit (CPU) for processing data and instructions, (3) a main (or core) memory unit for temporarily storing data and instructions, (4) an auxiliary storage unit (a floppy or a hard disk drive, along with a diskette) for saving data, instructions, and results, and (5) two output devices (a video display monitor and a printer). Exhibit 1-1 is a picture of a complete IBM PC microcomputer system. Here the video display monitor is sitting on top of the system unit, which contains the central processing unit, the main memory, and the disk drives. The printer is on the right.

Data and instructions are entered through the keyboard, which is shown in detail in Exhibit 1-2. Notice that the center section of the computer keyboard is similar to the keyboard of a typewriter, but it does include several additional keys. The keys with numbers on the right side of the keyboard are called the numeric pad; for 1-2-3 users, the keys in this section are primarily used to move around the worksheet. On the left side are ten function keys, numbered F1 through F10; they perform specialized functions in Lotus 1-2-3. Exhibit 1-3 provides a list of what the function keys do in 1-2-3; we will discuss each of them in detail in later sections.

===

Exhibit 1-1
IBM PC Microcomputer System

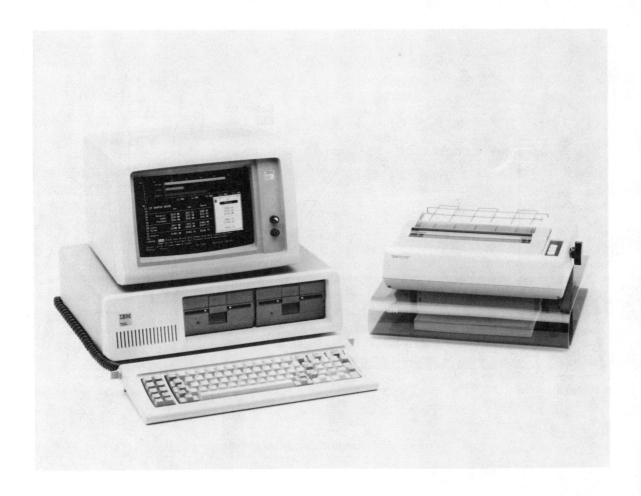

Source: Courtesy of International Business Machines Corporation.
===

===

Exhibit 1-2
An IBM PC Computer Keyboard

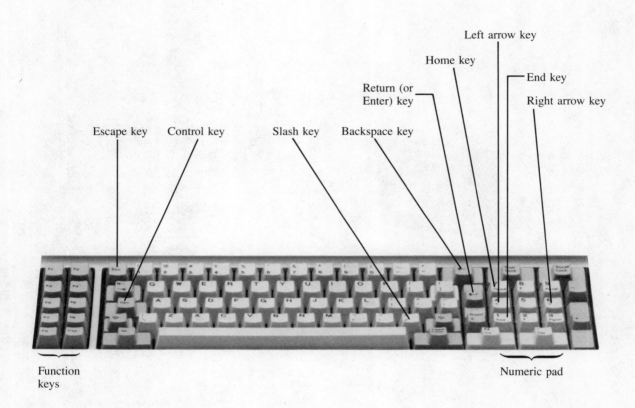

The center portion of the keyboard resembles
a typewriter keyboard.

Source: Courtesy of International Business Machines Corporation.
===

Exhibit 1-3
Function Keys

F1 = Help	F2 = Edit
F3 = Name	F4 = Abs
F5 = GoTo	F6 = Window
F7 = Query	F8 = Table
F9 = Calc	F10 = Graph

Note: With other software packages these keys may serve other functions.

==

    As data and instructions are typed on the keyboard,
they go into the computer's main memory. The central processing unit takes information from the main memory, works
with it as specified in the programmed instructions, and
then sends the results back to main memory. The results are
displayed as output on the video display monitor, and they
can also be printed to obtain a "hard copy" and/or stored on
either a floppy diskette or a hard disk for later use.
    There are two types of main memory: ROM and RAM. ROM
stands for read only memory; it refers to a portion of the
main memory which has permanent instructions that were in-
stalled by the manufacturer to control the computer. RAM
stands for random access memory; it is the section of main
memory used to store data and instructions entered from the
keyboard or read from a floppy or hard disk. The amount of
RAM in a PC determines the amount of data and special
instructions that can be processed within the computer. RAM
is measured in units called bytes. A byte can store one
character--a letter, a number, or a symbol. Memory size is
usually expressed in terms of kilobytes, where 1 kilobyte =
1,024 bytes. Thus, a 64K PC has 64 kilobytes of memory and
can store 64 X 1,024 = 65,536 characters, while a PC that
has been upgraded to 512K can store 524,288 characters.
Lotus 1-2-3, Release 2, requires at least 256K of RAM
memory.
    Information is stored only temporarily in RAM: when
the computer is turned off, RAM is erased, and all information stored there is lost. Therefore, data that will be
used again must be stored permanently on an auxiliary
storage device. For the IBM PC, this storage device is a

floppy diskette, while the XT and AT use both floppy diskettes and a hard or fixed storage disk with up to 20,000K of
memory. The floppy disk is inserted into one of the PC's
two disk drives, or into the XT's single floppy disk drive,
when information is to be recorded on it. The terms "disk"
and "diskette" are generally used interchangeably. When PCs
came on the scene, their 5 1/4" plastic disks were called
"floppy diskettes" because they are both flexible and small
compared to the larger metallic disks used on mainframe
computers

   The PC's disk drives can be seen in Exhibit 1-1--they
are the black rectangular boxes with the horizontal openings
located on the front of the system unit. On the XT, a
single floppy disk opening is on the left,.and the hard disk
is built in on the right. The left drive on the PC is
referred to as Drive A; the one on the right is Drive B. In
general, the diskette from which a program such as Lotus
1-2-3 will be read is placed in Drive A, and the diskette on
which data and results will be stored is placed in Drive B.
Thus, Drive A is called the source drive and Drive B the
target drive.

   The XT generally has only one physical drive for flop-
pies; that drive can be designated either A or B by a keyboard command, and the fixed disk is designated Drive C.
With the XT, Drive A is the source drive from which programs
are read, and the drive is then redesignated as Drive B and
used as the target drive to store data and results on floppy
diskettes. In other words, you could put a program diskette
into the floppy disk drive, read the program information
into main memory, remove the diskette, type a command which
transforms the drive to Drive B, then insert a blank
diskette, and finally have the computer transfer the information to the blank diskette. Drive C (the hard disk) is an
alternative target or storage disk.

   Note: It is important to store diskettes properly when
   they are not being used. A speck of dust blown in by
   the air conditioner, a fingerprint, or a magnetized
   paper clip that brushes against a diskette can ruin it
   and cause you to lose anything stored on it. Also,
   your Lotus 1-2-3 System disk should normally be stored
   with a write-protect tab over the notch; otherwise, you
   might write on it or format it (as one of us once did),
   either of which will effectively destroy the contents
   of the disk.

Getting Started

If you have your own computer, you will have to install
certain information on your Lotus 1-2-3 diskettes to tell
1-2-3 what kind of printer and other equipment you are
using. The Lotus manual provides good, easy-to-follow
installation directions. If you are using the computer in a
lab, the operators should have already taken care of that
task. Throughout this book we assume that the computer has
been set up according to the instructions in the Lotus
Manual. However, since people configure their computers for
their own convenience--for example, a user may install 1-2-3
in a subdirectory of his or her computer rather than in the
main directory--some of the procedures we describe may not
work on the computer you are using. This is particularly
true of the procedure for accessing 1-2-3. If a procedure
does not work, you should ask your lab operator for the
correct procedure for your machine.

Some people will be reading this chapter while sitting
in front of a computer. That's best, but it's not abso-
lutely necessary. Our students at Florida have to sign up
to use PCs in the computer lab, and they are limited to one
hour's use at a time. Therefore, they read the chapter in
advance to become somewhat familiar with the process and
thus get the most out of their hour when they do get on the
computer. We have tried to write this book so that it will
make sense whether or not you are sitting in front of a
computer.

If you are in front of a computer as you read the
following sections, we recommend that you type in only what
we tell you to type. These commands are set off with one
extra space before and after. At times, you'll wonder what
would happen if you did something else. Resist the
temptation to find out, because you may get into a box that
you cannot get out of; that is, you may not be able to get
back on the "right track." However, if you do yield to
temptation (or make a mistake), you can always turn off the
machine and start over. That will cause you to lose every-
thing--but in this first lesson, you will not have anything
in memory worth saving anyway.

The Lotus 1-2-3 Package

The Lotus 1-2-3 package consists of a detailed reference manual, two smaller manuals, and these six diskettes:

1. The 1-2-3 System disk, which is used to create and print worksheets and to create graphs.

2. The 1-2-3 System Backup disk, which is simply a copy of the System disk and which serves as a replacement if the System disk is lost or damaged.

3. The PrintGraph disk, which is used to print graphs.

4. The 1-2-3 Utility disk, which is used to prepare both the System disk and the PrintGraph disk for use on your personal computer.

5. A View of 1-2-3, which provides an overview of what 1-2-3 does.

6. The Install Library disk, which is used to install 1-2-3.

Before using the 1-2-3 System, Backup, and the PrintGraph disks for the first time, you must prepare them for use by (1) transferring your computer's disk operating system (DOS) to the Lotus disks and then (2) using the 1-2-3 Utility disk to add short programs called "drivers" to the information on the other disks. If you have your own computer and a copy of Lotus 1-2-3, you will need to read the section of the Lotus manual that gives instructions for preparing the disks for your computer; we do not explain the disk preparation process in this book. When you prepare the Lotus disks for use on an XT, you actually copy the diskettes onto the hard disk and then add the drivers to these copies. If the System disk is copied into the directory of Drive C using the Copyon program, the 1-2-3 program will automatically be loaded without using the System disk; otherwise, the system disk must be in Drive A for the 1-2-3 program to be accessed. This procedure is described in the pamphlet How to Start 1-2-3 Directly from a Hard Disk, which accompanies Release 2.

Note that you should prepare the disks only once; preparing already prepared disks can ruin them. If you are uncertain as to whether your disks have been prepared, try to call up 1-2-3 according to the procedures in one of the following two sections for either the PC or the XT. If you can access 1-2-3, your disks are prepared and ready to use; if not, read the relevant section of the 1-2-3 Manual.

If you are using 1-2-3 in a computer lab or on a borrowed PC, the disks should already be prepared and ready to go. In any event, when the disks have been prepared, you will be ready to use 1-2-3 to create worksheets.

If you know how to format disks and how to get the 1-2-3 spreadsheet on your screen, you may skip directly to Page 22, "Using the 1-2-3 Worksheet."

Using 1-2-3 on the IBM PC
(Skip to the XT section if you have an XT.)

As you sit in front of the IBM PC, you will see a keyboard, a video monitor, and a microcomputer system that contains two floppy diskette drives. Recall that the drive on the left is referred to as Drive A and the one on the right as Drive B. The PC stores information on magnetic floppy disks, which are inserted into the disk drives whenever information is to be stored or when previously stored information is to be retrieved. You will need one or more diskettes on which to store your 1-2-3 spreadsheets; since these disks are used to store information, they are called storage disks.

The operations of the PC are controlled by the disk operating system (DOS), which is a group of programs that controls the way the PC uses all other programs, including Lotus. DOS is a basic part of the PC operation--anyone purchasing a PC or XT must also purchase DOS as the number-one, most critical piece of software. DOS provides the set of instructions used for organizing and storing information on diskettes, calling this information into the main memory for processing, and transferring processed information back to diskettes for storage and later use. Thus, DOS allows you to call up 1-2-3, and it controls the way 1-2-3 stores worksheets and graphs on your diskettes. Appendix A at the end of this book explains how to use basic DOS commands to do things like format diskettes, copy diskettes, store files, and the like.

<u>Accessing 1-2-3 on a PC</u>. Lotus uses the term "access" to mean "read the information on the 1-2-3 System disk into main memory" (others might say "load the 1-2-3 System disk into main memory"). To begin accessing Lotus, insert the 1-2-3 System disk into Drive A (the "source drive") before turning on the power, holding it at the label end and inserting it label-side up. Place the formatted storage diskette, the one on which you will save worksheets and graphs, into Drive B (the "target drive"). Information goes from the diskette in the source drive to the main memory, where it is processed, and the results of these operations are then stored on the diskette in the target drive.

With the 1-2-3 System diskette in Drive A, turn on the computer. (If you have a color monitor, you will also have to turn that on.) After the machine warms up, it will "beep" and tell (or "prompt") you to type the date and time of day (see Exhibit 1-4, Lines 2 and 4). You now type in the date and then press the RETURN (or Enter) key, which on the IBM PC is designated by the symbol ↵ ; then, when you save your work, the date will be saved automatically. (Note: You could skip the date by simply pressing the RETURN key. We don't recommend this--you ought to get into the habit of dating your work. This simple step will often help you identify the most recent version of a file or model.) After you have typed in and entered the date, a beep will prompt you to enter the time. Type the time as 24-hour international time, press the RETURN key, and 1-2-3 will display standard time.

Note: The symbol ↵ cannot be typed out, so in this book we identify the Enter, or RETURN, key by the word RETURN. Incidentally, Release 1 of 1-2-3 called this key "the Enter key," while Release 2 calls it "the RETURN key." The DOS manual uses the term "Enter." We generally use the terms RETURN and RETURN key.

===

Exhibit 1-4
Time and Date Computer Screen

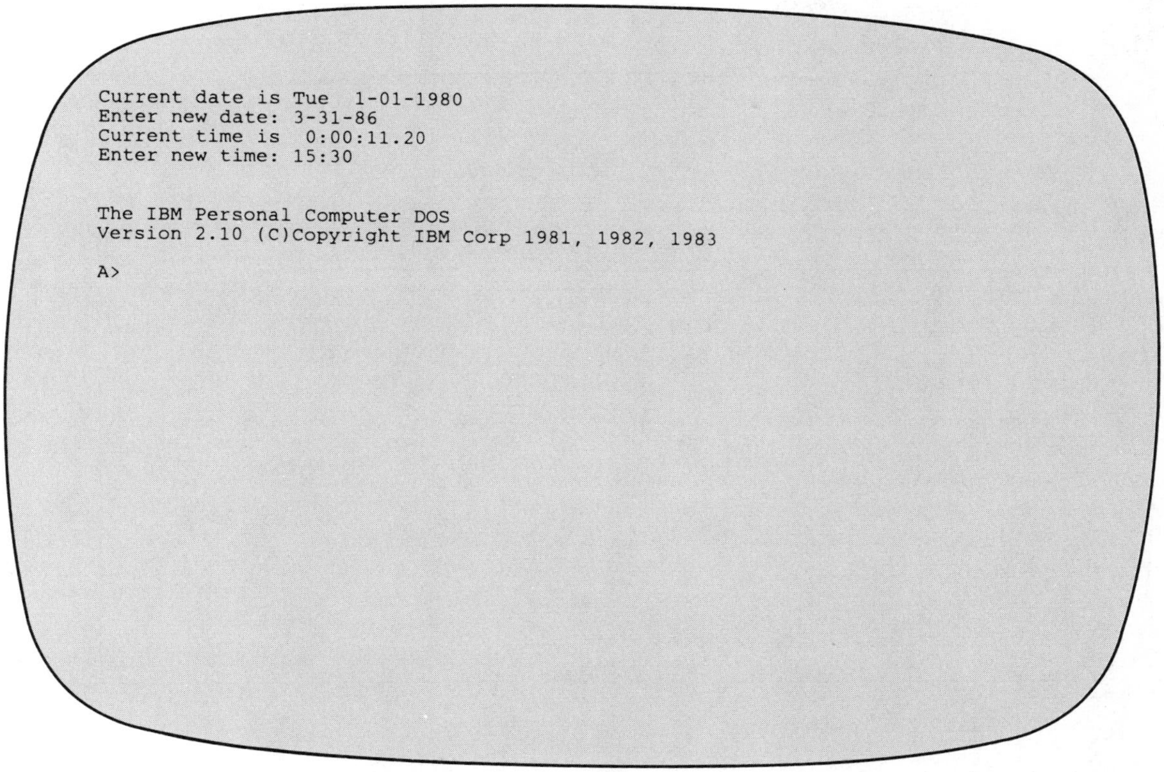

```
Current date is Tue  1-01-1980
Enter new date: 3-31-86
Current time is  0:00:11.20
Enter new time: 15:30


The IBM Personal Computer DOS
Version 2.10 (C)Copyright IBM Corp 1981, 1982, 1983

A>
```

===

After you have entered the date and time, the computer
will indicate that it is ready with the Lotus Access System,
which permits you to load one of the Lotus subprograms into
main memory. Exhibit 1-5 shows a picture of the monitor
screen, which at this point gives a menu, or listing, of the
six Release 2 Access System subprograms as given on the line
just below the double solid lines: 1-2-3, PrintGraph,
Translate, Install, View, and Exit.

===

Exhibit 1-5
1-2-3 Access System Menu

```
┌─────────────────────────────────────────────────────────────┐
│ ┌─────┐                                                       │
│ │1-2-3│ PrintGraph  Translate  Install  View  Exit            │
│ └─────┘                                                       │
│ Enter 1-2-3 -- Lotus Worksheet/Graphics/Database program      │
│                                                               │
│ ┌───────────────────────────────────────────────────────────┐│
│ │                 1-2-3 Access System                        ││
│ │             Lotus Development Corporation                  ││
│ │                   Copyright 1985                           ││
│ │                  All Rights Reserved                       ││
│ │                      Release 2                             ││
│ │                                                            ││
│ │ The Access System lets you choose 1-2-3, PrintGraph, the Translate utility, ││
│ │ the Install program, and A View of 1-2-3 from the menu at the top of this  ││
│ │ screen.  If you're using a diskette system, the Access System may prompt   ││
│ │ you to change disks.  Follow the instructions below to start a program.    ││
│ │                                                            ││
│ │ o  Use [RIGHT] or [LEFT] to move the menu pointer (the highlight bar at    ││
│ │    the top of the screen) to the program you want to use.  ││
│ │                                                            ││
│ │ o  Press [RETURN] to start the program.                    ││
│ │                                                            ││
│ │ You can also start a program by typing the first letter of the menu        ││
│ │ choice.  Press [HELP] for more information.                ││
│ └───────────────────────────────────────────────────────────┘│
└─────────────────────────────────────────────────────────────┘
```

===

The top part of Exhibit 1-6 provides a diagram of the Access System menu, and the five-point list below describes what the menu is and explains how to access a menu item. The pointer, or highlighter, initially covers the item "1-2-3." The line that appears below the menu listing on the screen describes what the highlighted menu item, in this case 1-2-3, does. The item 1-2-3 provides access to the Lotus spreadsheet, graphics, and database programs as indicated on the line just above the double solid lines. You will do 99 percent of your work with this menu item; that is, you will work with PrintGraph, Translate, Install, View, and Exit only about 1 percent of the time.

By pressing the right-arrow key on the right-hand side of the keyboard (this key is also labeled with the number 6), you can move the pointer successively over each of the six access subprograms as explained in Item 2 of Exhibit 1-6. As the highlighter is moved, the line on the screen beneath the menu changes to describe each item as it is highlighted; for example, with the highlighter on "1-2-3," pressing the right-arrow key will move the highlighter to "PrintGraph," and the second line will automatically change from the description of 1-2-3 to the description of Print-Graph. To make a selection of a menu item, move the pointer using the right- or left-arrow key until that item is highlighted, and then press the RETURN key.

Alternatively, you may select menu items by typing the first letter of the name. For example, to select Print-Graph, you could type p . As soon as you type the first letter of a program, 1-2-3 will access that program.

Normally you will want 1-2-3, so you will simply press the RETURN key. If you are at the setup shown in Exhibits 1-5 and 1-6, move the pointer so that it covers the 1-2-3 (if it is not already there), and press the RETURN key. A 1-2-3 symbol will appear to let you know that 1-2-3 has been accessed, and then a blank Lotus 1-2-3 spreadsheet will appear as shown in Exhibit 1-7. (Note that the current time and date appear at the bottom of the worksheet in Exhibit 1-7. We turned this feature off on other exhibits by typing /WGDOCNQ. The slash called up the main menu, and we then pressed W for Worksheet, G for Global, D for Default, O for Other, C for Clock, N for None, and Q for Quit. Soon, you will become familiar with these and other commands.) Before going on, it may be helpful to review what you have learned so far. To help you recall everything, Exhibit 1-8 provides a summary of the steps necessary for accessing 1-2-3 on a PC.

==

Exhibit 1-6
Access System Menu

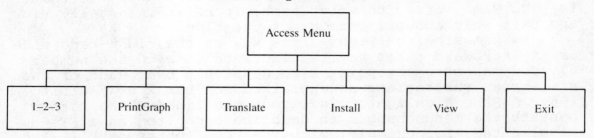

1. This Access Menu comes up when you first access the 1-2-3 system.

2. You choose one of the six items either (1) by using an arrow key to move the highlighter to that item and then pressing the RETURN key or (2) by typing the first letter of the item.

3. A description of each menu item follows:

   1-2-3: This selection calls up the Lotus spreadsheet/graphics/database program.

   PrintGraph: This selection calls up the Lotus graphics printing system.

   Translate: This subprogram allows files to be converted from Release 1 to Release 2 or from other programs to Lotus.

   Install: This subprogram is used to install 1-2-3, or to tell 1-2-3 if you have changed some of your equipment, such as your printer.

   View: This item gives you a quick view of some of 1-2-3's features; that is, it gives you an overview of what 1-2-3 will do.

   Exit: This sends you back to the PC's regular operating system.

4. As you press the right-arrow key to move the highlighter from 1-2-3 to PrintGraph to Translate and so on, the line below the Access submenu changes to display a description of the item being highlighted.

5. Spreadsheets are created using the 1-2-3 subprogram. Move the highlighter to 1-2-3, press the RETURN (or Enter) key, and follow the instructions on the screen to access the 1-2-3 subprogram. A blank worksheet will appear on the screen.

==

===

Exhibit 1-7
Blank 1-2-3 Worksheet

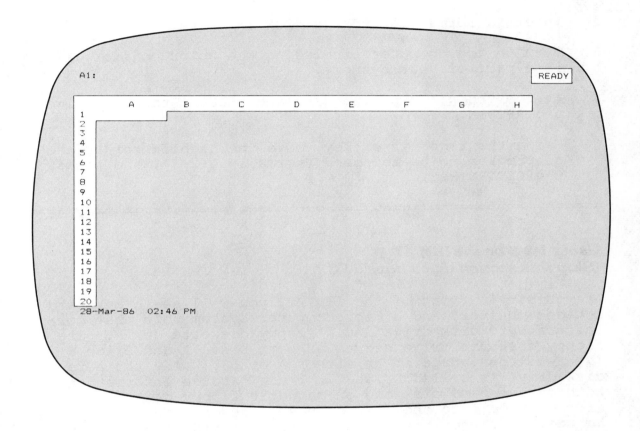

===

==

Exhibit 1-8
Summary of Steps for Accessing 1-2-3 on a PC

1. Insert the Lotus 1-2-3 System disk into Drive A.

2. Insert a formatted storage disk in Drive B.

3. Turn on the computer (including the color monitor, if it
    is a part of your system).

4. At the "beep," type the date and RETURN, then the time
    and RETURN.

5. Using the right arrow key, move the highlighter to the
    subprogram to be accessed (normally 1-2-3), and press
    the RETURN key.

==

Using 1-2-3 on the IBM XT
(Skip this section if you have a PC.)

As you sit in front of the IBM XT, you will see a keyboard,
a video monitor, and a microcomputer system unit that contains a hard disk drive and a floppy diskette drive. The
floppy diskette drive serves as both Drive A and Drive B
(you will designate it as either A or B), while the hard
disk drive is called Drive C. The XT stores information
both on the hard disk and on magnetic floppy disks, which
are inserted into the disk drives whenever information is to
be stored or when previously stored information is to be
retrieved. You will need one or more floppy diskettes on
which to store your 1-2-3 spreadsheets; since these disks
are used to store information, they are called storage
disks. In general, when the computer asks you to insert the
diskette for Drive A, it is prompting you to insert a diskette with programmed information, that is, one of the Lotus
disks, in the floppy diskette drive; if it asks for the
diskette for Drive B, insert one of your own storage
diskettes, including a blank but formatted diskette.

Note: If you are using 1-2-3 on an IBM AT with two
floppy disk drives, you place your 1-2-3 System disk in
Drive A and your storage diskette in Drive B. In this
respect, the process is similar to that used for the PC,
even though the AT also has a hard disk and therefore
more closely resembles the XT.

   The operations of the XT are controlled by the <u>disk
operating system (DOS)</u>, which is a group of programs that
controls the way the XT uses all other programs, including
Lotus. DOS is a basic part of the XT operation--anyone
purchasing a PC or XT must also purchase DOS as the number-
one, most critical piece of software. DOS provides the set
of instructions used for organizing and storing information
on diskettes, for calling this information into the main
memory for processing, and for transferring processed information back to diskettes for storage and later use. Thus,
DOS allows you to call up 1-2-3, and it controls the way
1-2-3 stores worksheets and graphs on your diskettes.
Appendix A explains how to use basic DOS commands to do
things like format diskettes, copy diskettes, store files,
and the like.
   On an XT, the DOS programs are stored in Drive C. The
Lotus diskettes are also normally copied onto the hard disk,
so that the Lotus program can be run without having to keep
the System diskette in Drive A. However, the original
System diskette must be in Drive A at the time the 1-2-3
subprogram is accessed.

<u>Accessing 1-2-3 on an XT</u>. Lotus uses the term "access" to
mean "read the information on the 1-2-3 System disk into
main memory" (others might say "load the 1-2-3 System disk
into main memory"). To begin accessing Lotus, make sure
that Drive A is empty before turning on the power; then,
when you turn on the computer, it will read the DOS programs
stored in Drive C. Turn on the computer. (If you have a
color monitor, you will have to turn it on too.) After the
machine warms up, it will "beep" and tell (or "prompt") you
to type the date and time of day (see Exhibit 1-4 in the
section on the PC). You now type in the date and then press
the RETURN (or Enter) key, which on the IBM XT is designated by the symbol ←⏐ ; then, when you save your work, the
date will be saved automatically. (Note: You could skip
the date by simply pressing the RETURN key. We do not

19

recommend this--you ought to get into the habit of dating your work. This simple step will often help you identify the most recent version of a file or model.) After you have entered the date, a beep will prompt you to enter the time. Type the time as 24-hour international time, press the RETURN key, and 1-2-3 will display standard time.

Note: The symbol ⟵ cannot be typed out, so in this book we identify the Enter, or RETURN, key by the word RETURN. Incidentally, Release 1 of 1-2-3 called this key "the Enter key," while Release 2 calls it "the RETURN key." The DOS manual uses the term "Enter." We generally use the terms RETURN and RETURN key.

After you have entered the date and time, the computer will indicate that it is ready with the Lotus Access System, which permits you to load one of the Lotus subprograms into main memory. Exhibit 1-5 (in the preceding section on the PC) shows a picture of the monitor screen, which at this point gives a <u>menu</u>, or listing, of the six Lotus Access System subprograms as given on the line just below the double solid lines: 1-2-3, PrintGraph, Translate, Install, View, and Exit.

Note that if you copied the Lotus disks into a subdirectory when you prepared them, you will need to change the directory of Drive C to the subdirectory by typing <u>cd\name of subdirectory</u>; for example, at the C prompt (C>), type cd\1232 if you stored 1-2-3 in a subdirectory called 1232 (for Lotus 1-2-3, Release 2). Then, at the next C prompt, enter the word Lotus, and the Lotus Access System will appear on the screen. If you are working on an XT in a computer lab, you will need to find out the exact access procedure for your computer from a lab assistant.

The top part of Exhibit 1-6 (in the preceding section on the PC) provides a diagram of the Access System menu, and the five-point list below the diagram describes what the menu is and explains how to access a menu item. The pointer, or highlighter, initially covers the item "1-2-3." The line that appears below the menu listing on the screen describes what the highlighted menu item, in this case 1-2-3, does. The item 1-2-3 provides access to the Lotus spreadsheet, graphics, and database programs as indicated on the line just above the double solid lines. You will do 99 percent of your work with this menu item; that is, you will work with PrintGraph, Translate, Install, View, and Exit only about 1 percent of the time.

By pressing the right-arrow key on the right-hand side of the keyboard (this key is also labeled with the number 6), you can move the pointer successively over each of the six access subprograms as explained in Item 2 of Exhibit 1-6. As the highlighter is moved, the line on the screen beneath the menu changes to describe each item as it is highlighted; for example, with the highlighter on "1-2-3," pressing the right-arrow key will move the highlighter to "PrintGraph", and the second line will automatically change from the description of 1-2-3 to that of PrintGraph. To make a selection of a menu item, move the pointer using the right or left-arrow key until that item is highlighted, and then press the RETURN key.

Alternatively, you may select menu items by typing the first letter of the name. For example, to select Print-Graph, you could type "p". As soon as you type the first letter of a program, 1-2-3 will access that program.

Normally you will want 1-2-3, so you will simply press the RETURN key. You must insert the System disk into Drive A in order to access the 1-2-3 subprogram. If you are at the setup shown in Exhibits 1-5 and 1-6, move the pointer so that it covers the 1-2-3 (if it is not already there), and press the RETURN key. A 1-2-3 symbol will appear to let you know that 1-2-3 has been accessed, and then a blank Lotus 1-2-3 spreadsheet will appear as shown in Exhibit 1-7 in the section on using a PC. If your file directory is set on Drive B, you will be told to insert the diskette in that drive. Remove the System diskette, and insert your storage diskette in the floppy diskette drive. Removing the System disk will not affect the display on your screen, because the 1-2-3 program has been read into memory. After you have inserted your storage diskette, press any key, and the spreadsheet will be put in READY mode. (Note that the current time and date appear at the bottom of the worksheet in Figure 1-7. We turned this feature off on other exhibits by typing /WGDOCNQ. The slash called up the main menu, and we then pressed W for Worksheet, G for Global, D for Default, O for Other, C for Clock, N for None, and Q for Quit. Soon, you will become familiar with these and other commands.) Before going on, it may be helpful to review what you have learned so far. To help you recall every-thing, Exhibit 1-9 provides a summary of commands for accessing 1-2-3 on an XT.

===

Exhibit 1-9
Steps for Accessing 1-2-3 on an XT

1. With Drive A empty, turn on the computer (including the color monitor, if one is a part of your system).

2. At the "beep," type the date and RETURN, then the time and RETURN.

3. Insert the Lotus 1-2-3 System disk into Drive A.

4. Using the right-arrow key move the highlighter to the subprogram to be accessed, and press the RETURN key. Normally, you will want 1-2-3, so you can just press RETURN.

5. Remove the System diskette; insert your storage diskette; then press any key.

===

Using the 1-2-3 Worksheet

The spreadsheet, or worksheet, shown on the screen and pictured in Exhibit 1-7 in an earlier section is a matrix of rows and columns. Notice that eight columns (A through H) and 20 rows are indicated along the borders on the top and left sides. You cannot tell it now, but each column on a blank worksheet when it first appears is nine characters wide; we will vary the column widths later on. The worksheet actually has 256 columns and 8,192 rows, but the monitor can display only a limited number at any one time. The full set of columns is labeled A...Z, AA...AZ, BA...BZ, and so on until IV (which is the 256th column). The rows are numbered consecutively from 1 to 8,192. The intersection of each row and column is called a cell. Thus, there are 256 X 8,192 = 2,097,152 cells in a worksheet. Each cell has an address which is identified by the column letter and row number: A1, B25, and CZ210 are cell addresses. Each cell holds an item of information--an _entry_--which can include up to 240 characters (numbers, symbols, letters, or blank spaces). For example, one could enter a formula that was 180 characters long into Cell C20, and the PC would display the final value of the formula on the screen in that cell.

Any rectangular block of cells is called a _range_. As shown in Figure 1-10, a range can be a single cell, a group of cells across a row or down a column, or a rectangular group of cells encompassing several rows and/or columns. A range is defined by naming two diagonally opposite cells or, in the case of a single-cell range, by naming an individual cell. Where more than one cell is involved, a period must separate the diagonal cells. Thus, B3.C3 defines the range indicated as Range A in Exhibit 1-10; B5.B10 defines Range B; D4 defines Range C; and D6.F13 defines Range D. Because Lotus 1-2-3 will accept any two diagonally opposite cells as a range definition, Range D, for example, could also be defined as D13.F6, F13.D6, or F6.D13.

At any given time, exactly 20 rows of the worksheet will be visible, but since the screen has a width of 72 characters, the number of columns displayed depends on the width of each column. When 1-2-3 is called up, the blank worksheet initially displays 8 columns, each 9 characters wide. However, as we noted above, you can adjust the width of the columns as desired. You should also keep in mind that each cell can contain up to 240 characters, even though a maximum of 72 can be displayed on the screen at any one time. The nondisplayed characters are retained in the computer's memory, and if they are part of a number or formula, they will be used in the program's operations.

At Cell A1 (the upper left corner), you will see a highlighted rectangle called the _cell pointer_. The pointer is always at A1 when 1-2-3 is initially accessed. Notice also that the address of the highlighted cell is shown above the worksheet proper in the upper left corner of the screen. The area above the worksheet is called the _control panel_. If data is entered in a cell, that information is displayed on Line 1 of the control panel, following the pointer location, as well as in the cell itself. Type in the word Now and press RETURN to see what we mean. Leave the word "Now" in Cell A1 for a while. We will come back to it later.

===

Exhibit 1-10
Cell Ranges on a 1-2-3 Worksheet

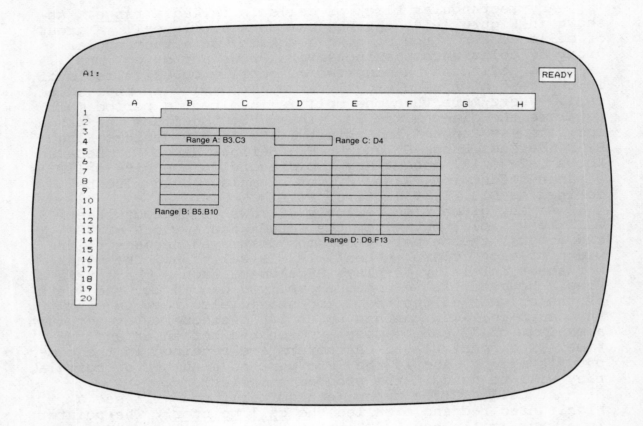

===

1-2-3 Commands

1-2-3 can accept a large number of <u>commands</u>, or instructions
to do particular tasks, within the 1-2-3 subprogram. You
will use commands in every 1-2-3 session to perform such
functions as these:

24

1. Saving and retrieving the worksheet.

2. Copying, moving, and deleting data from the worksheet.

3. Changing column widths.

4. Printing the worksheet.

5. Creating and saving graphs.

     To issue a command, you must press "slash" (/), located just above the right corner of the space bar. You must be in READY mode, as indicated in the upper right corner of the control panel, to issue a command.
     Now go ahead and press / , and 1-2-3 will display the main command menu keywords on the second line of the control panel, as shown in Exhibit 1-11. The word MENU in the upper right corner of the control panel shows that you are in MENU mode. 1-2-3's menu shows you your choices and displays subcommands or explanatory phrases about the highlighted command on the third line of the control panel, as shown in Exhibit 1-11. If you press the right arrow to move the pointer to a different command, the submenu on the third line of the control panel changes to that of the newly highlighted command.
     The mode indicator will display READY whenever 1-2-3 is ready to accept a piece of data or an instruction. There are several other mode indicators; they tell you what the program is doing. For example, if MENU is the indicated mode, this means that part of a command has been issued, but the command has not been completed. WAIT signals that the computer is processing a command. VALUE says that the piece of data being entered is a number or a formula, rather than an alphabetic string (or a word), which would be indicated by the mode LABEL. Exhibit 1-12 lists and defines all of 1-2-3's mode indicators.

==

Exhibit 1-11
Main Command Menu Keywords and Subcommands

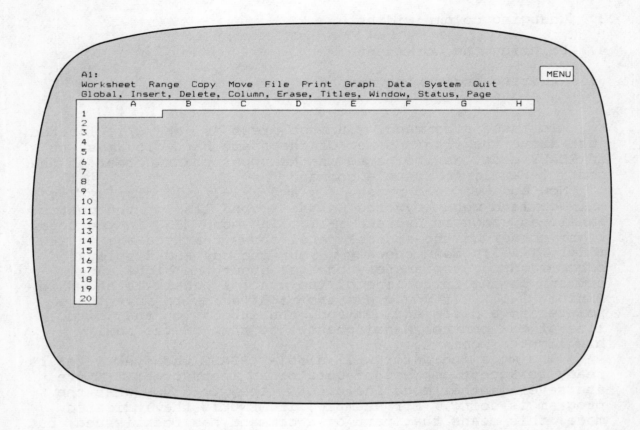

```
A1:                                                              MENU
Worksheet  Range  Copy  Move  File  Print  Graph  Data  System  Quit
Global, Insert, Delete, Column, Erase, Titles, Window, Status, Page
        A          B         C         D         E         F         G         H
 1
 2
 3
 4
 5
 6
 7
 8
 9
10
11
12
13
14
15
16
17
18
19
20
```

==

```
===================================================================
```

Exhibit 1-12
Mode Indicators

EDIT   The entry in the highlighted cell is being edited, or contains an error and thus needs to be edited.

ERROR   An error has occurred. This may be a programming error, such as erasing the contents of a cell used in a formula, or an equipment error, such as failing to put a storage diskette in Drive B before saving a file. Press ESCAPE to return 1-2-3 to READY mode, and then correct the error.

FILES   A listing of the files on a diskette is being displayed, such as during a File Retrieve or File Save operation.

FIND   A /Data Query Find operation is being executed.

HELP   A Help menu is being displayed.

LABEL   The data being entered will be treated as a label.

MENU   A command is being issued.

POINT   This menu item appears when a command requires that a range be specified. When 1-2-3 is in POINT mode, you may change the indicated range by using the arrow keys.

READY   1-2-3 is ready for the next entry or command.

VALUE   The data being entered is numeric and will be treated as a number or formula.

WAIT   Do not enter any data or issue a command; 1-2-3 is executing a previously issued command. For long calculations, the WAIT indicator may flash for several minutes.

```
===================================================================
```

You select a command from the command menu either by typing the first letter of the command or by moving the pointer to the command and pressing the RETURN key. When you press RETURN, the submenu for the selected command will move up from the third to the second line of the control panel, and the submenu for the first entry will then appear on the third line. By selecting a sequenced set of command keywords, you build up a command one keyword at a time. At some point during a command sequence, 1-2-3 may prompt you to supply some information such as a file name or a range; simply type in the information and press the RETURN key, and at that point 1-2-3 will execute the command or prompt you either to select another keyword or to enter additional information.

Exhibit 1-13 presents a tree diagram of the subcommands under the main command entry "Worksheet." Similar diagrams have been drawn to detail the subcommands under Range, Copy, Move, and so forth; these diagrams are provided in Appendix B. Exhibit 1-14 describes in detail the command sequence you would use if you had numbers in your worksheet and you wanted to show all numerical entries with commas and to two decimal places.

At any point in a command sequence, but before the command is actually executed, the command can be stopped by pressing the Escape (ESC) key. Doing so returns you to the previous menu or, if the main command menu is shown, to the READY mode. Thus, you can "back out" of a command sequence such as that in Exhibit 1-14 one step at a time by pressing ESC the required number of times. Press ESC now to return to READY mode.

```
================================================================
```

Exhibit 1-13
A Tree Diagram of the Subcommands under "Worksheet"

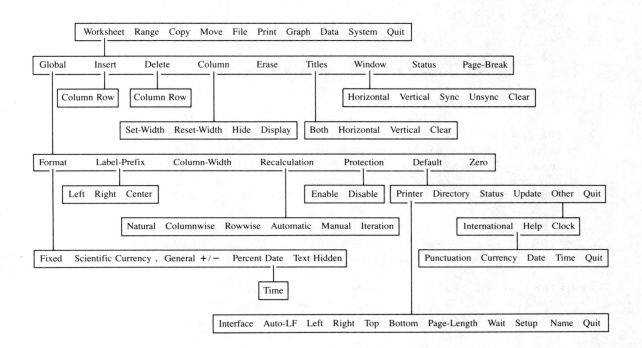

Source: Lotus Development Corporation 1986.   Used with permission.

```
================================================================
```

==

Exhibit 1-14
Command Sequence to Display Numeric Entries
with Commas and 2 Decimal Places

1. From the Access menu, enter 1-2-3 by pressing the RETURN key. This
    gives you a blank worksheet.

2. Now type a slash (/), which gives you the "Main Command Menu" in
    the <u>control panel</u> above the worksheet. The main command menu is
    shown on the second line of Exhibit 1-11 and the first line of
    Exhibit 1-13, with Worksheet at the left, followed by Range, and so
    on, across to Quit.

3. The bottom line in the control panel (see Exhibit 1-11) gives the
    submenu to the highlighted main menu item, Worksheet: Global
    Insert Delete Column Erase Titles Window Status Page. If
    you press the right arrow to move the pointer from Worksheet to
    Range, the submenu changes to that for Range, and so forth.

4. With the pointer on Worksheet, press the RETURN key; the Worksheet
    menu is now shown in the second line of the control panel, and what
    the first entry, Global, does is shown on the third line.

5. Press RETURN with the pointer on Global, and Global's submenu
    appears on Line 2. Global's submenu items are: Format Label-
    Prefix Column-Width Recalculation Protection Default Zero.

6. From Global's submenu, select Format by pressing RETURN. This
    command will allow you to specify the way you want numbers dis-
    played in the worksheet. Since the command is Global, it will
    affect the display of all numbers in the worksheet.

7. When you selected Format, a new submenu appeared: Fixed Scienti-
    fic Currency ,(comma) General +/- Percent Date Text Hidden.
    We would like to display all numbers in the worksheet with commas
    and two decimal places. Therefore, we select , (comma) by pressing
    a comma.

8. At this point, 1-2-3 asks you to enter the number of decimal
    places. A 2 will be shown above the blinking cursor, so just press
    RETURN. The command is now completed, so 1-2-3 displays all
    numbers in the worksheet with commas and two decimal places. Also,
    since this is the end of the menu chain, 1-2-3 returns the

30

worksheet to READY mode, as indicated in the upper right corner of the control panel.

9. You could have moved down some other branch of the menu set forth in Exhibit 1-13. 1-2-3 performs many commands--you just have to move down the correct menu chain. In this sense, 1-2-3 is a "menu-driven" program.

10. If at any point you change your mind about which branch of the menu chain you want, just press the Escape (ESC) key, and 1-2-3 will move you up the chain by one level. If you continue to press ESC, you will eventually get back to READY mode.

==

When you have a worksheet in the READY mode and press /, the 1-2-3 "Main Menu" commands which you can issue are these:

1. Worksheet, which controls the overall appearance of the worksheet.

2. Range, which affects the display of a single cell or a range of cells.

3. Copy, which reproduces entries in one cell or a range of cells in some other cell or cells.

4. Move, which moves entries from one location to another.

5. File, which allows you to save your worksheet, to retrieve a worksheet previously stored on a diskette, and to obtain a listing of the files on a diskette.

6. Print, which prints the worksheet in one of several ways.

7. Graph, which creates and displays graphs using data contained in a worksheet.

8. Data, which allows manipulation, such as ranking of worksheet data. Regression analysis can also be performed with the Data command under Release 2.

31

9. <u>System</u>, which is available only in Release 2, lets you go back to the DOS system temporarily to do things like format storage diskettes.

10. <u>Quit</u>, which ends the 1-2-3 session and returns you to the Lotus Access menu.

These Main Menu commands are also shown on Line 2 of Exhibit 1-11 and on Line 1 of Exhibit 1-13, while a complete listing of 1-2-3's command structure is given in Appendix B at the end of this book.

Moving Around the Worksheet

The position of the cell pointer determines where data is entered on the worksheet. There are three ways to move the pointer:

1. <u>Arrow Keys</u>. You can move the pointer up and down and side-to-side, one cell at a time, by pressing one of the four <u>arrow keys</u>, which are the same as the 2, 4, 6, and 8 keys on the numeric pad on the right-hand side of the keyboard. For instance, you move one row to the right by pressing the <u>right-arrow</u> key, which is also numbered "6." Experiment by moving the pointer with the arrow keys. Notice that if you attempt to go up from Row 1 or to the left of Column A, the computer simply "beeps," telling you that you must stay within the 256 columns and the 8,192 rows. Notice also these points: (1) If you hold down an arrow key, the pointer will continue to move until you either hit a boundary and start the computer beeping or release the key; (2) as you move to the right more than 8 columns, the column headings start changing; (3) moving down more than 20 rows causes the displayed row numbers to change; (4) if you want to go back to Cell A1, you can do so by moving to the left and up until you get there. Of course, you can stop at any cell and enter data, then move on. For example, your Cell A1 should contain the label "Now". Move from A1 to A2, type in is , and press the RETURN key. Then go to A3, type in the , and press RETURN and to A4 and type in time then press RETURN . If you make a typing error, don't worry--we'll show you how to fix it later.

2. <u>Big Moves</u>. If you have a large worksheet with many rows and columns, you will often want to move down several rows and/or across several columns at a time, and using the arrow keys will be too slow. Here are some ways to make big moves:

   a. <u>Big Left and Big Right</u>. If you hold down the Control key--the one just left of A marked Ctrl-- and then press the left- or right-arrow key, you will move one full screen to the left or right. For example, if Columns A through H are on your screen, and you press Ctrl -->, the screen will move over to the right, and Columns I through P will then be displayed. This is called Big Right. Note that regardless of where the pointer is located when the command is issued, it will end up in the left column of the new screen.
   Another way to move one full screen to the left or right is to use the Tab key located just to the left of Q and designated ⊢⟶ . To move to the right one screen, you press the Tab key. To move to the left one screen, you press (simultaneously) the Shift key (just above the Caps Lock key) and the Tab key.

   b. <u>Page Up and Page Down</u>. Keys marked PgUp and PgDn are given just above and below the right-arrow key. These keys shift the screen up or down 20 rows at a time. The pointer maintains its relative position on the screen; for example, if it is on Cell A4 and you press PgDn, it will move to A24.

   c. <u>Home</u>. The Home key, which is located just above the left-arrow key, returns the worksheet to its original position, with A1 in the upper left corner and the pointer on A1.

   d. <u>End</u>. The End key, located just below the left arrow, is used in conjunction with the Home key or an arrow key. Pressing End and then Home moves the screen and pointer to the lower right-hand corner of the worksheet matrix. For example, if your right-most column is J and your longest column goes down to Row 50, then pressing (sequentially) End and then Home will give you a screen with J50 in the lower right corner and the pointer on that cell.

When used with an arrow key, the End key moves you up or down, or left or right, to the next filled cell that is adjacent to an empty cell or else to the boundary. (See the Users Manual, pages 37-38, for other uses of the End key. Since we rarely use them, we decided not to explain them to avoid confusing you with details.)

3. GoTo Function Key. The pointer can be moved directly to any cell by pressing the function key F5 at the left side of the keyboard. F5 is the 1-2-3 GoTo function key. (Note that this is different from the cell address F5, which you would use by entering an F followed by a 5.) After you press the F5 function key, the message "Enter address to go to:" will appear on the second line of the control panel, along with the cell you are now in. The blinking light, or cursor, in the highlighted cell is prompting you to enter the cell address (column letter and row number) to which you would like the pointer to move. To illustrate, after pressing function key F5 , type in A7 , then press the RETURN key; the pointer automatically jumps to Cell A7, and that address also appears in the upper left part of the screen (the control panel). Type in good here, and press RETURN .

Practice moving the pointer around the worksheet. As you do, notice that the location of the pointer is always shown in the control panel, and it changes as you move the pointer.

Entering Data

Now that you know how to move around the worksheet, we need to enter some real data and then watch 1-2-3 process it. First, though, let's get rid of the things you typed in while reading the last section. The spreadsheet (or worksheet--we use the terms interchangeably) can be erased, like a blackboard. To erase it, first type a slash (/), the general command key. The main command menu will be displayed in the control panel, and the word "Worksheet" will be highlighted. Since you want to do something with the

whole worksheet, press RETURN . A subsidiary menu appears
with the submenu item "Global" highlighted. You want to
erase the worksheet, so press the right arrow four times to
move over to Erase, and then press RETURN , or type E .
The word "No" will appear, highlighted. This gives you a
chance to reconsider whether or not you really want to erase
the worksheet. Since you do, you want "Yes"; move over one
space and press RETURN , or type Y . The worksheet goes
blank. You had nothing of value on it, but if you had, it
would be gone. We'll show you how to save worksheets
shortly, but let's first enter something worth saving.

The word READY appears in the mode indicator in the
upper right corner of the control panel above the now blank
worksheet. When the mode indicator says READY, 1-2-3 is
ready for you to type a data entry. (Once we have some data
in, and the computer is computing, the mode indicator will
switch from READY to WAIT.) Data can be entered as labels,
values, or formulas.

1. Labels. A label can be one or more words or some
    combination of letters, symbols, or numbers. A label
    must begin with a letter, a blank space, or a label
    prefix. A label prefix indicates to 1-2-3 that the
    entry which follows is to be treated as a label even if
    it is a number, like 1/1/85 (meant as January 1, 1985),
    and it tells 1-2-3 not to do anything except display
    the label within the cell as indicated. (If no prefix
    had been used, 1-2-3 would have divided 1 by 1, then
    divided the result by 85, and finally displayed the
    number 0.011765.) The label prefixes used by 1-2-3
    are:

    a. Apostrophe (') = left-aligned label.

    b. Quote (") = right-aligned label.

    c. Caret (^) = centered label. (The caret is found
        over the number 6 in the center of the keyboard.)

    d. Backslash (\) tells 1-2-3 to fill the cell with the
        next character typed. For example, typing \-RETURN
        will fill the cell with dashes, which serve as
        underlines in 1-2-3. Typing \= provides a double
        underline, and * gives you a line of stars.

If no prefix is used for an entry that begins with a letter, like Year, the label is automatically aligned on the left side of the cell. Note also that as soon as you type a letter or a label prefix, the mode indicator changes from READY to LABEL. Type Y to see this change, then ESC to go back to READY.

If you do not specify otherwise, labels will automatically be aligned to the left of a cell. As you will see shortly, typing labels can be a pain and entering label prefixes a special bother. However, there is a way to simplify entering label prefixes; we will show you how to left align, center, or right align a whole group of labels at once in Chapter 3.

2. Values. Values are numbers, and the 1-2-3 program causes arithmetic operations to be performed on them. Any entry that begins with a digit is automatically treated as a value (unless a label prefix is used), as is any entry preceded by one of the characters +, -, ., @, #, (, or $. For example, 125 is a value, and so is +B4, because the "+" sign in front of B4 tells 1-2-3 that "B4" is a value (the value in the Cell B4) and not a label. As soon as you type either a number or one of the value-indicating characters, the mode indicator changes from READY to VALUE. Try it by typing a + , and then type ESC to return to READY.

3. Formulas. A formula is a special type of value entry, because a value results from a formula. Formulas can be used to express relationships among values in a worksheet in terms of the worksheet cell addresses. The operators +, -, *, and / mean add, subtract, multiply, and divide when used in a formula. A caret (^) designates an exponent. For example, the formula +B2+B3 tells 1-2-3 to add the contents of Cell B2 to the contents of Cell B3; this sum will be stored in the current cell (the cell which contains the pointer). 2*72/8 is also a formula. If you type this formula, and then press RETURN, the computer will first multiply 2 by 72, then divide the result by 8, and finally display 18 as the "answer" in the cell that is highlighted.

2+72/8 is also a formula. If you type this formula, 1-2-3 will first divide 72 by 8, then add 2, and then display 11 as the answer. If you actually wanted to add 2 to 72, and then divide by 8, you would have to use parentheses and write the formula as (2+72)/8; then 1-2-3 would display 9.25 as the answer rather than 11. These results occur because 1-2-3 performs calculations within parentheses first, then does exponentiation, then does multiplication and division from left to right, and finally does addition and subtraction from left to right. If you wrote 2*2^2, Lotus would first square the second 2 (because exponentiation is the very first operation performed if no parentheses are used), then multiply 4 by 2 to produce an answer of 8. If you actually wanted 2 times 2, squared, you would write (2*2)^2 and get the answer 16.

Remember: parentheses first; then exponentiation; then multiply and divide; then add and subtract; and all operations at a given level begin at the left and proceed toward the right. Notice also that when you type in a formula and press the RETURN key, the formula is displayed in the control panel but the value which results from it is displayed on the worksheet.

If formulas are to be recognized as values by 1-2-3, they must begin with a digit or one of the special characters that tells 1-2-3 that the entry is a value. Suppose you wanted to divide the contents of Cell B5 by the contents of Cell A5 and then store the result in Cell C5. First, put the highlighter on Cell C5, then type +B5/A5 , and then press RETURN . Lotus 1-2-3 will display the answer in Cell C5 (and the formula in the control panel whenever the cell pointer is on C5). If you had forgotten to precede the B5/A5 with a +, Lotus 1-2-3 would have treated B5/A5 as a label and displayed it in Cell C5, because the entry began with a letter. To avoid this problem, type a plus sign before the formula to indicate to 1-2-3 that you are entering a value.

Now let's enter a label, some data, and a formula and then evaluate the data. If your worksheet is not blank, press / , RETURN to select Worksheet, move to Erase, press RETURN , move to Yes, and press RETURN . Alternatively, you could use the following four keystrokes: /WEY . Whenever items are displayed in a menu, you can select an item by either using the arrow to highlight it and then

37

pressing RETURN, or simply by typing in the first letter of the item you want, such as E for Erase or Y for Yes.

After using either procedure, a blank worksheet will appear. Go to Home (A1), type in the word Units , and press the RETURN key. (If you make a mistake and want to correct it, skip to the next section to learn how.) You now have a left-aligned label. Now press the right arrow to go to B1, type in 1000 , and press RETURN .

> Note: <u>Never type commas in values</u>. They are permitted in labels but not in values. Also, with a regular typewriter, you can use the lowercase letter L for 1. However, with a computer, L is L and 1 is 1, so you must be sure to use the 1 on the top row of the keyboard.

Now go to A2 and type in Price , but <u>do not</u> press RETURN-- rather, hit the right arrow, which simultaneously enters Price as a label and moves you to Cell B2, thus saving you a keystroke. Now type in 30 , which is the price per unit, and press the down arrow and then the left arrow to both enter the 30 and get to Cell A3. Type in Sales and then the right arrow to get to B3. Now type this formula, but don't hit the RETURN key yet:

> +B1*B2 (or, alternatively, +b1*b2 . You may use upper- or lowercase letters in cell addresses; 1-2-3 automatically converts lowercase to uppercase for cell reference purposes).

Look at the control panel above the worksheet (see Exhibit 1-15). The address of the highlighted cell is shown in the upper left corner. The mode indicator VALUE is shown in the upper right corner; if you had not put in the + sign, the word LABEL would have been displayed. The formula is given on the second line; again, it can be in either upper- or lowercase letters (B or b)--it makes no difference to Lotus 1-2-3. Now press RETURN . Cell B3 shows the value 30000. The control panel shows your formula--now capitalized even if you typed it in lowercase--and the mode indicator reads READY, indicating that 1-2-3 is ready for you to continue building your spreadsheet.

===

Exhibit 1-15
Partial Worksheet

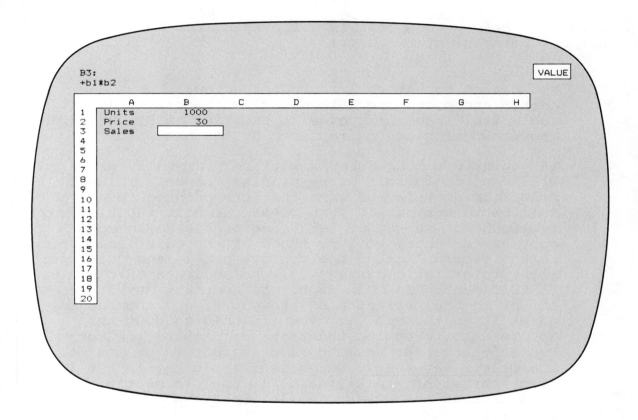

===

Correcting Errors

No matter how careful you are when entering data or formulas, you will invariably make some mistakes. If you
notice a mistake <u>before you press the RETURN key</u>, you can

correct it by depressing the Backspace key (<--), which is on the top row of the keyboard just over the RETURN key. The Backspace key erases the last character typed. Continue backspacing until all the errors have been erased, then retype the entry correctly. Alternatively, you can press the Escape key (ESC), which is on the top row just to the left of the 1, to cancel the entry and return the mode indicator to READY, and then type the entry correctly.

If the cell contents have already been entered into the worksheet before the error is discovered, the entry may be corrected in one of two ways:

1. You can go to the cell to be corrected, type a new entry, and press the RETURN key. In other words, if you write a new entry over an existing entry, the old one disappears and is replaced by the new one.

2. If you have a long formula with only a small error, you will want to correct it by placing the cell in EDIT mode. To do this, be sure that the pointer is at the cell to be corrected, then press the edit function key, F2, found on the upper left side of the keyboard. A copy of the entry will be shown on the edit line, which is the second line of the control panel, and the upper right corner will display EDIT to indicate that you are in EDIT mode. In EDIT mode, the Home key moves the cursor to the beginning of the entry, and the End key moves it to the end. If you are holding down the Control key, pressing the left- or right-arrow keys causes the cursor to move five characters at a time. The Delete key (DEL), which is the big key in the lower right corner of the keyboard, is used to delete the character at the cursor, while the Backspace key (<--) erases the character preceding the cursor. Typing a character adds the character at the location of the cursor and shifts the character that was at the cursor and all that follow it to the right to make room for the character or characters that are being added. Finally, pressing the RETURN key places the corrected entry in the worksheet and returns the mode indicator to READY.

Note: You could also have gone into EDIT mode
before the incorrect formula had been entered,
corrected it, and then entered it. You should do
this if you have typed a long statement which
has just a small error.

Now let's illustrate the editing process. First, go to
Cell B4, type in a backslash (\ ) and a dash (--), and
then hit RETURN to get an underline. Now go to Cell A5,
and type in Unites Cort , which is "Unit Cost" misspelled,
and press RETURN . Now press function key F2 , which puts
you into EDIT mode. The cursor is blinking just to the right
of the "t." Use the left arrow to go back to the "e" in
"Unites". Press the Delete key (DEL) twice to get rid of
the unwanted "es". Before going on, type the " es " back in,
going back to "Unites". Then hit the Backspace key twice;
you will see that it does the same thing as the DEL key. Now
use the right arrow to move the cursor to the "r" in "Cort."
Press the DEL key, obtaining "Cot." Now type an " s " to
get "Cost." (You could have used the Backspace here, too.)
You now have the correct label, so you can press the RETURN
key to complete the operation.
We will go into this later, but when you had "Unites
Cort" as the label, it took up 11 spaces, including the
space between the words. The column width, however, is only
9 spaces. Lotus 1-2-3 permits you to enter up to 240 characters per cell, and it will display them in the proper
space if there is no entry in the next column that requires
the space. If we had something in Cell B5, the entry in A5
would have been truncated to 9 characters.
It is also worth noting that 1-2-3 permits a cell to be
completely filled if it is a label, but if a value is in a
cell, one space must be left blank so that numbers can be
distinguished when they are displayed in adjacent columns.
Thus, if your worksheet has 9-character columns, you can
enter only 8-character numbers; if you want 9 digits, you
must widen the columns to 10 characters. Changing the
column width is discussed in Chapter 2.
To continue with our example, go to B5 and type in
 20 , but do not enter it. Suppose you realize the correct
entry is 15, not 20. You could press the Escape key to
clear the entry in the control panel, then type in 15 and
press RETURN. Alternatively, you could use the Backspace or
Delete keys or go into EDIT mode and make the correction.

Now suppose you have already entered 20 in Cell B5 before learning that you really want 15, so go ahead and press RETURN . Then, with B5 highlighted and the mode indicator set on READY, type 15 and press RETURN . The 20 is replaced by 15.

One other type of correction should be noted. Go to B7, type in 100 , and press RETURN . Suppose this was a mistake--you really wanted B7 to be blank, so now you want to completely delete the entry. You might try pressing F2 to enter EDIT mode, then Backspace to wipe out the 100 on the edit line of the control panel, and then press RETURN, hoping to see the 100 disappear. If you did, the 100 would still be there; that operation would not work. The way Lotus 1-2-3 blanks out an entry is as follows: Press / , then R for Range, E for Erase, and then enter the range to be erased, for example, B7, or press RETURN to erase the highlighted cell. To repeat, the keystrokes to blank out a cell are:

/RE(Range) RETURN

In later chapters, we will use a variation of that set of strokes to erase large sections of the worksheet as well as single cells.

Summary

In this chapter, we have discussed some of the basics of Lotus 1-2-3. You should know how to access the 1-2-3 sub-program, how to move around the worksheet, how to enter data into the worksheet, and how to correct errors. Soon you will be able to perform these operations automatically, but for a while you will need to refer back to Chapter 1 frequently to refresh your memory. In the next chapter, we will demonstrate more 1-2-3 features as we construct a sample worksheet. If you are going to take a break now, just remove your diskette and turn off your machine, then start it up for the next session just as you did for this one.

Chapter 1 Exercises

1-1   (Editing) Get a blank worksheet on the screen, then
       enter the following labels and values in the indicated
       cells and complete the requirements given below.

                   A1   Rte
                   B1   3
                   A2   Unt
                   B2   900
                   A3   cost

       Requirements:

       a.   Using the EDIT mode, correct Cell A1 to read "Rate"
            by inserting the letter a between the R and the t.

       b.   Correct Cell A2 to read Units by retyping the cell.

       c.   Correct Cell A3 so that cost begins with a capital
            C.

       d.   Type a formula in Cell B3 that multiplies Cell B1
            by Cell B2.

1-2   (Writing formulas) Use /WEY RETURN to get a blank
       worksheet on your screen, then enter the following
       labels and values in the indicated cells and complete
       the requirements given below:

                   A1   Order of Operations:
                   A2   '1. Parentheses (Note: you must type the
                               label prefix ('), but it will not appear
                               on the screen.)
                   A3   '2. Exponentiation
                   A4   '3. Multiplication and division from left
                               to right
                   A5   '4. Addition and subtraction from left to
                               right

Requirements:

a. In Cell A8, multiply 2 times 6, then add 4, and then divide the result by 2. (Answer: (2*6+4)/2 gives 8)

b. In Cell A9, add 2 plus 6, then multiply by 4, and then add 2 to the result. (Answer: (2+6)*4+2 gives 34)

c. In Cell A10, add 2 plus 6, then multiply the result by the sum of 12+3, and then square the result. (Answer: ((2+6)*(12+3))^2 gives 14400) Note that the * must be used to designate multiplication.

d. In Cell A11, add 7 plus 6; then divide by 3; then add to the result the product of 6 times 2, raised to the third power (that is, $(6*2)^3$); and finally divide the result of the preceding steps by 4. (Answer: 433.0833)

e. In Cell A12, add the contents of Cell A8 to that of A9. (Answer: +A8+A9 gives 42)

f. In Cell A13, add the contents of Cell A9 to that of A10, and then multiply that sum by the contents of Cell A8. (Answer: 115472)

g. Now go back to Cell A10, use the Edit key (F2) to go into EDIT mode, and change the multiply sign (*) to a divide sign (/). What is the new result? (Answer: 0.284444)

h. Now go back to Cell A12, go into EDIT mode, press the Home key to go to the beginning of the equation, press the Delete key to remove the + sign, and then press the RETURN key. What happened?

i. Now go to Cell A14 and add the contents of Cells A8 to that of A13. (Answer: 282.2755)

j. Now go to Cell A15 and add the contents of Cell A14 to that of A8. (Answer: 290.2755)

k. Now go back to Cell A8. Type 500 and press RETURN.
    What happened to Cells A13, A14, and A15? Why did
    they change?

l. Now go to (or stay in) Cell A8, and type X and
    RETURN. What happened to Cells A13, A14, and A15?
    (You got an ERR message because you were adding a
    label (the X in A8) to a number.) Replace the X in
    A8 with 8 to remove the ERR messages.

m. Now go to (or stay in) A8, and type /RE RETURN.
    What happens to Cells A13, A14, and A15? Why?
    (Hint: Cell A8 is now blank, and 1-2-3 interprets
    a blank as a zero. Move the pointer to Cell A13
    and look at the formula in the control panel.)

Chapter 2
A Sample Worksheet

Table of Contents

Constructing a Spreadsheet Model   48
    Column Width   49
    Functions   51
    Formatting the Balance Sheet   53
    Inserting Rows and Columns   55
Saving and Retrieving Files   58
    Saving the Worksheet   58
    Exiting 1-2-3   59
    Retrieving the Worksheet   60
Printing   61
    Printing the Balance Sheet   61
    Printing to a File   62
    Copy Command: Forecasting   63
    Printing Again   67
Sensitivity and Other Topics   68
    Sensitivity Analysis: What if?   68
    Specifying Growth Rates   70
    Titles   74
    Windows   76
Summary   79
Summary of Commands   80

- -

In this chapter, we illustrate many of the features of 1-2-3 with data for the West Corporation. We first construct a balance sheet for the year ending December 31, 1985, after which we convert this statement to a forecast for the years 1986 through 1995.

    The diskette that accompanies this book contains files for most of the spreadsheets displayed in this and subsequent chapters. Initially, you should totally ignore our diskette, create your own models, and store them on your own diskette. In later chapters, you will want to call up and work with our models rather than typing in your own models from scratch. Also, if you mistakenly erase a model you have created, you may want to call up our model rather than recreate your lost one.

Constructing a Spreadsheet Model

Exhibit 2-1 shows the balance sheet for West Corporation for the year ending December 31, 1985. We will convert this balance sheet into a computer spreadsheet, after which we will use it as the basis for forecasting future balance sheets under different sets of assumptions.

===

Exhibit 2-1

West Corporation's Balance Sheet, 1985   (LB2X1)

                                        1985

    Current assets $1,000.00
    Fixed assets   1,000.00

    Total assets $2,000.00
                                   ===========

    Current liabilities $500.00
    Long term debt   500.00
    Common equity   1,000.00

    Total liabilities and capital $2,000.00
                                   ===========

===

Column Width

To begin, follow the procedures discussed in Chapter 1 to
get a blank 1-2-3 worksheet on your monitor screen. Look at
Exhibit 2-2; you will need to type the information shown on
that exhibit into your computer. Column A will be used for
such labels as "Current assets," and Column B will be used
for the 1985 amounts, in dollars. Note, though, that
several of the balance sheet labels contain more than 9
characters and, therefore, they will not fit into Column A.
Although we could let the labels extend into Columns B and
C, a better procedure is to change the width of Column A to
accommodate the longer labels before typing them in. <u>1-2-3
allows you to change the width of any column individually or
to change all columns at once.</u>
     We want to change only Column A at this point. To do
so, move the highlighter, or pointer, to Cell A1 if it is
not already there. Then type a slash (/) to invoke the
1-2-3 main command menu. The 1-2-3 main menu commands will
appear on your control panel, with the item Worksheet
highlighted. Just below, you will see the subparts of the
Worksheet command menu, including the word Column. With
Worksheet highlighted, press the RETURN key (or type a
 W). Now you are in the Worksheet menu, and the middle
line of the control panel lists some operations you can
perform on the worksheet. Global, the first operation,
causes whatever command you execute to affect the entire
worksheet; you would press G or RETURN at this point if you
wanted to change the entire worksheet. However, you want to
change only the width of Column A, so move across to the
fourth submenu item, Column, and press RETURN (or press
 C , the first letter of Column).
     The Column-Width menu which appears offers the choices
Set-Width and Reset-Width (along with Hide and Display),
with the pointer originally at Set-Width. Set-Width allows
you to specify the width of the current column to be 1 to
240 characters wide, while Reset-Width automatically changes
the width of the current column to the default column width
of the worksheet. (The default column width is generally 9
characters wide, but it may be changed by going to the main
menu with a slash, selecting Worksheet, then Global, and
then Column.) We want to expand the width of Column A to
accommodate about 30 characters (count the characters in the
longest label), so choose Set-Width by typing RETURN or
 S . This prompt will appear:

Enter column width (1..240): 9

==

Exhibit 2-2
Data for West Corporation's Balance Sheet

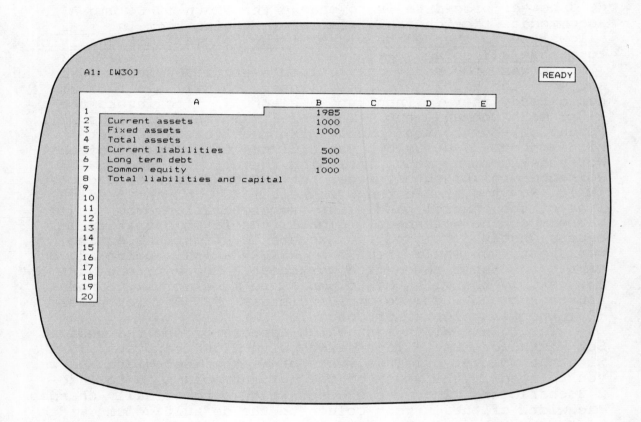

```
A1: [W30]                                                         READY

                                A              B       C       D       E
    1                                         1985
    2      Current assets                     1000
    3      Fixed assets                       1000
    4      Total assets
    5      Current liabilities                 500
    6      Long term debt                      500
    7      Common equity                      1000
    8      Total liabilities and capital
    9
   10
   11
   12
   13
   14
   15
   16
   17
   18
   19
   20
```

==

The (1..240): 9 tells you that you can set the column
width at from 1 to 240 characters and that the current width

50

is 9. You want 30 characters, so type 30 ; you will see that
30 replaces 9 in the control panel. Now press the RETURN
key. Notice that the pointer, or highlighted area in Cell
A1, expands to 30 characters. Notice also that Columns F,
G, and H disappear from the screen: They were "pushed off."
The mode indicator also returns to READY, showing that you
are ready for the next step.

Move to Cell A2, and then type the labels in Cells A2
through A8 exactly as they are shown in Exhibit 2-2, beginning with Current assets . For now, type the labels without
leaving any blank rows; we want them this way so that later
on we can show you how to add blank lines to clean up the
appearance of your worksheet. Also, after you type in the
label Current assets in Cell A2, press the down arrow; that
will both enter the label and move the pointer to Cell A3.

Now go up to Cell B1 and put in the year 1985 . You can
enter it as either a label or a value; but, as you will see,
it is often more efficient to enter years as values, so
simply type 1985 in Cell B1, then press the down arrow,
which will enter 1985 in B1 and simultaneously move the
pointer to B2. Now enter the 1985 data for Current assets,
Fixed assets, Current liabilities, Long term debt, and
Common equity, without decimal places or dollar signs, just
as we show in Exhibit 2-2.

We can now total up the assets and liabilities, using
1-2-3 commands to do the addition. Total assets is the sum
of Current assets and Fixed assets, so enter the formula
 +B2+B3 in Cell B4. Make sure you typed a + before B2, and
then press the RETURN key; the value 2000 will appear in
Cell B4, with the formula being given in the control panel.
Now go to Cell B8. Total liabilities and capital is the sum
of Current liabilities, Long term debt, and Common equity,
so you can enter the formula +B5+B6+B7 in Cell B8. Do
that (making sure you typed a + before B5), and then press
the RETURN key. The value 2000 will appear in Cell B8.

Functions

In our example, we had to add only a few items, so our
formulas (+B2+B3 and +B5+B6+B7) were not hard to write out.
However, in many instances we will want to add literally
hundreds of items, and it would be tedious to write
+B1+B2+...+B100. Lotus 1-2-3 therefore provides a "function
command" that can be used to automatically sum numbers--

indeed, 1-2-3 provides a number of very useful built-in functions. In 1-2-3, functions always begin with the "at" symbol, @ (found at the top of the keyboard on the 2 key). Then comes the name of the function, followed by the function parameters typed within parentheses. For example, if you typed @SUM(B5.B7) RETURN in Cell B8, you would get exactly the same result as you would from +B5+B6+B7 RETURN.

Lotus 1-2-3 contains a total of 51 functions. We introduce several functions in this book as they are needed in models; for a complete listing of 1-2-3's functions, see Chapter 4 of the Lotus Manual. Some examples include:

@SUM(B2.B124)	Sums Cells B2 through B124.
@NPV(discount rate,E6.E15)	Finds the net present value, discounted at a rate which you specify, of Cells E6 through E15.
@SQRT(A6)	Finds the square root of the value in Cell A6.
@STD(A5.A20)	Finds the standard deviation of the values in Cells A5 through A20.

To use the Sum function, type @SUM and then, in parentheses, the first and last cells in that part of the row or column to be summed, and then press the RETURN key. Now in your worksheet type @SUM(B5.B7) in Cell B8 and press the RETURN key. You should find the value in Cell B8 to be 2000 using either formula. Note also that you could use either uppercase or lowercase letters for Sum, and that you need to use only one period to set off the parameters (that is, B5.B7) even though the Lotus Manual and worksheet formula show two periods; 1-2-3 will add the second period for you. Finally, to demonstrate another way of typing this formula, type @SUM(in Cell B8 and move the pointer to B7, type a period , then move the pointer to B5 and type a right parenthesis , and then press RETURN . Typing the period at B7 "anchored" that end of the range, and moving the pointer specified the remainder of the range to be summed.

Formatting the Balance Sheet

Your 1985 balance sheet should now be complete, but it is not very pretty--we need to fix it up, or <u>format</u> it better. Note that formatting in this sense is quite different from formatting a diskette. Formatting a diskette refers to setting up a mechanism to organize the way files are stored on the diskette, while formatting a worksheet refers to specifying the way cells' contents are displayed in the worksheet and, later on, printed out on paper.

First, we will format all of the cells in the worksheet so that they have two decimal places, and we shall add dollar signs to certain cells. Formatting changes which affect the entire worksheet are done using the Worksheet Global Format command series, while those affecting only a portion of the worksheet are executed by the Range Format command.

First, we will add decimal places. Since all numbers in the entire worksheet will be affected by this format change, we type /WGF to access the Command Worksheet Global Format submenu. From this submenu, select Fixed by pressing the RETURN key or typing F, and then specify the number of decimal places each cell should display. The prompt tells us to enter from 0 to 15 as the number of decimal places, and 1-2-3 suggests two places by having the cursor blinking at the "default decimal places," 2. Since this is the number of decimal places you want, press RETURN. As soon as you do so, the worksheet will change to conform to your specifications. If you had wanted three decimal places, you would have typed 3 and then pressed RETURN. (This option allows the user to set a fixed number of decimal places to be displayed; if this option had not been used, then cells would be displayed with as many significant decimals places as will fit in the column, which can sometimes look very strange.)

Formatting changes only the way cell contents are displayed on the screen, not the way they are stored. Regardless of the formatting, all values are stored in the computer to 15 decimal places. Also, if the true value were 15.626 and you specified a two-decimal-place format, the number would appear as 15.63; that is, 1-2-3 rounds to the nearest number: 15.624 would be rounded to 15.62, but 15.625 would appear as 15.63.

Now notice that the date 1985 has decimal places. Since we don't want that, put the pointer on Cell B1 and then type /RFF0 RETURN to format this cell as an integer (be sure to use "zero" rather than "oh" for the 0). Then press the RETURN key again in response to the prompt "Enter range to format". Recall that a range is either a single cell or a rectangular block of cells, which is defined by naming two diagonally opposite cells. Therefore, our series of commands gets rid of the decimal point in Cell B1 but lets decimal points remain elsewhere. This example points out that you can override the Global command within a specified range using the Range Format command. It does not matter if the Range command is entered before or after a Global command. Once entered, the format specified by a Range Format command can be changed only with another Range command, because <u>Range commands override Global commands</u>.

The Format submenu contains several other options, permitting you to express entries in dollars and cents, as percentages, with commas, or in exponential notation. We want to add dollar signs to the first item in each category, and to our totals and subtotals. To add dollar signs, first go to Cell B2 and then type /RF to access the Range Format submenu. Then, type a C to select Currency, which adds dollar signs and commas to the cell. You will be asked to specify the number of decimal places; the default value, 2, is displayed, so agree by pressing the RETURN key. You will now be asked to specify the <u>range</u> to which this format applies. Since you want to format Cell B2 only, press RETURN .

When you hit the last RETURN, a set of asterisks appeared in Cell B2. What happened is that you have a 9-character-wide column; when you went to Currency format, you added a dollar sign, a comma, a period, and two extra zeros, for a total of 9 characters. 1-2-3 requires at least one space between columns of numbers, and it will not let you "overflow" a column. To solve the problem, we can use the Global Column-Width command and change all columns (except A, which was formatted separately with the range command) to 10-character width. Do that by typing /WGC10 RETURN . The asterisks will go away, and $1,000.00 will appear in B2.

Now you can use the same procedure to add dollar signs and commas to the other cells. Type this series of commands, moving sequentially to the proper cell, beginning with Cell B3, before executing each command:

```
/RF, RETURN B3 RETURN
/RFC RETURN B4.B5 RETURN
/RF, RETURN B6.B7 RETURN
/RFC RETURN B8 RETURN
```

This goes a long way toward cleaning up your balance sheet,
but we can do still better. First, though, look at Exhibit
2-3, which provides a summary of the Format options available under Release 2 and tells you what they do. These
options can be used with either the Global or Range
commands.

Inserting Rows and Columns

At this point, your balance sheet looks quite cramped. We
can add a title, and also some spaces and underlines, to
make the balance sheet easier to read. First, let's add a
title in Row 1. To do this, we need to insert two lines
above the information already contained in Row 1. Put the
pointer on Cell A1, and then type / to get the main command menu. "Insert" is a Worksheet command, so type WIR
for Worksheet Insert Row. Notice that 1-2-3 prompts you to
enter the current cell (A1..A1) as the range. You can
accept this by pressing the RETURN key. However, we want to
insert two rows, so press the down arrow once, which respec-
ifies the range to A1.A2. Then, press the RETURN key,
which instantaneously inserts two blank rows as Rows 1 and 2
and moves all the previous rows down two spaces. (Note that
you could have typed A1.A2 rather than move the pointer to
specify the range of inserted rows. Using this procedure,
the cursor can be at any cell in the worksheet, and the rows
you add will be inserted in the specified range.)
      Now type this label: West Corporation's Balance
Sheet, 1985 (LB2X1) in Cell A1. The title will be displayed in Columns A, B, and C; had there been an entry in
Cells B1 or C1, the title would have been truncated. The
(LB2X1) in the title is a file name; it is not necessary to
include it in the title, but we always do to help us identify our files. We will leave Row 2 blank to separate our
title from the balance sheet.

55

==

Exhibit 2-3
Format Options under Global and Range Commands

Fixed: Assigns a fixed number of decimal places (0-15) either
                to cells within a specified range or globally.

Scientific: Scientific notation; assigns a fixed number of decimal
                places times a power of 10.

Currency: Adds dollar signs and commas, gives a fixed number of
                decimal places, and puts negatives in parentheses.

, (comma):   Adds commas, gives a fixed number of decimal places,
                and puts negatives in parentheses.

General: No fixed number of decimal places; suppresses trailing
                zeros; uses scientific notation for very small or very
                large numbers.

+/- (.) :   Symbol output; "+" for positive, "-" for negative, and
                "." for zero. -7 would appear as 7 minus signs, while
                +3 would appear as 3 plus signs.

Percent: Assigns a fixed number of decimal places followed by a
                percent sign.

Date: Dates are shown in regular format but utilized as
                "serial numbers" within 1-2-3 for calculations between
                dates.

Text: Inputs are shown as entered, that is, as formulas or
                numbers.

Hidden: The contents of the specific range do not appear on the
                screen, although they are retained in the computer's
                memory. To unhide after hiding using Global Format,
                type /WGFF RETURN or some other non-hidden format.

Reset: Found only on Range Format menu, not on Global. Re-
                stores the specified range to the default format. Used
                to redisplay a hidden range.

==

Now move to A4 and type /WIR RETURN . That set of
entries inserts a blank row at the current cell, A4, to
separate the date from the assets. Notice (1) that the
entire balance sheet, beginning with the row on which the
pointer was located, has moved down 3 rows in total and (2)
that the new row was inserted into the range that was recom-
mended in the prompt and that you accepted by pressing
RETURN.

Now move the highlighter to Cell B7 and notice that the
formula shown in the control panel has been changed from the
+B2+B3 that you typed in earlier to +B5+B6; thus, Total
assets is still the sum of Current assets and Fixed assets.
Whenever a row or column is added or deleted, most formulas
in the worksheet are automatically changed to maintain the
relationships which existed prior to the change. The principal exception involves the summation function, @SUM, as we
explain later in the chapter.

The procedure for inserting a column is similar to that
for inserting a row. We don't want you to do it now, but
you could type /WIC and then specify the range in which the
column or columns are to be inserted. For example, /WIC
C1.D1 RETURN would insert two columns after Column B, and
the old Column C would become the new Column E. Rows and
columns are deleted in the same manner, except that the
worksheet command Delete is chosen instead of Insert. Be
very careful when deleting rows and columns--when you delete
information from the worksheet, it is gone forever.

Now let's go on with cleaning up the balance sheet. Go
to Cell B7 and type /WIR RETURN , then type a backslash
(\ ) followed by a hyphen (the lowercase symbol on the
top row of keys, just to the right of 0), and then press the
RETURN key. As we saw earlier, that command causes a label
consisting of dashes to fill the cell; we use it in 1-2-3 as
an underline.

Now move down to B9 and add two rows by typing /WIR↓
RETURN . We have now separated the assets from the liabilities. We can add a double underline by typing the backslash and equal signs: \= RETURN .

Go to B14 and type /WIR RETURN followed by \-
RETURN in Cell B14; then go to B16 and type \= RETURN .
You should now have a nicely formatted balance sheet for
1985.

Saving and Retrieving Files

Saving the Worksheet

You have done a lot of work which you should keep, so it would be advisable to save your worksheet now. Make sure your storage diskette is in Drive B on the PC or the floppy drive on the XT. If this is the first time your storage diskette has been used, you will need to prepare, or <u>format</u> it using the <u>disk operating system</u>, or DOS, program before you can store information on the diskette. If you have never formatted a diskette, then you might want to read the relevant section of Appendix A at this point; it is only two pages. If you do have prior experience formatting, then charge ahead! <u>WARNING: Never format the 1-2-3 System disk (or a previously formatted diskette if it has information you want to keep) since formatting will erase any information which was stored on the diskette</u>. To format your blank storage diskette, make sure it is in Drive B, then type /S . This will put you in DOS. Then type format b:RETURN . You will receive a message to place the new diskette to be formatted in Drive B and then to press the RETURN key when ready. After a few seconds, you will be told that your diskette has been formatted, and you will be asked if you want to format another diskette, type N for no, press the RETURN key, then type EXIT to return to 1-2-3.

Now you are ready to save your worksheet, so type / and choose File from the command menu by typing an F (you are going to save your worksheet in a worksheet file on your diskette). From the File submenu, select Save by typing an S . To repeat the command thus far, you have typed /FS.

<u>File Names</u>. When you typed the S, this prompt appeared:

Enter save file name:

You must name your worksheet in order to save it. Your diskette is like a file cabinet, and files are like file

folders that are placed in file cabinets. Efficiency
demands that file folders be labeled before being placed in
file cabinets, and the same thing holds true for files saved
on diskettes. Therefore, you must name your file before
saving it.

File names must begin with a letter, can contain no
more than 8 characters, and can contain only numbers,
letters, and selected characters. (See Appendix A for permitted characters if your system is using DOS 3.1. If your
system uses DOS 2.1, you can use only numbers, letters, and
the underline character for a file name. Blanks are never
permitted in a file name.) For this example, we use as the
file name LB2X1, typed in lowercase letters; therefore, type
 lb2x1 RETURN . The red light on the disk drive will come on,
a whirling noise will sound, the lowercase letters will be
changed to caps, and your worksheet will then be on the
storage diskette. The name "LB2X1" stands for Lotus Book,
Chapter 2, Exhibit 1. This same convention will be used for
naming other models outlined in this book; thus, LB4X8 is
the file for Exhibit 8 in Chapter 4.

In summary, to save your worksheet on the storage
diskette, type /FSlb2x1 RETURN.

Exiting 1-2-3

At this point, you deserve a break. Before ending a 1-2-3
session, make sure you have saved all of your work on a
storage diskette as described above. While you are working
on a spreadsheet, the information is being stored in the
main memory. When the computer is turned off, all the
information in the main memory will be lost forever unless
it was previously saved on a storage diskette.

You can exit 1-2-3 in three ways:

1. If you are completely finished, just turn off the
    computer (after saving your worksheet).

2. If you want to use the computer but not 1-2-3, exit
    from 1-2-3 by typing a slash (/), then Q for Quit,
    and then Y in response to "Do you wish to end the
    1-2-3 session?" You will then be returned to the
    Access System menu. To exit the Access System, type
     E for "Exit." The prompt A> (or C> if you are using

an XT or AT) will appear on the screen, indicating that the computer has returned to the disk operating system. Remove the diskettes from their drives and put them in their folders, and you will be finished with the 1-2-3 lesson.

3. If you want to use the DOS system--for example, to format a storage diskette and then return to 1-2-3, type /S , which takes you to DOS. You can return to 1-2-3 by typing EXIT at the DOS prompt.

Retrieving the Worksheet

Once you have created and saved a worksheet on your storage diskette, you can recall the worksheet to make changes to it if needed, to use it in forecasting, for "what-if" (or sensitivity) analysis, to print it, or to make graphs of your results. If your computer is not on, turn it on and access the Lotus 1-2-3 spreadsheet program according to the procedures discussed earlier. Get a blank worksheet on the screen with the mode indicator at READY, and put your storage diskette in Drive B.

Now, to retrieve your file, type /FR for File Retrieve. A listing of all 1-2-3 worksheet files saved on your storage diskette will appear on the third line of the control panel, while the second line (1) prompts you to enter the name of the file to retrieve and (2) lists the name of the current file directory. 1-2-3 suggests the name of the first file in the list by highlighting it. At this point you probably have only one file, LB2X1, but later on you will have several. If you do have only LB2X1 on file, then accept 1-2-3's suggestion as to which file to retrieve by simply pressing the RETURN key. To select a different file if more were on your diskette, you could either type in the file name or move the highlighter to the file name and press the RETURN key. If you have more files on the diskette than the five that can be shown in the control panel, pressing the right arrow will cause new files to appear at the right and old ones to slide out of view to the left. When all file names have been displayed, the first one will reappear. Alternatively, pressing the down arrow will, if you have more than five files on the disk, display a second row of file names in the control panel.

Printing

Printing the Balance Sheet

At this point, assuming your computer has a printer, you
should print a copy of your balance sheet. If you do not
have a printer, read this section anyway, as we will explain
later how to set things up on your storage diskette so you
can print your output on another computer attached to a
printer.

With LB2X1 retrieved and on the screen, press the Home
key to move the pointer to A1. Notice that you have information as far to the right as Column C and down to Row 16.
Thus, you will want to print everything in the range A1.C16.
(Nothing has been typed into Column C, but your label in A1
extended over to Column C.) Now type / and select Print
on the main command menu list by typing the letter P or by
moving the pointer over Print and pressing the RETURN key.
Press P again to choose Printer, since you want the desti-
nation to be the printer and not a storage file on a diskette. On the Printer menu, select Range from the menu
listing by typing R . A print range is defined by typing
the cell address of the upper-left-most cell and the lower-
right-most cell of the matrix to be printed. For the range,
you know you want to print the matrix that starts with A1
and goes to C16. Therefore, in response to the prompt
"Enter print range:", type A1.C16 RETURN .

At this point, be sure that your printer is turned on,
has paper, and is on-line. If you do not have a printer,
type Q to quit the Print command and then save your file;
your print range (and any options specified) will be saved,
so you may later print your file without re-entering the
print range and options. If you do have a printer, type A
for Align so that the top of the worksheet will be printed
at the top of the printer's page. Next, press G for Go to
send the worksheet to the printer. The worksheet will be
typed as it appeared on the screen; see Exhibit 2-4 for an
example. When the worksheet has been printed, type Q for
Quit to leave the Print command and return to READY mode.

At this point, you may be ready to take another break.
If so, after making sure you saved your worksheet on the

storage diskette, type / and select Quit from the command
menu by typing Q . Then type Y for Yes to confirm your
choice. Note that when you save your file, the print range
and options are also saved. (Note that when you saved your
worksheet again, now with the print specifications, you were
asked if you wanted to cancel your command or replace the
worksheet. In this case you would press R for Replace.)
The next time you access this file, you may print by typing
/PPAGQ .

===

Exhibit 2-4

West Corporation's Balance Sheet, 1985   (LB2X1)

                                                    1985

Current assets $1,000.00
Fixed assets   1,000.00

Total assets $2,000.00
                                    =============

Current liabilities $500.00
Long term debt   500.00
Common equity   1,000.00

Total liabilities and capital $2,000.00
                                    =============

===

Printing to a File

In the preceding section we used the command /PP, which told
1-2-3 we wanted to transmit to a printer. We could have
used /PF, which would have caused the worksheet to be
printed to a "print file." You would use the Print File
command if you wanted to insert your worksheet into a report
that was being written in a word processing language such as
WordStar. You would print to a file on the storage

diskette, then (separately) read this file into your word processing file for insertion into your report. (Note that if you did print to a file, the file is not a Lotus file and its file name would not be displayed on a Lotus File Retrieve command. However, the filename would be displayed in DOS under a directory listing command.) In this book, we will never use the Print File command (although we did use it when we were writing the book).

Copy Command: Forecasting

If you quit at the end of the last section, you will need to retrieve your file. After turning on the computer and accessing the 1-2-3 worksheet, type /FR and, if LB2X1 is the only file in the directory on Row 3 of the control panel and hence is highlighted, press RETURN to put the balance sheet back on the worksheet. (If you had several files on your diskette, they would appear on Line 3. You would move the pointer to LB2X1, then press RETURN . Also, if you have somehow lost your saved worksheet, you can insert our diskette and type in /FR LB2X1 RETURN . Then remove our diskette, insert yours, type /FS RETURN to save the spreadsheet on your diskette, and proceed.)

Thus far, 1-2-3 has served only as an intelligent, correcting typewriter--we typed in some information and got the computer to do some simple addition, but it would have been easier to type up the balance sheet with a plain type-writer. In this section, though, we will start to see the real power of 1-2-3. Let's assume that West's sales have been growing at a rate of 10 percent per year and that we expect this growth rate to continue in the future. Now we want to forecast balance sheets for 1986 through 1995. Our forecast, printed to show only 1985, 1986, 1987, and 1995, is given in Exhibit 2-5. The procedure for developing it is given below.

First, let's put in the years. Move the pointer to Cell C3 and type +B3+1 RETURN . At this point, 1986--but formatted incorrectly--appears in C3. We'll correct the format in a minute, but first let's fill in the remainder of the years, using 1-2-3's Copy command. To use this command, start with the pointer on C3 and type the following:

/C	This tells 1-2-3 that you want to copy something. The prompt in the control panel suggests that you copy from C3.
RETURN	You do want to copy the formula in C3, so press the RETURN key.
D3.L3	You want to put the formula in C3 into cells D3 through L3--those are the 10 cells that will represent 1986 to 1995. You can either type in D3.L3 or use 1-2-3's "pointing system." Notice that when you pressed RETURN in the step above, the mode indicator switched to "Point." You now could use the right arrow to move to D3, the first cell you want to copy into, type a period (.) to "anchor" the pointer, and then continue using the right arrow (or Big Right, Ctrl -->), to move the pointer out to L3. At this point, the control panel will show the "To:" range to be D3.L3, and it will be highlighted.
RETURN	Now press RETURN, and the formula +B3+1 will be copied into the range C3.L3. However, as the copying process proceeds, 1-2-3 automatically changes the B to a C, then a D, and so forth, as it moves across the worksheet. Thus, the formula in D3 is +C3+1, the formula in E3 is +D3+1, and so forth. Put the pointer on various cells in Row 3 to confirm this. Since numeric values for formulas appear in the cells themselves, in C3 we have +B3+1 = 1985+1 = 1986, and so on, for the other cells.

Now put the pointer back on Cell C3, and then type

/RFF0 RETURN C3.L3 RETURN

This puts the years in the proper format. Use "Big Right," which means press Ctrl and, simultaneously, the right arrow (or the Tab key located to the left of Q), to see that you do indeed have years for 1985-1995. Use Big Left to get back to the left screen.

==

Exhibit 2-5

West Corporation's Balance Sheet, 1985-1995   (LB2X5)

	1985	1986	1987	1995
Current assets	$1,000.00	$1,100.00	$1,210.00	$2,593.74
Fixed assets	1,000.00	1,100.00	1,210.00	2,593.74
Total assets	$2,000.00	$2,200.00	$2,420.00	$5,187.48
Current liabilities	$500.00	$550.00	$605.00	$1,296.87
Long term debt	500.00	550.00	605.00	1,296.87
Common equity	1,000.00	1,100.00	1,210.00	2,593.74
Total liabilities and capital	$2,000.00	$2,200.00	$2,420.00	$5,187.48

==

Now let's make a forecasted balance sheet for 1986, with each item growing by 10 percent. Go to cell C5, for the first forecasted year, and type as follows:

+B5*1.1 RETURN   This formula increases the value in B5 by 10 percent.

/C RETURN   With the pointer still on C5, this command tells 1-2-3 that you want to copy the formula in C5, and 1-2-3 gives you a prompt asking into what range to copy it.

C6.C15 RETURN   Type C6.C15, or use the pointer system, to tell 1-2-3 that you want to copy C5 into the range C6.C15. When you then press RETURN, this increases all the numbers by 10 percent. You get ERR messages in certain cells and 0.00 in C10.

Move the pointer to C7 and type   \- RETURN . This changes
the ERR to an underline. Do the same thing in C14, and then
type   \= RETURN   in C9 and C16. Finally, with the pointer
on C10, type   /RE RETURN   to erase the 0.00.
     Your balance sheet now looks correct; however, if you
put the highlighter on Cell C8 you will see the formula
+B8*1.1. Since C8 should be the total of C5 and C6, change
C8 by typing   +C5+C6 RETURN   with C8 highlighted. Then move
to C15 and type   @SUM(C11.C13) . Alternatively, you could
copy B8 into C8 and B15 into C15. If you do these two
copies, the format is also copied--the copy command also
copies the format in the copied cell.
     Now let's complete the forecasted balance sheets. Begin
with the pointer on Cell C5, and type as follows:

/C C5.C16 RETURN   This tells 1-2-3 you want to copy the
                         range C5-C16, and 1-2-3 gives you a
                         prompt asking what range you want to
                         copy to. You could, after the /C, have
                         pressed the down arrow 11 times, thus
                         using 1-2-3's pointing system to estab-
                         lish the "Copy From" range. Notice that
                         the first cell does not need to be an-
                         chored--this is done automatically in
                         Copy From.

D5.L16 RETURN   This tells 1-2-3 you want to copy the
                         1986 formulas into the columns for 1987
                         to 1995. When you press the RETURN key,
                         1-2-3 increases each item by 10 percent
                         per year to complete your forecasted
                         balance sheets. Use Big Right to see
                         that you do indeed now have 10 years of
                         forecasted balance sheets.

You could add commas by typing   /WGF, RETURN   and some
dollar signs by typing these statements:

                    /RFC RETURN C5.L5 RETURN
                    /RFC RETURN C8.L8 RETURN
                    /RFC RETURN C11.L11 RETURN
                    /RFC RETURN C15.L15 RETURN

Note: When you copy a cell or range of cells, the cells into which you copy will take the format of the cells from which you copy. Therefore, had you formatted Column C before copying it into the range D5.L16, it would have come out already formatted with commas and dollar signs in the proper places.

To complete the worksheet, change your title to read 1985-1995 and change the worksheet name to LB2X5 . It would also be a good idea to save your work, so at this point type /FS LB2X5 RETURN to save the completed worksheet. (Get into the habit of saving your work frequently, as any sort of power failure will cause RAM to be lost. As we were working on this section of the book, someone tripped over the power cord and caused the PC to lose power. If we had not just saved the file, we would have lost a good deal of work. Also, in Florida we get a lot of thunderstorms, so on cloudy days we save especially often.)

Printing Again

Now let's print out our new forecasted balance sheet. This presents us with a bit of a problem, because we have used 30 spaces for Column A and 10 x 11 = 110 spaces for Columns B through L, or 140 spaces in total, and most printers can generally handle only 76 characters. Let's print anyway, to see what happens. Type /PPRA1.L16 RETURN AG . If your printer was set up correctly, it should have printed out balance sheets for 1985-1988 on one sheet and those for 1989-1995 on a second sheet. Had you skipped the A in the commands above, the sets of balance sheets would not have been printed on separate pages.

If you are using a wide printer that can handle 140 spaces, you can go to the "Options" entry of the Print menu and then to "Margins" by typing /PPOM . By typing L you can set the left print margin; we generally use 4, which means we leave four blank spaces on the left. After entering 4 (or whatever you choose), type M to get back to Margins and then R for Right. With narrow paper, we would type 76 RETURN , which allows us to fit 72 characters on a line. With wide paper, we would type 138 RETURN , which sets the right margin 138 spaces from the left boundary and allows us to fit 134 characters on a line. In

er 4 we will tell you how to print in small type and
et more columns on a page.
         Once you have your printed output, type Q for Quit to
et back to READY mode.

Printing Borders. When a printout will not fit on one page,
it is often desirable to print the row labels (Column A) on
each page. This can be done using the Borders option of the
Print command. When you specify a border range, it is
printed first on each page, followed by as much of the print
range as will fit on the page. Therefore, the border range
should not be included in the Print range. In our example,
we want to specify Column A as a border and Columns B
through L as the print range, so type

             /PPRB1.L16 RETURN OBCA1.A16 RETURN QAG

Here O stands for the Print command Options, B stands for
Borders, C stands for Columns, A1.A16 is the range which
will be printed as a border, and Q stands for "Quit Print
command Options". If your printer uses narrow paper, it
should print the balance sheets for 1985-1988 on one sheet,
those for 1989-1992 on a second sheet, and those for 1993-
1995 on a third. The border will be printed on each sheet.
We will extend our discussion of printing later, and pages
99-110 of the 1-2-3 Manual provide a complete explanation of
all the Print options.

Sensitivity and Other Topics

Sensitivity Analysis: What-If?

You ought to be convinced at this point that Lotus 1-2-3 is
useful for forecasting, and you ought to be able to visualize other types of operations in financial management for
which the 1-2-3 commands can save you time, increase your
accuracy, and provide you with easy-to-read output. But to
really convince yourself of its power, suppose your boss

comes in and tells you that she made a mistake--the growth rate is projected to be 15 percent, not 10 percent. If you had done your forecast with a calculator and then typed it up, you would really be steamed--think of doing all that work over again! But with Lotus, it's as easy as 1-2-3.

Move the pointer to Cell C5. You will see in the control panel the formula +B5*1.1, which indicates a 10 percent growth rate. We want to change the growth rate to 15 percent. Therefore, press the function key F2 on the upper left part of the keyboard to go into EDIT mode. Type a 5 after 1.1, making the formula read +B5*1.15 on the second row (the "edit line") of the control panel, and then press the RETURN key. Repeat this process in the Cells C6, C11, C12, and C13. At this point, you will have a revised 1986 balance sheet, but you will still have to revise the 1987-1995 data. To make these revisions, use the Copy command by typing /C C5.C16 RETURN D5.L16 RETURN . WAIT will flash in the mode indicator, and then READY will reappear. Your forecasted balance sheets will be revised to reflect a 15 percent growth rate; Exhibit 2-6 shows the data for 1985-1987 and 1995.

===

Exhibit 2-6
Forecast with 15% Growth

West Corporation's Balance Sheet, 1985-1995   (LB2X6)

	1985	1986	1987	1995
Current assets	$1,000.00	$1,150.00	$1,322.50	$4,045.56
Fixed assets	1,000.00	1,150.00	1,322.50	4,045.56
Total assets	$2,000.00	$2,300.00	$2,645.00	$8,091.12
Current liabilities	$500.00	$575.00	$661.25	$2,022.78
Long term debt	500.00	575.00	661.25	2,022.78
Common equity	1,000.00	1,150.00	1,322.50	4,045.56
Total liabilities and capital	$2,000.00	$2,300.00	$2,645.00	$8,091.12

===

It is worth noting that to print Exhibit 2-6 and have displayed only 1985-1987 plus 1995, we used the Border option in a somewhat different way: We established the border as the range A1.D16, and we used as the print range only L1.L16, the column for 1995. The full Print command was:

                /PPR L1.L16 RETURN OBCA1.D16 RETURN QAG

This can also be done (in Release 2 only) using the Column Hide command. Type /WCH E1.K1 RETURN to hide Columns E through K. Then, Columns A through D and Column L will appear on the screen and can be printed using this command:

                /PPR A1.L16 RETURN AG

If you wanted to print just the data for 1985, 1990, and 1995, you would have to use the Column Hide command twice, first to hide Columns C through F and then to hide Columns H through K, leaving Columns A, B, G, and L on the screen. After printing, you would use the command /WCD(Range) to redisplay the columns you had hidden.

Specifying Growth Rates

The revisions in the preceding section were not too difficult to make, but if we needed to construct forecasted balance sheets at a number of growth rates--say, 0, 5, 10, 15, 20, and 25 percent--it would be a pain to have to do as much editing as we did. Fortunately, 1-2-3 offers an easier way, but you have to plan for it. To be specific, if you know (or think) that you will have to revise some particular value in your worksheet, such as the growth rate in our forecasted balance sheet, then you can set the growth rate up as a variable in your formulas. We will take you through the process:

70

1. Print and then save your existing worksheet, the one with the 15 percent growth forecast. The print is not essential, but the save is. Save it as LB2X6. (Make sure that you change the file name to LB2X6 before saving the worksheet.)

2. Now go to Cell A2, and insert a blank row by typing /WIR RETURN . With the highlighter in the new Cell A2, type "Growth = RETURN to get a right-aligned label. (Be sure to type the quotation sign; remember, it is the label prefix for "right-align.")

3. Move to Cell B2, and type .05 to specify a new growth rate. We will change this later on.

4. Now go to Cell C6, and put the worksheet in EDIT mode by pressing the F2 key. Backspace to delete the 1.15, and then type in (1+B2) RETURN to make the formula in Cell C6 read +B6*(1+B2). Pressing the RETURN key will cause $1,050.00 to appear in Cell C6; this is the same value that you would have obtained using the formula +B6*1.05.

5. Replace the 1.15's in Cells C7, C12, C13, and C14 with (1+B2). This revises the 1986 forecast to reflect a 5 percent growth rate.

6. Now type /C C6.C17 RETURN D6.L17 RETURN to copy the above changes into the columns for 1987 through 1995.

7. This should have revised the worksheets for Years 1987-1995 to reflect the 5 percent growth rate, but it did not; let's see what went wrong.

    a. Put the pointer on C6. The formula in the control panel tells us that C6 = B6*(1+B2). Since B6 = $1,000 and B2 = 0.05, C6 is equal to $1,050. Now move the pointer one space to the right, to D6. The formula now includes C2. This cell is blank; hence, it is assigned a value of zero, yet C2 represents the growth rate in our formula when the pointer is moved to D6. So no growth is reflected in the years beyond 1986.

Actually, we want the value for B2, or .05, to remain constant and to be used in our calculations in the remaining years. With the 1-2-3 program, values may be held constant, or treated as <u>absolutes</u>, by placing the symbol $ in front of the cell address that we want to keep constant.

b. We can correct our problem by going back to Cell C6, going into EDIT mode by pressing function key F2 , using the left arrow to place the cursor on the B in B2, and then typing a $ sign. Now press RETURN , and the formula will read +B6*(1+$B2). The dollar sign in front of the B tells 1-2-3 to keep the absolute value of B if the formula in Cell C6 is copied into some other cell. Otherwise, the B would be changed to C, D, and so forth, and this would result in zero growth rates for years beyond 1986. There are instances where we want to maintain <u>relative</u> as opposed to <u>absolute</u> cell positions when we copy, but in this case (and many others), we need to copy the absolute value of Cell B2 into the formulas for all the columns. We will discuss relative and absolute copying in more detail in Chapter 3.

c. Add a dollar sign in front of B2 in the formulas for Cells C7, C12, C13, and C14.

d. Now type the Copy command /CC6.C17 RETURN D6.L17 RETURN . The worksheet recalculates, and this time everything grows at a 5 percent rate, as in Exhibit 2-7.

e. You now have an extremely powerful forecasting model--by changing just one value, the growth rate in Cell B2, you can obtain 10 years of forecasted balance sheets. Try it--put the pointer on B2 and type .1 RETURN . Almost instantly you will have forecasted the balance sheets at a 10 percent growth rate. Save this worksheet as LB2X7.

```
===============================================================

                        Exhibit 2-7


West Corporation's Balance Sheet, 1985-1995    (LB2X7)
                   Growth =      0.10

                                 1985     1986      1987     1995

Current assets              $1,000.00 $1,100.00 $1,210.00 $2,593.74
Fixed assets                 1,000.00  1,100.00  1,210.00  2,593.74
                            --------------------------------------
Total assets                $2,000.00 $2,200.00 $2,420.00 $5,187.48
                            ======================================

Current liabilities           $500.00   $550.00   $605.00 $1,296.87
Long term debt                 500.00    550.00    605.00  1,296.87
Common equity                1,000.00  1,100.00  1,210.00  2,593.74
                            --------------------------------------
Total liabilities and capital $2,000.00 $2,200.00 $2,420.00 $5,187.48
                            ======================================


===============================================================
```

    We could at this point go on to make other modifications to our forecasted balance sheet. For example, we could let growth rates vary from year to year by putting a growth rate for each year at the top of the column and building those rates into the formulas. If we did so, and we wanted to modify the model--for example, to increase the growth rate in each year by 5 percent--we would have to change each growth rate individually. As each change was made, 1-2-3 would automatically recalculate the entire worksheet. In a small spreadsheet, such as West Corporation's balance sheets, 1-2-3 would take only a few seconds to recalculate the spreadsheet. However, if the worksheet were large it would take longer, and it would be unnecessarily time consuming to wait for the worksheet to be updated after each change.

    1-2-3 allows you to stop the automatic recalculation process by issuing the command /Worksheet Global Recalculation Manual, that is,/WGRM RETURN. You can make all your changes and then tell 1-2-3 to recalculate the balance sheet by pressing the F9 key, which is the <u>Calc</u> function key. If you do set up a worksheet for manual calculations and then change a data item like the growth rate, the word CALC will appear at the bottom of the screen, but the effect of the growth rate change will not be reflected in your worksheet until you press the F9 key. To go back to automatic recalculation, press /WGRA RETURN.

　　　　We could also use different growth rates for different asset and liability items. However, by doing this our balance sheet might not balance, so we might have to add a "surplus or deficit of capital" item. You actually have all the tools necessary for making such extensions yourself at this time, but efficiency will be better served if we proceed more systematically. We will look at a few other commonly used operations in this chapter, then take another break.

Titles

Retrieve your forecasted balance sheet for 1985-1995, LB2X7, by typing /FRLB2X7 RETURN . Press the Home key to get to A1. Now press the right arrow repeatedly. As you advance to years beyond 1988, you will no longer be able to see the balance sheet labels in Column A. If you are actually working in such a position, this can be confusing. 1-2-3 helps you overcome that problem by fixing the labels, or titles.

　　　　To see how the Titles command works, put the pointer on Cell B5. Now type / to bring up the Main Command Menu, and a W to bring up the Worksheet submenu. The sixth entry is "Titles"; press T to bring it up. On Line 2 of the control panel, these words appear: Both Horizontal Vertical Clear

Both. With the cell highlighter on B5 and the control panel highlighter on "Both", pressing RETURN will cause both the rows above the pointer and the columns to the left of it to be frozen on the screen, so Rows 1-4 and Column A will be frozen. Press RETURN . The mode indicator will return to READY. Now press the right-arrow key. As the columns shift out toward 1995, the vertical axis labels remain in view-- you can tell what the numbers in the 1989-1995 columns mean, whereas you could not before you invoked the Titles command.

Now press the down arrow 16 times (from Row 5). That will move you to Row 21, but only 20 rows can be displayed on the screen; therefore, a row will drop off to make room for Row 21. Ordinarily, Row 1 would move up out of view, but since we froze Rows 1-4, Row 5 is dropped. As you continue to press the down arrow, Row 6 will disappear to make room for Row 22, and so forth.

Now press the Home key. The pointer will go to Cell B5--it will not go to A1 because the titles are frozen. When the Titles command is used, the frozen portion of the worksheet becomes part of the boundary area, and the high-lighter cannot be moved there.

Note that if you had issued the command /WTB with the pointer on Cell C3, Rows 1 and 2 and Columns A and B would have been frozen. Also note that you cannot issue this command with the pointer on Row 1 or in Column A.

Clear Titles. With the cell pointer at any location, but with the mode indicator at READY, press /WT to bring up the Titles submenu. Now press C , and the Titles will no longer be frozen. Press Home and then the right-arrow key to see that you are back to the unfrozen titles position.

Horizontal/Vertical. Put the cell pointer back on B5. Press /WT to bring up the Titles submenu once more. You could freeze the rows above the cell pointer--that is, freeze Rows 1-4--by pressing H for Horizontal or the columns to the left of the pointer--that is, freeze Column A--by pressing the V for Vertical. Immediately upon pressing H or V, either rows or columns are frozen, and the mode indicator goes to READY. Again /WTC clears (unfreezes) the titles.

We will have occasion to use the Titles command often when we get into more complex models later in the book. However, there will be instances in which we would like to move into the frozen area to make changes but cannot. In these cases, we can use the Windows command, discussed below.

Windows

If your forecasted balance sheet worksheet, LB2X7, is not on the screen, retrieve it. Press the Home key to go to A1, then move to B2. Now change the entry in B2 from 0.10 to 0.05 . You should be able to see immediately the effects of this change in the growth rate on the balance sheets for 1985-1988 because Columns A through E should be showing on the screen. But how did this change affect the 1995 balance sheet? We can find out by pressing the End and Home keys to move the highlighter to Cell L17. Alternatively, we can use the Windows command to divide the worksheet into two sections, one in which Column B will be displayed and one in which Column L will be displayed. The Windows command will divide the worksheet into two parts by splitting it either vertically or horizontally. This command is particularly useful in finance applications, in which we often want to change a variable in the first column of the spreadsheet (Column B) but are primarily interested in seeing how the change affects the final column.

To see how the Windows command works, move the high-lighter to Cell C5. Then type / to bring up the Main Command Menu, a W to bring up the Worksheet menu, and a second W to select Windows from the Worksheet menu. The Windows option allows you to select either vertical or horizontal windows and to scroll the windows in sync or not in sync (that is, cause rows or columns to move in one window but remain fixed in the other window as the arrow keys are pressed repeatedly).

Vertical Windows. With the highlighter on C5 and the Windows submenu displayed on the control panel, type V to cause the screen to be split vertically into two windows. Notice that a column of row numbers has been inserted to the right of the cell highlighter (between Columns B and C), the cell pointer has moved to Cell B5, and the mode indicator has returned to READY. This is shown in Exhibit 2-8. Do not do anything else to your screen yet.

Vertical windows allow you to view two different groups of columns at the same time. The set of columns that con-tains the cell pointer (now A and B) can be scrolled, but the other set of columns remains frozen. Try it by pressing the left and right arrow keys, and then press Home . You can move the pointer from one group (window) to the other by

76

pressing F6 , or the <u>window function key</u>. The pointer
should jump to C1. Now press the right-arrow key
repeatedly, stopping when only Column L appears in the right
window.

===

Exhibit 2-8

```
 B5:                                                        READY

        ┌───────────────A──────────────B──┐┌───C────────D────────E──┐
      1 │West Corporation's Balance Sheet, 1985-1││  995    (LB2X7)         │
      2 │               Growth =      0.05  ││2                        │
      3 │                                   ││3                        │
      4 │                             1985  ││4     1986     1987     1988  │
      5 │                          ┌──────┐ ││5                        │
      6 │Current assets           $1,000.00 ││6 $1,050.00 $1,102.50 $1,157.63│
      7 │Fixed assets              1,000.00 ││7  1,050.00  1,102.50  1,157.63│
      8 │                         ─────────── ││8 ──────────────────────────────│
      9 │Total assets             $2,000.00 ││9 $2,100.00 $2,205.00 $2,315.25│
     10 │                         ========== ││10 ============================== │
     11 │                                   ││11                       │
     12 │Current liabilities        $500.00 ││12  $525.00  $551.25  $578.81│
     13 │Long term debt             500.00  ││13   525.00   551.25   578.81│
     14 │Common equity             1,000.00 ││14  1,050.00  1,102.50  1,157.63│
     15 │                         ─────────── ││15 ──────────────────────────────│
     16 │Total liabilities and capital $2,000.00 ││16 $2,100.00 $2,205.00 $2,315.25│
     17 │                         ========== ││17 ============================== │
     18 │                                   ││18                       │
     19 │                                   ││19                       │
     20 │                                   ││20                       │
        └───────────────────────────────┘└─────────────────────────┘
```

===

     Now press the F6 key again to return to the left win-
dow, and move the pointer to B2, the growth rate indicator.
Type 0 RETURN in this window setup. You can see what

happens to the 1995 balance sheet and compare it to the 1985 balance sheet. Type .15 and a few more growth rates, and observe the changes. (If growth exceeds 0.17, an overflow occurs in Column L. You would have to press the F6 key to jump into the right window, then increase column widths, in order to read the balance sheet numbers.)

Clear Windows. Now, with the cell pointer at B2 and the mode indicator at READY, press /WW to bring up the Windows submenu. Press C , and the right window will disappear. The left window will expand to the right to fill the monitor screen, and the cursor will remain at B2. The windows will be gone.

Horizontal Windows. Horizontal windows are used when you have a long worksheet and want to view different rows in each window simultaneously. Again the highlighter is moved between windows by pressing the F6 key. You clear horizontal windows exactly like you do vertical windows--by pressing /WWC.

Sync/Unsync. When the worksheet is divided into vertical windows, you can view different columns in each window, but you will normally see the same rows in both windows. To see this, with no window on the screen, move the pointer to Column B and press /WWV to set up vertical windows. Then press the down arrow repeatedly. Once the rows start scrolling, rows in both windows normally move. (If on your machine they do not, we will explain why in a minute.) This result occurs because the movements of vertical windows are synchronized so that the same rows are seen in each window. Similarly, horizontal windows are normally synchronized so that the same columns but different rows are seen in each window.

However, there will be instances in which you would like the windows to be unsynchronized. For example, in a capital budgeting analysis, you might enter certain pieces of data, such as the cost of capital, in a section of the worksheet preceding the actual analysis. Suppose you wanted to change the cost of capital, which you had entered in Cell B6, and then to see the impact of this change on the project's NPV, which was calculated in Cell J42. You would

need to create <u>unsynchronized</u> vertical windows by typing
/WWV/WWU. If you typed the last command, /WWV, your worksheet should already have vertical windows. Now, to create
unsynchronized windows type /WWU . To resynchronize the
windows, type /WWS . Here U and S stand for the Window
commands Unsync and Sync. Note that the Clear command
clears the windows, but if your last window was in Sync,
your next window will also be in Sync, and vice versa.

Summary

We have covered a number of important 1-2-3 operations and
commands in this chapter. You should now know how to
create, edit, modify, save, retrieve, and print a
spreadsheet. Thus, you should be familiar with the basics
of 1-2-3, and you should be getting comfortable with spreadsheet operations. In the following chapters, we shall discuss other features of 1-2-3 and also develop a series of
spreadsheet models that can be used in various practical
applications. We will develop prototype, or "template"
models into which you can insert data for your own company
or companies and quickly do complex ratio analyses, capital
budgeting studies, and a wide variety of other things. As
we go through these chapters, you will see why it is
becoming virtually impossible for a firm--or a student in
the job market--to be competitive without a knowledge of
computer spreadsheets and how to use them.

Chapter 2
Summary of Commands

Command	Function	Page
Column width: /WCS(Size of column width) RETURN	Change width of a single column	49
Copying: /C(Range to be copied) RETURN (Range to be copied to) RETURN		65
Exiting 1-2-3: /S	Return to DOS and still be able to go back to Lotus Worksheet.	58
/QYE	Return to DOS.	59
Formatting a worksheet: /WGFF(# of decimal places) RETURN	Global command for fixed decimal	53
/RFC(# of decimal places) RETURN (Range) RETURN	Range command for currency (Note: A Range command overrides a Global command.)	54
Functions: @SUM(Range)	Sums a range of cells.	52
@NPV(Rate, Range)	Finds the net present value.	52
@SQRT(Argument)	Finds the square root.	52
@STD(Range)	Finds the standard deviation.	52
Insert/Delete: /WIR RETURN	Insert row	55
/WDC RETURN	Delete column	57
Manual recalculation: /WGRM RETURN	Change from automatic to manual recalculation	73

Command	Function	Page
Automatic recal- culation: /WGRA RETURN	Change from manual to automatic recalculation	74
Printing a file: /PPR(Range) RETURN AGQ		61
Printing a file with a column border: /PPR(Range Excluding Border Range) RETURN OB(Border range) RETURN QAGQ		68
Retrieving a file: /FR(Filename) RETURN	Note: If saving or retrieving from a file not in the default drive, precede the file name with the drive designator and a colon, e.g., b:LB2X1.	60
Saving a file: /FS(Filename) RETURN		58
Titles: /WTH /WTV /WTC	Set horizontal title Set vertical title Clear either vertical or hori- zontal titles	75 75 75
Underlining: \- RETURN \= RETURN	Single underline Double underline	57 57
Window: /WWV /WWH /WWC /WWS /WWU	Vertical window Horizontal window Window clear Synchronize windows Unsynchronize windows	76 78 78 79 79

Chapter 2 Exercises

2-1 (Creating spreadsheets) With a blank worksheet on the screen, enter the following data exactly as given in the indicated cells and then complete the requirements given below in the exact sequence specified.

A1 Capital Equipment, Ltd. (LB2EX1) A9 Taxable income
A2 Pro Forma Income Statements   A10 Taxes
A3 1985-1988   A11 Net income
A5 Sales Revenue   B4 1985
A6 Operating costs   B5 10000
A7 Operating income   B8 400
A8 Interest   C4 +B3+1

Requirements:

a. Convert the item in Cell A3 to a left-aligned label. Press the Edit key (F2) and Home to position the cursor at the beginning of the line and type the appropriate label prefix.

b. What happened to the label in Cell A5 when you entered 10000 in B5? Why is there no problem with the other labels? Can you anticipate future problems?

c. Increase the column-width for Column A to accommodate Operating income without overflowing into Column B.

d. Extend the row of years to 1988 using the Copy command. (Hint: In C4 put +B4+1 and then copy that formula.)

e. Format the worksheet globally to display commas and 2 decimal places using the Worksheet Global Format command.

f. Format the years as integers with no commas using the Range Format command and the right-arrow key. (Hint: /RFFO RETURN --> --> --> RETURN)

g. Increase the width of the other columns to 12 characters using the Worksheet Global Column-Width command.

h. In Column B, enter the proper formulas using cell addresses so that:

1. Operating Costs = Sales * 0.72

2. Operating Income = Sales - Operating Costs

3. Taxable Income = Operating Income - Interest

4. Taxes = Taxable Income * 0.46

5. Net Income = Taxable Income - Taxes (Answer: 1,296.00)

i. Clean up the worksheet by separating the 3-line title from the table with 2 blank rows, and the years from the data with 1 blank row. Now sales revenues should be on Row 8. Then format sales revenue and net income with a dollar sign and 2 decimal places.

j. Copy the five formulas in question h across their respective rows. Hint: Only two copy commands need to be issued. In the first, the From range is B9.B10 and the To range is C9.E10.

k. Project the following relationship for the years 1985-1988. Hints: In C8 type +B8*1.1 RETURN /C RETURN --> . --> RETURN . With the pointer on B11, type /C RETURN C11.E11 RETURN .

1. A 10% growth in sales per year, and

2. A 0% growth in interest

l.   Notice that the values in Row 14 have dollar signs but all those in Row 8 do not. Why? (Hint: Think what cells you copied from.) Now format Cells C8 to E8 so these cells have dollar signs.

m.   Underline data for Operating costs, Interest, and Taxes within the data of the worksheet. Insert the needed rows first. Use \- and then copy it. Then underline the Net Income results with a double line (=).

n.   Save the file under the name LB2EX1.

o.   Print the file, if you have access to a printer.

p.   Use /WEY to erase the worksheet, and then retrieve LB2EX1.

2-2   (Sensitivity analysis) Retrieve File LB2EX1. In Cell A4 type Growth = and in B4 type 0.1. Then do the following:

a.   Change the formula in C8 to +B8*(1+$B4).

b.   Copy the formula in C8 across to 1988.

c.   Your income statements should look exactly the same as they did before. Would they have remained the same if you had not included the $ in the formula +B8*(1+$B4)? Why, and what would have happened?

d.   Now put the pointer on B4 and substitute in these growth rates: 0, .05, .25, 1.0. End with .1.

e.   Now use /RFP RETURN RETURN to format B4, and then repeat question d. What happens if you enter the growth rate for ten percent as (1) .1, (2) 10%, and (3) 10?

2-3   (Windows) Retrieve the file LB2EX1, from Exercise 2-1, and extend the Pro Forma Income Statements to meet the following requirements.

Requirements:

a. Use the Vertical Window command to help with inputting. (Hint: Place the highlighter on Cell B1 and type /WWV. Then, press the F6 key to move the highlighter into the right half of the screen.)

b. Extend the rows out to 1990 using the Copy command. Notice that the formatting instructions entered in Exercise 2-1 have also been copied into the new cells.

c. Project the following relationships for the years 1989 and 1990:

   1. A 20% growth in sales per year.

   2. A 10% growth in interest per year.

d. Clear the Window option.

e. Save the file as LB2EX2.

f. Print the file, if you have a printer, utilizing the Border option so that Column A appears on each printed page. Remember, the print range should NOT include the border cells.

g. Print the spreadsheet so that only the data for 1985 and 1986 appear.

Chapter 3
DCF Analysis

Table of Contents

Relative and Absolute Values: An Example   88
    Rules for Copying   91
    Abs Function Key   92
    Special Copying Methods   93
    Label Prefixes the Easy Way   95
Using the Spreadsheet for DCF Analysis   96
    Future Value   96
    Present Value   100
    Future Value of an Annuity   101
    Present Value of an Annuity   102
More on DCF Analysis and Financial Functions   104
    NPV   104
    IRR   107
    Lotus versus Financial Calculators   109
    Other 1-2-3 Financial Functions   110
    @CTERM(k,FV,PV)   110
    @PMT(PV,k,TERM)   110
    @RATE(FV,PV,TERM)   111
    Amortization Schedules   111
    Non-Annual Compounding   116
    Continuous Compounding   116
Summary   117
Summary of Commands   118

- -

The preceding chapter covered many of 1-2-3's basic features. In this chapter we expand our discussion of 1-2-3's
features and show how 1-2-3 can be used for various types of
discounted cash flow (DCF) analyses. We begin with a more
detailed discussion of the use of relative and absolute
values when copying formulas, and then we show how one can
create present and future value interest tables.

Relative and Absolute Values: An Example

Recall that in our growth example in Chapter 2, we put a $ sign in front of the B in the equation +B6*(1+$B2) because we wanted to keep the growth rate designated in B2 constant as we moved across to the various columns. We did not need to put a $ sign in front of the row designator, 2, in that example because we were copying across the rows--for instance, from B6 into C6 into D6, and so on. However, if we had been copying down the column--say, from B6 into B7, B8, and so forth--and if we had wanted to keep the cell address we were copying constant, we would have had to make the row designator absolute by using B$2. If we had wanted to keep rows and columns constant, we would have used $B$2.

Let's do an example where the row designator must be kept constant. Get a blank worksheet on the screen by typing /WEY . Assume you plan to deposit $100 in a bank time deposit on January 1, 1986, and to leave it in the account, earning a 10 percent interest rate, through 1991. You want to know how much interest you will earn during each year, and you also want to know your total balance (old beginning amount plus accumulated interest) at the beginning of each year. Exhibit 3-1 presents the data, but let's see how to solve the problem with Lotus 1-2-3 and how absolute values are used in the process. Here are the steps:

1. Type the heading only as shown in Exhibit 3-1 in Cell A1.

2. Type Interest rate = in Cell A3.

3. Type .10 in Cell B3 and type /RFF RETURN RETURN to format this cell to 2 decimal places.

4. Type /WGC15 RETURN to make the columns 15 characters wide.

5. Type labels in Columns A, B, and C, in Rows 5, 6, and 7, as shown in Exhibit 3-1. Type /RLR A5.C7 RETURN to make the labels right-aligned. In this command, the first R stands for Range, L for Label, and the second R

for right-align. The Range Label command is used to align a range of labels without having to type a label-prefix in front of each one. We will discuss this command later in the chapter.

6. Put the cell pointer on A9, and type 1986 .

7. Move the pointer to A10, and type +A9+1 to get 1987.

8. With the pointer on A10, type /C RETURN A11.A14 RETURN to complete the years. At this point, your screen should look like Exhibit 3-1 except for the dollar amounts.

9. Go to Cell B9 and type 100 .

10. With the pointer still on B9, type /RFF RETURN B9.C14 RETURN . This will format the range; see that the 100 now reads 100.00.

==

Exhibit 3-1

SAVINGS ACCOUNT 1986-1991   (LB3X1)

Interest rate =   0.10

	Beginning Amount in Bank	Interest Earned
Year		
1986	$100.00	$10.00
1987	110.00	11.00
1988	121.00	12.10
1989	133.10	13.31
1990	146.41	14.64
1991	161.05	16.11

==

11. Now go to C9 and type +B9*B3 RETURN . The $10 of interest will appear as 10.00.

12. Go to B10, and type +B9+C9 RETURN to get $110, the deposit at the beginning of 1987.

13. With the pointer still on B10, type /C RETURN B11.B14 RETURN . $110 will appear in Cells B11 through B14. This is an intermediate step, and the numbers will change in a moment.

14. Go to Cell C9 and type /C RETURN C10.C14 RETURN . You expect to see some dollars of interest, but you get only zeros and ERRs.

15. Move the pointer to C10, and observe on the control panel that the formula is +B10*B4. The B10 part is correct, but B4 is a blank, which 1-2-3 reads as zero, so interest is zero. A similar situation holds in the other years.

16. Move back to C9. Press the F2 key to go into EDIT mode, move the cursor back to the 3, and type a $ sign so that the formula reads +B9*B$3. Press RETURN .

17. With the pointer still on C9, type /C RETURN C10.C14 RETURN . This will cause new, correct values to appear in Column C, and these will be used to produce correct values in Column B.

18. Complete your worksheet by typing /RFC RETURN B9.C9 RETURN . This will add $ signs to the 1986 amounts.

19. Go to Cell B3, and type .05 RETURN ; this will show how your position would change if the interest rate changed from 10 percent to 5 percent. Type in .15 , .20 , and some other interest rates to see how easy it is to calculate the effects of a change in interest rates. Similarly, go to Cell B9 and type in 500 RETURN to see the effect of a change in your initial deposit.

The point of this exercise was to demonstrate the use of relative and absolute designators when employing the Copy command. We copied the formula in Cell C9 down a column. That formula contained the term B3; as it was copied into lower and lower cells, the row numbers changed to B4, B5, B6, and so on to maintain a _relative_ position. However, we wanted an _absolute_ position--we wanted the formula value to remain constant at B3. We accomplished this by writing the term as B$3.

We could have written the term as $B$3, but that was not necessary because, when we copied, we went _down a column_, so the B part of the formula remained constant even without the $. Had we been copying _across a row_, as we were in the West Corporation example in Chapter 2, it would have been necessary to put the dollar sign before the B but not before the 3.

Rules for Copying

It would be nice to state some simple rule for the use of relative and absolute designators, but that is not possible. However, here is a not-too-complicated set of rules:

1. You need to worry about designators mainly when (1) you have some value like the interest rate in the bank account example or the growth rate in the West Corporation example which is used in a number of different years and (2) you use the Copy command. However, since this situation occurs _very often_, you will need to worry about designators frequently.

2. When copying _down a column_, you'll need to hold the _row designator_ constant. When copying _across a row_, the _column designator_ must be held constant.

3. It is tempting to just use the $ sign in front of both the row and the column, but that will not always work, because there will be times when you want one to be relative and the other absolute.

4. In the final analysis, the best thing to do is _think through the problem_ and then place the dollar signs where they logically belong.

91

Abs Function Key

We should note that in Lotus 1-2-3, the F4 function key is called the <u>Abs</u>, or <u>absolute</u>, <u>function key</u>. In long, complicated formulas, which you will encounter later in the book, the Abs function key can be useful. The Abs key works like this:

1. Go to the cell with the formula to be copied which needs an absolute designation--in our example, C9.

2. Press the F2 key to go into EDIT mode.

3. Move the cursor to the location just past the cell address in the formula; in our example, the cursor should be just beyond the 3 in +B9*B3.

4. As you repeatedly press the Abs function key, F4 , dollar signs will appear or disappear, cycling, before the B and the 3. With no $ present, the first press of F4 puts $ signs in front of both the B and the 3. The second press removes the $ in front of the B but leaves the one in front of the 3. The third press puts a $ before the B and removes the one before the 3. The fourth press deletes both $ signs. Try it, but be sure to end up with B$3.

5. Use the left arrow to move the cursor to the *, and press the F4 key. You will see that this affects the first cell designator in the formula. Be sure to end up with no $ signs in the B9 term.

6. Finish by saving this file as LB3X1. Since we will be using this file again, make sure the interest rate is .10 and the amount in Cell B9 is $100 before you save this file.

Relative and absolute copying may still be a little unclear to you. The best way to become familiar with them is to use them and to recognize that you must be careful because it is easy to make a mistake. You will get some practice later in the chapter, when we use relative and absolute copying to create interest factor tables for use in DCF analysis.

Special Copying Methods

<u>Converting a Formula to a Value</u>. Many times it is useful to determine a value using a formula and then convert the formula to its resulting numeric value so that the cell will not be recalculated when the worksheet is modified. For example, suppose that in conducting a what-if analysis we would like to change some variables in the model and keep a record of the results obtained under each scenario. In Releases 1 and 1A you can do this only by using the File Extract command (which we will discuss later) to extract the value and then using the File Combine command to put it back into the original file. Release 2, however, allows you to convert a formula to a value in one step using the Range Value command. We will illustrate this command using the interest rate spreadsheet that we created in the last section.

1. Retrieve the worksheet saved as LB3X1.

2. Enter the label Scenario Analysis in A18, the label '1. Int. rate = in A19, the label '2. Int. rate = in A20, the label '1991 balance = in C19, and the label '1991 balance = in C20.

3. Now put the pointer on B19 and enter +B3 , and then go to D19 and enter +B14 .

4. Now we want to change the interest rate in B3 and show the results on Row 20. Begin by going to B3 and entering .2 . That recalculates the worksheet, but it changed the values on Row 19, which you wanted to keep.

5. Now let's fix things. First, with .2 entered in Cell B3, put the pointer on B3 and type /RV RETURN , then move the pointer to B19 and press RETURN . You copied the value in B3 to B19, rather than entering +B3 in B19. Now put the pointer on B14, type /RV RETURN , move the pointer to D19, and press RETURN . This step

93

has enabled you to enter the 1991 balance, with a 20 percent interest rate, as a value rather than a formula, so D19 will not change if we modify the worksheet. We should also note that you could use the Range Value command to copy an entire range as a set of values, rather than just a single cell. We will use the /RV Copy command often in scenario analyses.

6.   Now move the pointer to B3, and change the interest rate back to .10 . The balance in B14 is again recalculated, but B19 and D19 do not change.

7.   With the pointer on B3, type /RV RETURN B20 RETURN . Then move the pointer to B14, type /RV RETURN D20 RETURN . This will save the interest rate for this scenario in B20 and the 1991 balance in D20.

===

Exhibit 3-2

SAVINGS ACCOUNT 1986-1991   (LB3X2)

Interest rate =   0.10

Year	Beginning Amount in Bank	Interest Earned
1986	$100.00	$10.00
1987	110.00	11.00
1988	121.00	12.10
1989	133.10	13.31
1990	146.41	14.64
1991	161.05	16.11

Scenario Analysis
1. Int. rate =   0.20 1991 balance =   248.83
2. Int. rate =   0.10 1991 balance =   161.05

===

You could have typed the interest rate and 1991 balance values into the scenario analysis cells each time you made a change to the worksheet, but by using the /RV command, you save time and also reduce the possibility of typing errors. Change the title to LB3X2 and save this worksheet as LB3X2.

Copying Labels. You can copy labels just as you would copy formulas using 1-2-3's Copy command. A label will be copied exactly as it was typed in the FROM range. This procedure can save you a lot of typing time if you use the same label often. However, if you have used a label in several locations in a worksheet and you then change the label, you will have to recopy the changed label into each cell where it was used. Therefore, it is often more efficient to reference labels using cell formulas than to copy them. For example, suppose you are planning to make a balance sheet, an income statement, and several other statements for West Corporation, and also for 10 other companies. You plan to use the statements for West, but with necessary changes, for the other companies. The companies' names will appear in Cells A1, A20, and A40. You can type the company name in A1, and then enter +A1 in both A20 and A40. Then, when you change the company name in A1, A20 and A40 will automatically change. We use cell referencing frequently in our later model chapters to avoid having to retype or copy labels that were used several times within one model.

Label Prefixes the Easy Way

Before we leave this section, we need to discuss one more command which was introduced earlier in the chapter: /Range Label. Rather than assign a label prefix to each label as you type it, you can do the following, using the Range Label command:

1. Type in all the labels for a series of columns. By default, they will all be left-aligned.

2. You can then use a Range command to center or right-align all the labels within the range. Here are the keystrokes to center all labels in the range A3.F5:

/RLCA3.F5 RETURN

You must enter the labels and then center them; you cannot use the Range command, enter labels without prefixes, and expect them to be centered.

We used the Range label command to right align columns when we created savings account model, LB3X1. Retrieve File LB3X1 and highlight Cell B5. You will see that the label "Beginning" is right-aligned (and has a ") even though you typed it in without a label prefix. All of the column headings were right-aligned when you issued the command /RLRA5.C7 RETURN.

If you want all, or most, of your labels to be centered or right-aligned, you could, at the start of the 1-2-3 session, use a global command to adjust labels: /WGLC to center them and /WGLR to make them right-aligned. Again, the Range command will override this global command. Note that the Global Label command differs from the Range Label command. The Global Label command allows you to enter the command first then the labels, while with the Range Label command you must enter the labels first then the command.

Using the Spreadsheet for DCF Analysis

Future Value

Capital budgeting, bond and stock valuation, lease analysis, and many other aspects of finance employ discounted cash flow (DCF) techniques, which involve finding future and present values, and implied interest rates. Interest rates are applied to cash flows (CF), discounting to find the value of these cash flows today (present value, PV) or compounding to find their value in the future (future value, FV). When present values are found, the interest rate is called a discount rate; when future values are found, the interest rate is called a compounding rate.

A savings deposit can be used to illustrate compounding. A deposit of $100, earning a return of k = 0.12 = 12 percent per year for n = 10 years, will grow to a FV of $310.58 by the end of Year 10, as found by the future value formula:

$$FV = PV(1 + k)^n \qquad\qquad (3\text{-}1)$$

Since the caret (^) denotes an exponent in 1-2-3 language, and since a parenthesis is not enough to denote multiplication, the FV equation is written as follows:

$$PV*(1+k)\char`^n \qquad\qquad (3\text{-}1a)$$

Use the command /WEY to get a blank worksheet on your screen and then put 100 in Cell A1, 0.12 in B1, 10 in C1, and then, with the cell pointer on D1, enter this formula:

$$+A1*(1+B1)\char`^C1$$

The value 310.5848, the FV of 100 compounded for 10 years at 12 percent, now appears in Cell D1. Changing the values in Cells A1, B1, or C1 would result in a new value being calculated for the future value in D1.
    We can use the future value formula to create a future value interest factor (FVIF) table as shown in Exhibit 3-3. With a blank 1-2-3 worksheet on the screen, type the label FUTURE VALUE OF \$1 AT THE END OF N PERIODS (LB3X3) in Cell A1. Move the highlighter to A3 and enter the label PERIODS . Enter the value 0 (zero) in Cell A4; enter the formula +A4+1 in Cell A5; and copy the formula in A5 into Cells A6 through A14 using the command sequence /CA5 RETURN A6.A14 RETURN . This produces numbers in Column A which will serve both as labels and as the number of periods, n, in the future value equation, 3-1a.
    Now we need to input interest rates across Row 3. Again, these values will serve both as labels for the columns and as inputs for the future value equation. Move the highlighter to B3, enter the value .01 , enter the formula +B3+.01 in Cell C3, and copy C3 into Cells D3 through H3, using the command /C RETURN D3.H3 RETURN . Now type /RFP RETURN B3.H3 RETURN to format the Row 3 values as percentages. The interest rates 1.00% to 7.00% should be displayed

in Row 3. Thus, we will create an interest factor table for 10 periods (generally years) with interest rates ranging from 1 to 7 percent.

We now go to Cell B4, and we will enter the future value formula. Note that the interest rate for Column B, 1 percent, is stored as a percent in B3, and zero, the number of periods for Row 4, is in A4. Therefore, in a moment we will have you write the future value formula in B4 as (1+B3)^A4. We will shortly copy this formula into Cells B5 through B14 and then copy the range B4.B14 into the range C4.H14. However, we must be careful to copy the formula correctly.

==

Exhibit 3-3

FUTURE VALUE OF $1 AT THE END OF N PERIODS (LB3X3)

PERIODS	1.00%	2.00%	3.00%	4.00%	5.00%	6.00%	7.00%
0	1.0000	1.0000	1.0000	1.0000	1.0000	1.0000	1.0000
1	1.0100	1.0200	1.0300	1.0400	1.0500	1.0600	1.0700
2	1.0201	1.0404	1.0609	1.0816	1.1025	1.1236	1.1449
3	1.0303	1.0612	1.0927	1.1249	1.1576	1.1910	1.2250
4	1.0406	1.0824	1.1255	1.1699	1.2155	1.2625	1.3108
5	1.0510	1.1041	1.1593	1.2167	1.2763	1.3382	1.4026
6	1.0615	1.1262	1.1941	1.2653	1.3401	1.4185	1.5007
7	1.0721	1.1487	1.2299	1.3159	1.4071	1.5036	1.6058
8	1.0829	1.1717	1.2668	1.3686	1.4775	1.5938	1.7182
9	1.0937	1.1951	1.3048	1.4233	1.5513	1.6895	1.8385
10	1.1046	1.2190	1.3439	1.4802	1.6289	1.7908	1.9672

==

Type (1+B3)^A4 into Cell B4, and use the command /C RETURN B5.B14 RETURN to copy it into Cells B5 through B14. You will get a lot of error messages, so something is obviously wrong. Now move the highlighter to Cell B5. The formula (1+B4)^A5 is displayed in the control panel, but that is not what we wanted. The interest rate should remain constant as we move down Column B, that is, the formula should read (1+B3)^A5, not (1+B4)^A5. To keep the interest rate constant, we need to hold row number B3 constant, or at its absolute value, so we need to use a $ sign. Thus, the formula written into Cell B4 should read (1+B$3)^A4. To make this change, put the pointer on Cell B4, press the F2 function key to go into EDIT mode, use the left-arrow key to put the cursor under the caret (^), and then press the F4 function key (the Abs key) twice to cause the formula to read (1+B$3)^A4. (It is not necessary to use the Abs key; you could have put the cursor under the 3 and typed in a $ sign.) Now press RETURN , and then type /C RETURN B5.B14 RETURN . This gives you a correct set of interest factors in Column B.

Now we need to fill in the rest of the table. Our first thought is to copy the formulas in Column B into Columns C through H by typing /CB4.B14 RETURN C4.H14 RETURN . Do that, and then put the pointer on Cell C4. Notice that the formula reads (1+C$3)^B4, but it should read (1+C$3)^A4. As we copied Column B across Columns C to H, the column numbers changed so as to retain their <u>relative</u> positions, whereas we wanted the <u>absolute</u> value, A, so that A4 would be the exponent in formulas all across the row. Thus, the formula in Cell B4 should have read (1+B$3)^$A4; then, the A4 would have remained constant as we copied across the columns.

To correct the error, put the pointer on B4, press the F2 function key to go into EDIT mode, and then press the F4 function key three times to cause a $ sign to be placed before the A; then press RETURN . Now the equation in B4 should read (1+B$3)^$A4. Type /C RETURN B5.B14 RETURN followed by /CB4.B14 RETURN C4.H14 RETURN .

Your interest factor table is now complete, but to make it look better, format the worksheet to display all values with four decimal places using the command sequence /WGFF4 RETURN . Notice that the interest rates across Row 3 remain in percentage format--you specified them using the Range command, which takes precedence over the Global command. Notice also that the periods (years) in Column A now are displayed with four decimal places. However, they would look better with no decimal places, so format them using the Range command /RFF0 RETURN A4.A14 RETURN . Your future value interest factor table should now look like the one in Exhibit 3-3. Save this worksheet under the name LB3X3 by typing /FS LB3X3 RETURN .

Present Value

The present value of a cash flow to be received at the end
of a future time period is found using this formula:

$$PV = FV(1.0+k)^{-n} \qquad\qquad (3-2)$$

The exponent -n is equivalent to $1/n$, so the present value
interest factor, $PVIF = (1.0 + k)^{-n} = 1/(1.0 + k)^{n}$, is the
reciprocal of $FVIF = (1.0 + k)^{n}$.

We can create a PVIF table by following procedures
similar to those used to create the FVIF table developed
above. Retrieve the future value interest factor worksheet,
if it is not displayed on your monitor, by typing /FR LB3X3
RETURN . We will create the present value table simply by
changing the interest factor formula. First, move to Cell
A1, go into EDIT mode by pressing the F2 key, and change
the title to PRESENT VALUE OF $1 DUE AT THE END OF N
PERIODS (LB3X4) . Next, move the highlighter to Cell B4 and
enter the formula 1/(1+B$3)^$A4 . You can do this by
hitting F2 to go into EDIT mode, then hitting Home , and
then typing 1/ RETURN . Now copy this formula into Cells
B5 through B14, using the command series /C RETURN B5.B14
RETURN , and then copy Column B into Columns C through H,
using the command /CB4.B14 RETURN C4.H14 RETURN . The
interest factor table is immediately converted from future
values to present values. Finally, save the table as LB3X4.
This worksheet is shown in Exhibit 3-4.

100

```
=============================================================
```

Exhibit 3-4

PRESENT VALUE OF $1 DUE AT THE END OF N PERIODS (LB3X4)

PERIODS	1.00%	2.00%	3.00%	4.00%	5.00%	6.00%	7.00%
0	1.0000	1.0000	1.0000	1.0000	1.0000	1.0000	1.0000
1	0.9901	0.9804	0.9709	0.9615	0.9524	0.9434	0.9346
2	0.9803	0.9612	0.9426	0.9246	0.9070	0.8900	0.8734
3	0.9706	0.9423	0.9151	0.8890	0.8638	0.8396	0.8163
4	0.9610	0.9238	0.8885	0.8548	0.8227	0.7921	0.7629
5	0.9515	0.9057	0.8626	0.8219	0.7835	0.7473	0.7130
6	0.9420	0.8880	0.8375	0.7903	0.7462	0.7050	0.6663
7	0.9327	0.8706	0.8131	0.7599	0.7107	0.6651	0.6227
8	0.9235	0.8535	0.7894	0.7307	0.6768	0.6274	0.5820
9	0.9143	0.8368	0.7664	0.7026	0.6446	0.5919	0.5439
10	0.9053	0.8203	0.7441	0.6756	0.6139	0.5584	0.5083

```
=============================================================
```

Future Value of an Annuity

A constant cash flow of X dollars per period--for example, $100 per year for 5 years--is defined as an <u>annuity</u>. The <u>future value</u> of an annuity is the summation of the compounded payments. Future value interest factors for annuities ($FVIFA_{k,n}$) could be calculated on a 1-2-3 spreadsheet using this formula:

$$FVIFA_{k,n} = \sum_{t=1}^{n} (1 + k)^{n-t} = \frac{(1 + k)^n - 1}{k} = ((1 + k)\hat{\ }n - 1)/k \qquad (3-3)$$

However, 1-2-3 has a built-in function, @FV, which computes the future value of an annuity directly:

@FV(Payment, interest rate as a decimal, term)

You must enter the periodic payment, the interest rate, and the term (or number of periods) as parameters in the function. For example, to find the future value of a 5-year annuity of $1 per year if the interest rate is 7 percent, move to an empty cell on your worksheet--say, B16--and type @FV(1,.07,5) RETURN . The answer, 5.7507, appears. Alternatively, we could enter the parameters as cell addresses rather than values, such as @FV(B1,H3,A9), if you had previously stored the periodic payment in B1, the interest rate in H3, and the number of periods in A9. Use /RE to clear B16 before going on.

Again, we can create an interest factor table for annuities by simply changing the interest factor formula in our previous worksheets. Retrieve your FV table, which was saved as LB3X3. Change the label in A1 to FUTURE VALUE OF $1 PER PERIOD FOR N PERIODS (LB3X5) . Then go to B4 and enter the function @FV(1,B$3,$A4) in B4, and then copy it, first in B5.B14 and then in C4.H14. You should produce the table shown in Exhibit 3-5. Now save the table under the file name LB3X5.

Present Value of an Annuity

Lotus 1-2-3 also has a present value function, @PV, which computes the present value of an annuity; this function works just like the @FV function:

@PV(Payment, interest rate as a decimal, term)

To create an interest factor table for the present value of an annuity, retrieve your future value of an annuity worksheet, LB3X5; use the Edit key (F2) to change the word FUTURE to PRESENT and LB3X5 to LB3X6 in your Cell A1 label; then use the Edit key to change the F in Cell B4 to a P , producing @PV(1,B$3,$A4); and then copy this cell into the other cells. The result is the table shown in Exhibit 3-6. Save it as LB3X6.

==

Exhibit 3-5

FUTURE VALUE OF $1 PER PERIOD FOR N PERIODS (LB3X5)

PERIODS	1.00%	2.00%	3.00%	4.00%	5.00%	6.00%	7.00%
0	0.0000	0.0000	0.0000	0.0000	0.0000	0.0000	0.0000
1	1.0000	1.0000	1.0000	1.0000	1.0000	1.0000	1.0000
2	2.0100	2.0200	2.0300	2.0400	2.0500	2.0600	2.0700
3	3.0301	3.0604	3.0909	3.1216	3.1525	3.1836	3.2149
4	4.0604	4.1216	4.1836	4.2465	4.3101	4.3746	4.4399
5	5.1010	5.2040	5.3091	5.4163	5.5256	5.6371	5.7507
6	6.1520	6.3081	6.4684	6.6330	6.8019	6.9753	7.1533
7	7.2135	7.4343	7.6625	7.8983	8.1420	8.3938	8.6540
8	8.2857	8.5830	8.8923	9.2142	9.5491	9.8975	10.2598
9	9.3685	9.7546	10.1591	10.5828	11.0266	11.4913	11.9780
10	10.4622	10.9497	11.4639	12.0061	12.5779	13.1808	13.8164

==

==

Exhibit 3-6

PRESENT VALUE OF $1 PER PERIOD FOR N PERIODS (LB3X6)

PERIODS	1.00%	2.00%	3.00%	4.00%	5.00%	6.00%	7.00%
0	0.0000	0.0000	0.0000	0.0000	0.0000	0.0000	0.0000
1	0.9901	0.9804	0.9709	0.9615	0.9524	0.9434	0.9346
2	1.9704	1.9416	1.9135	1.8861	1.8594	1.8334	1.8080
3	2.9410	2.8839	2.8286	2.7751	2.7232	2.6730	2.6243
4	3.9020	3.8077	3.7171	3.6299	3.5460	3.4651	3.3872
5	4.8534	4.7135	4.5797	4.4518	4.3295	4.2124	4.1002
6	5.7955	5.6014	5.4172	5.2421	5.0757	4.9173	4.7665
7	6.7282	6.4720	6.2303	6.0021	5.7864	5.5824	5.3893
8	7.6517	7.3255	7.0197	6.7327	6.4632	6.2098	5.9713
9	8.5660	8.1622	7.7861	7.4353	7.1078	6.8017	6.5152
10	9.4713	8.9826	8.5302	8.1109	7.7217	7.3601	7.0236

==

More on DCF Analysis and Financial Functions

In the preceding section, we used 1-2-3 to create interest factor tables for annuities and single payments. However, many financial decisions involve uneven cash flow streams. For example, bonds generally promise an even stream of interest payments but then a large lump-sum maturity value; common stocks generally involve an increasing stream of dividends; and capital budgeting projects could involve either increasing or decreasing, or even positive or negative, cash flows in different years. Lotus 1-2-3 can help you analyze any of these uneven payment streams. In this section, we examine 1-2-3's built-in NPV and IRR function, along with several other functions.

NPV

The net present value (NPV) of a cash flow stream is found as the sum of the present values of the individual components of the stream. For example, suppose we need to find the net present value of an investment which costs $1,000 and pays $100 at the end of Year 1, $200 in Years 2 through 5, zero in Year 6, and $1,000 in Year 7, all discounted at a rate of 6 percent. Exhibit 3-7 shows our completed spreadsheet, generated using the following steps:

1. Get a blank worksheet on the screen by typing /WEY , then enter the following labels, values, and formulas.

2. A1:   Example of uneven cash flow analysis (LB3X7)

3. A3:   "Year

4. B3:   "Payment

5. C3:   ^X

6. D3:   "PVIF(k,n)

7. E3:   ^=

104

8. F3:   "PV of Payments

9. Now go to Cell D4, and enter   .06 .

10. Now go to A5, type   \- RETURN   to add an underline, and copy to B5.F5 by typing   /C RETURN B5.F5 RETURN .

11. Now go to A6, and enter   0 .

12. Now go to A7, enter   +A6+1 , and copy it to A8.A13.

13. Now enter these annual cash flows in Column B:

    B6:   -1000
    B7:   100
    B8:   200
    B9:   200
    B10:   200
    B11:   200
    B12:   0
    B13:   1000

14. Now enter this formula in D6:   (1/(1+$D$4))^A6 . Copy it to D7.D13.

15. Now enter this formula in F6:   +B6*D6 . Copy it to F7.F13.

16. Now go to F14, and type   \- RETURN   to produce an underline.

17. Now go to F15, and type   @SUM(F6.F13)   to find NPV, which is the sum of the PVs of the payments less the cost of the project.

18. Now go to E15, enter   "NPV=   to label the NPV; and then go to F16, and type   \= RETURN   to add a double underline.

```
================================================================
```

Exhibit 3-7

Example of uneven cash flow analysis (LB3X7)

Year	Payment	X	PVIF(k,n) 0.06	=	PV of Payments
0	($1,000)		1.0000		($1,000)
1	100		0.9434		94.34
2	200		0.8900		178.00
3	200		0.8396		167.92
4	200		0.7921		158.42
5	200		0.7473		149.45
6	0		0.7050		0.00
7	1,000		0.6651		665.06

```
                                      NPV=      $413.19
                                                ==========
                   NPV USING LOTUS FUNCTION =   $413.19
                                                ==========
```

```
================================================================
```

19. Now format as follows:

        /WCS11 RETURN (with pointer on Column F)
        /RFF4 RETURN D6.D13 RETURN
        /RFC0 RETURN B6 RETURN
        /RF,0 RETURN B7.B13 RETURN
        /RFC0 RETURN F6 RETURN
        /RF, RETURN F7.F13 RETURN
        /RFC RETURN F15 RETURN

     Cell F16 now shows the NPV of the cash flows. We could
also use a built-in Lotus 1-2-3 function to calculate the
NPV; here's how it is set up:

     @NPV(k, cash flow range for Years 1 to N) + CF_0

Here k is the cost of capital (or discount rate), and CF_0 is
the initial cash flow. <u>Note that the cash flow range specified within the parameters is for Years 1 to N, not 0 to N.</u>
This is different from the way most financial calculators
are programmed--if Lotus had been programmed like the

calculators, the NPV function's cash flow range would include CF_0. Here is the NPV setup for our problem, which you should enter in Cell F17:

$$@NPV(D4,B7.B13)+B6$$

Now format F17 by typing /RFC RETURN RETURN with the pointer on Cell F17. Next, enter "NPV USING LOTUS FUNCTION = in C17. Finally, with the pointer on F18, type \= RETURN to add a double underline. This completes Exhibit 3-7, so save the spreadsheet as LB3X7.

IRR

The <u>internal rate of return (IRR)</u> represents the rate of return you would earn if you invested $1,000 in our illustrative project and received the indicated cash flows. The IRR can be found using 1-2-3's IRR function, which is set up as follows:

$$@IRR(Guess\ as\ to\ actual\ IRR,\ cash\ flow\ range)$$

Thus, the @IRR function requires as parameters an initial guess as to the IRR value plus the range which contains both the initial cost (CF_0) and the periodic cash flows from the investment. For most real-life problems, 10 percent is a good guess. Lotus 1-2-3 determines the IRR through an iterative trial-and-error process, so the better your guess, the quicker 1-2-3 will find the IRR. If the result of this calculation is ERR, then 1-2-3 was unable to determine the IRR within 20 iterations. However, 1-2-3 will almost always be able to find the IRR if the initial guess is a value between 0 and 1.0, provided there are no multiple IRRs, as could result if negative cash flows occur during the project's life.

If you do not already have File LB3X7 on the computer screen, retrieve it now. In File LB3X7 the cash flow range is B6.B13, and we can use 0.10 as our guess for the IRR to illustrate the Lotus IRR function. Here is the complete IRR

function, which you should enter in Cell F19 of the model
LB3X7.

$$@IRR(.1,B6.B13)$$

The resulting answer shows that you would expect to make
0.139636, or 13.96 percent, on the investment. Enter
 "IRR= in Cell E19; format with /RFP RETURN F19 RETURN ;
and add a double underline in F20 by typing \= . Finally,
change the heading in Cell A1 to read LB3X8, save your
worksheet as LB3X8, and you will have finished with this
exercise. Your final worksheet should look like our Exhibit
3-8.

===

Exhibit 3-8

Example of uneven cash flow analysis (LB3X8)

Year	Payment	x	PVIF(k,n) 0.06	=	PV of payments
0	($1,000)		1.0000		($1,000.00)
1	100		0.9434		94.34
2	200		0.8900		178.00
3	200		0.8396		167.92
4	200		0.7921		158.42
5	200		0.7473		149.45
6	0		0.7050		0.00
7	1,000		0.6651		665.06

NPV = $413.19
============

NPV USING LOTUS FUNCTION = $413.19
============

IRR = 13.96%
============

===

108

Lotus versus Financial Calculators

NPVs are calculated often in financial management, and you are probably familiar with financial calculators. However, as noted above, calculators are programmed differently from the Lotus 1-2-3 NPV function, so it is worthwhile spending a little more time on NPV now to avoid confusion later. A "time line" of our project's cash flows follows, with worksheet cell addresses shown below each cash flow:

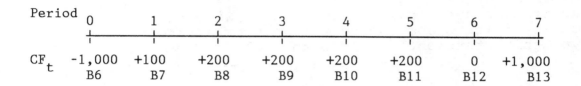

In Lotus 1-2-3, with Cell D4 containing the discount rate, we find the NPV as follows:

$$@NPV(D4,B7.B13) + B6$$

If Lotus had been programmed like a financial calculator, the formula would have been @NPV(D4,B6.B13). However, if we actually used that equation, we would discount each cash flow back one too many periods because Lotus, in its NPV function, assumes the first cash flow in the range is due at t = 1, not t = 0.

Note, though, that Lotus 1-2-3's IRR function is set up under the assumption that the first cash flow in the range occurs at t = 0, not t = 1 as in the NPV function. Thus, we find IRR as

$$@IRR(guess,B6.B13)$$

Keep this in mind when you use 1-2-3 to calculate NPVs and IRRs.

Other 1-2-3 Financial Functions

In addition to @FV, @PV, @NPV, and @IRR, 1-2-3 also has several other built-in financial functions.

@CTERM (k, FV, PV)

Here k is the interest rate (or, more generally, the growth rate), FV is the future value, PV is the present (or initial value), and the function calculates how many periods are required for PV to grow to FV at the rate k. For example, suppose you need to know how long it will take $10,000 to double if it is compounded annually at a rate of 7 percent. Type this statement in any blank cell:

@cterm(.07,20000,10000)

The result, 10.24477 years, will appear in the cell. Note (1) that the interest rate must be entered as a decimal fraction, (2) that you could have used FV = 2 and PV = 1, and (3) be sure to include the C in @CTERM; otherwise, you will get an incorrect answer.

@PMT (PV, k, TERM)

This function is used primarily to find the payment required to amortize a loan. The amount of the loan is PV, the interest rate is k percent, and the maturity is TERM periods. For example, suppose you borrowed $10,000 for 36 months at an interest rate of 1 percent per month. This function would find your monthly payment (since the value for TERM in the function is in months), $332.14:

@pmt(10000,.01,36)

110

@RATE (FV, PV, TERM)

Suppose for $5,000 cash you can buy a zero coupon bond which promises to pay $10,000 at the end of 10 years, and you want to know what rate of return you would receive if you made the purchase. This 1-2-3 function will give you the answer, 7.18 percent:

@rate(10000,5000,10)

Rate is, of course, the IRR of this zero coupon bond.
Lotus 1-2-3 also has built-in functions which calculate straight line, sum-of-years'-digits, and double declining balance depreciation. Since most companies now use ACRS, the fastest depreciation method permissible under the Tax Code, we do not use these 1-2-3 functions. They are discussed on pages 265-272 of the Lotus Manual.

Amortization Schedules

An important application of discounted cash flow analysis relates to loans and mortgages which are paid off in equal installments over time. Such loans are called amortized loans, and 1-2-3 is ideally suited for setting up amortization schedules which show the payment, interest component, principal repayment component, and ending loan balance for each period. To illustrate, suppose you borrow $10,000 to buy a new car. The bank offers to lend you the $10,000, and you must then make 36 monthly payments, with the first payment due one month from the day you take out the loan. Further, the bank states that the rate of interest on the loan is 1 percent per month on the unpaid balance, or 12 percent per year. (This is how many banks would quote the loan, even though one could argue that the annual rate should be stated as $[1 + 0.12/12]^{12} - 1.0 = [1.01]^{12} - 1.0 = 12.68\%$. We will discuss this topic further later in the chapter.) You can use 1-2-3 to first find the monthly payment and then set up a schedule to show your total payment, interest component, principal repayment component, and loan balance at the end of each month.

111

Now recall that an installment loan is the sum of the PVs of the (equal) payments, with each payment (PMT) discounted at the stated periodic interest rate, k:

$$\text{Loan} = \text{PV} = \sum_{t=1}^{n} \frac{\text{PMT}}{(1 + k)^t} = \text{PMT} \sum_{t=1}^{n} \frac{1}{(1 + k)^t} = \text{PMT}(\text{PVIFA}_{k,t}) \qquad (3\text{-}4)$$

If we know the interest rate (k), the loan amount (PV), and the number of periods, then we can solve Equation 3-4 for the payment:

$$\text{PMT} = \frac{\text{Loan amount}}{\text{PVIFA}_{k,t}} \qquad (3\text{-}5)$$

where PMT is the monthly payment and $\text{PVIFA}_{k,t}$ is the present value interest factor for the annuity. As noted above, Lotus 1-2-3 has a built-in function for finding the payment on a loan:

@pmt(Loan amt., int. rate expressed as decimal, no. of periods)

When we type the parameters @PMT(10000,0.01,36) into any blank cell, the value 332.1431 will appear in the cell; this tells you that $332.1431 is the monthly payment required to pay off a $10,000 loan over 36 months at an interest rate of 1 percent per month.

With this background, we can now specify the steps necessary to produce the loan amortization schedule shown in Exhibit 3-9. With a blank worksheet on the screen, first set column widths to 12 spaces with this command: /WGC12 RETURN . Then enter the following labels and formulas:

A1:   LOAN AMORTIZATION SCHEDULE (LB3X9)
A3:   Loan =
B3:   10000 ; after entering 10000, format to currency with
        2 decimals by these keystrokes: /RFC RETURN RETURN .
A4:   Interest =

B4:   .01 ; after entering .01, format to percent by these
        keystrokes: /RFP RETURN RETURN .
C4:   ^per month
A5:   Periods =
B5:   36
A8:   Month
B8:   Payment
C8:   Interest
D6:   Repayment
D7:   of
D8:   Principal
E7:   Remaining
E8:   Balance
E8:   After entering Balance, type   /RLCE8.A6 RETURN ; this
        Range Label command centers the column headings over
        the columns.
A9:   \- ; after entering, copy over range B9.E9 by typing
        /CA9 RETURN B9.E9 RETURN .
A10:   0
A11:   +A10+1 ; after entering, copy over range A12.A46.
        (Note: To calculate the endpoint in a long range such
        as this one, proceed as follows: (1) Observe that you
        need to go from 1 to 36 months, which means 36 cells;
        (2) the first cell in the range is A11; (3) now add
        35 additional cells to obtain the end cell: A11 + 35
        = A46.)
B10:   0
B11:   @pmt($B$3,$B$4,$B$5) ; after entering, copy over
        range B12.B46; format B11 to currency with 2 decimal
        places and format B12.B46 to comma with 2 decimals.
C10:   0
C11:   +$B$4*E10 ; after entering, copy over range C12.C46;
        format C11 to currency with 2 decimal places and
        C12.C46 to comma with 2 decimals. (Note: This column
        will compute when Column E is entered.)
D10:   0
D11:   +B11-C11 ; after entering, copy over range D12.D46;
        format D11 to currency with 2 decimal places and
        D12.D46 to comma with 2 decimals. (Note: This column
        will also compute correctly when Column E is entered.)
E10:   +B3
E11:   +E10-D11 ; after entering, copy over range E12.E46;
        format E10 to currency with 2 decimal places and
        E11.E46 to comma with 2 decimals.
B47:   \-

```
C47:     \-
D47:     \-
A49:     ^Totals
B49:     @SUM(B10.B46) ; after entering, copy over range
         C49.D49; format the range B49.D49 to currency with 2
         decimal places.
B50:     \=
C50:     \=
D50:     \=
```

Now press Home , then move the cell pointer to A12, and
press /WWH to split the worksheet into horizontal windows.
Then press the F6 key to go into the lower window, and
press the PgDn key until you can see Cell A50. You can
now see the critical parts of your worksheet.

You can easily change the worksheet to generate amortization schedules for different principal balances and
interest rates by simply changing the values in Cells B3 and
B4. Press the F6 key to go into the upper window, and
change the value in B4 to .015 , .02 , .03 , .05 ,
and .005 to see how easy it is to get new amortization
schedules at different interest rates. However, if you
wanted to change the number of periods, you would have to
modify the schedule to increase or decrease the number of
rows. Also, if you do make changes, remember that your
periodic interest rate must match your repayment schedule--
an annual interest rate for annual payments, a monthly
interest rate for monthly payments, and so forth.

To end this exercise, clear the window by typing
 /WWC , change the value in B4 back to .01 , and then save
the worksheet under the file name LB3X9.

===

Exhibit 3-9

LOAN AMORTIZATION SCHEDULE (LB3X9)

Loan = $10,000.00
Interest =   1.00% per month
Periods =   36

Month	Payment	Interest	Repayment of Principal	Remaining Balance
0	0	0	0	$10,000.00
1	$332.14	$100.00	$232.14	9,767.86
2	332.14	97.68	234.46	9,533.39
3	332.14	95.33	236.81	9,296.58
4	332.14	92.97	239.18	9,057.41
5	332.14	90.57	241.57	8,815.84
6	332.14	88.16	243.98	8,571.85
7	332.14	85.72	246.42	8,325.43
8	332.14	83.25	248.89	8,076.54
9	332.14	80.77	251.38	7,825.16
10	332.14	78.25	253.89	7,571.27
11	332.14	75.71	256.43	7,314.84
12	332.14	73.15	258.99	7,055.84
13	332.14	70.56	261.58	6,794.26
14	332.14	67.94	264.20	6,530.06
15	332.14	65.30	266.84	6,263.22
16	332.14	62.63	269.51	5,993.71
17	332.14	59.94	272.21	5,721.50
18	332.14	57.21	274.93	5,446.57
19	332.14	54.47	277.68	5,168.89
20	332.14	51.69	280.45	4,888.44
21	332.14	48.88	283.26	4,605.18
22	332.14	46.05	286.09	4,319.09
23	332.14	43.19	288.95	4,030.14
24	332.14	40.30	291.84	3,738.30
25	332.14	37.38	294.76	3,443.54
26	332.14	34.44	297.71	3,145.83
27	332.14	31.46	300.68	2,845.14
28	332.14	28.45	303.69	2,541.45
29	332.14	25.41	306.73	2,234.72
30	332.14	22.35	309.80	1,924.93
31	332.14	19.25	312.89	1,612.03
32	332.14	16.12	316.02	1,296.01
33	332.14	12.96	319.18	976.83
34	332.14	9.77	322.37	654.45
35	332.14	6.54	325.60	328.85
36	332.14	3.29	328.85	0.00
Totals	$11,957.15	$1,957.15	$10,000.00	

===

Non-Annual Compounding

Retrieve File LB3X9 if it is not on your screen. In our amortization example, the interest rate was stated to be 12 percent with monthly compounding, or 1 percent per month. If you were asked to convert that to an equivalent annual rate, you could use this equation:

$$\text{Equivalent annual rate} = (1 + \frac{k_{nom}}{m})^m - 1.0 \qquad (3\text{-}6)$$

or, in 1-2-3 terminology,

$$\text{Equivalent annual rate} = (1 + k_{nom}/m)\hat{\ }m - 1.0 \qquad (3\text{-}6a)$$

where k_{nom} is the stated annual rate, 12 percent, and m is the number of compounding periods per year, 12. Therefore, you could type this command in Cell E4 to find the equivalent annual rate:

$$(1+.12/12)\hat{\ }12-1 \qquad (3\text{-}6b)$$

and format to percent with 2 decimals. The answer is 0.1268, or 12.68 percent. For a more general equation, clear E4 with /RE RETURN, and then enter (1+B4)^12-1 in Cell E4. Now whenever you change B4, the annual equivalent rate will appear in E4.

Continuous Compounding

Now suppose you saw an ad stating that a bank would pay 12 percent interest with <u>continuous</u> compounding; what would the effective annual rate be? You could substitute a very large value for m in Equation 3-6a to obtain an approximation; for example, if you replaced the 12s in Equation 3-6b with

999999, the result would be 0.127496708 ≅ 12.75%. At the limit, this expression would result:

$$\text{Equivalent annual rate} = e^k - 1.0 \qquad (3\text{-}6c)$$

Lotus 1-2-3 has an exponential function for e, so you could substitute k = 0.12 into Equation 3-6c as follows:

$$@EXP(.12)-1.0$$

You would obtain the answer 0.127496851 ≅ 12.75%.

If you wanted to find out how much $1,000 deposited in an account that pays 12 percent compounded continuously would grow to over 5 years, this formula would do it:

$$FV = PVe^{kt} = 1000*(@EXP(.12*5))$$

$$= \$1,822.12$$

This compares with

$$FV = 1000*1.12\hat{}5 = \$1,762.34$$

with annual compounding.

Summary

The primary goals of this chapter were (1) to illustrate the use of relative versus absolute copying and (2) to show how 1-2-3 can be used to evaluate problems which involve the time value of money. In the process, we introduced several new functions--@FV, @PV, @PMT, @CTERM, @RATE, @IRR, and @EXP. In the following chapters, we will use the features covered in this chapter often.

Chapter 3
Summary of Commands

Command	Function	Page
Converting a formula to a value: /RV(Range to copy from) RETURN (Range to copy to) RETURN		93
Erasing the screen: /WEY	Provides a clean worksheet	88
Label prefixes for Range:		
/RLC(Range) RETURN	Centers labels	95
/RLL(Range) RETURN	Left aligns labels	95
/RLR(Range) RETURN	Right aligns labels	95
Global label prefixes: /WGLC	Centers all labels	95
/WGLR	Right aligns labels	95
/WGLL	Left aligns labels	95
More functions:		
Compounding periods calculated: @CTERM(Interest rate as decimal, future value, present value)		110
Exponent of e: @EXP(Exponent)		117
Future value of an annuity: @FV(Payment, interest rate as decimal, # of periods)		102

Command	Function	Page
Internal rate of return: @IRR(Guess as decimal, range for Year 0 to N)		107
Net present value: @NPV(Discount rate as decimal, range for Year 1 to N)-CF_0		106
Payment: @PMT(Loan, interest rate per period as decimal, # of periods)		110
Present value of an annuity: @PV(Payment, interest rate as decimal, # of periods)		102
Rate: @RATE (Future value, present value, # of periods)		111

Chapter 3 Exercises

3-1 (Interest Factors) Modify File LB3X3 so that the table
determines the future value of $1 at interest rates of
2%, 4%, 6%, 8%, 10%, 12%, and 14%. To do this, first
change the interest rate in Cell B3 to .02, then edit
the formula in Cell C3 to read +B3+0.02, and finally,
copy C3 into the range D3.H3. Save this file as
LB3EX1.

3-2 (Interest Factors) Retrieve File LB3EX1 and extend it
to calculate the future value of $1 at the end of 15,
20, 25, 30, 40, and 50 periods. To do this, first, add
the additional periods in Column A, and then copy
B14.H14 into B15.H20 with the Copy command. Format
appropriately. Save this file as LB3EX2.

3-3 (Amortization Schedule) Modify File LB3X9 to construct
an amortization schedule for a 15-year mortgage loan
with 180 monthly payments. The beginning loan amount
is $75,000, and the annual rate of interest on the loan
is 10 percent. To make the modifications, follow these
steps:

a. Enter the beginning loan balance in Cell B3.

b. Enter the formula 0.1/12 in Cell B4 to calculate
the monthly interest rate.

c. Enter the number of periods, (12x15 = 180), in Cell
B5.

d. The amortization schedule will be updated
automatically, but it will only cover the first 36
periods. To extend the schedule, move the
highlighter to Cell A46, then type /WIR A47.A190.
This will add 144 (180-36) rows to the spreadsheet.

e. Then, copy A46.E46 into A47.E190. It will take a
while for this to compute.

f. Finally, edit the functions on Row 193 to sum Rows 10 through 190.

If you did everything correctly, you should have determined the monthly payment to be $805.95, and the remaining balance in Cell E190 should be zero. Save this file as LB3EX3.

3-4 (Future Value at Different Compounding Periods) Construct a table which shows the amount to which $10,000 will grow over a 5-year period at a 10 percent annual rate using the following compounding periods: (1) annual, (2) semiannual, (3) quarterly, (4) monthly, (5) daily, and (6) hourly. The steps needed to do this are:

a. Get a blank worksheet on your screen and then enter the following labels and values in the indicated cells.

A1: Future Value at Different Compounding Periods
A4: Compounding
A5: Period
A6: \-
A7: Annual
A8: Semiannual
A9: Quarterly
A10: Monthly
A11: Daily
A12: Hourly
B4: Initial
B5: Investment
B6: \-
B7: 10000
C4: Periods
C5: per Year
C6: \-
C7: 1

C8: 2
C9: 4
C10: 12
C11: 365
C12: 365*24
D4: Periodic
D5: Rate
D6: \-
D7: .1
E4: Number
E5: of Periods
E6: \-
E7: 5
F4: Value in
F5: '5 Years
F6: \-

b. Change the column widths to 12 using the command /WGC12.

c. Center the column headings using the Range Label

121

command /RLC A4.F5.

d. Enter the formula +B7 in Cell B8. Copy into
B9.B12.

e. Enter the formula +D$7/C8 in Cell D8, and copy
this formula into D9.D12.

f. Enter the formula +E$7*C8 in Cell E8, and copy
this formula into E9.E12.

g. Enter the formula +B7*((1+D7)^E7) in Cell F7, and
copy it into F8.F12.

h. Format the entire worksheet to display commas and
2 decimal places using the command /WGF, RETURN.
Then change Cells B7 and F7 to currency with 2
decimal places, and then change the range D7.D12 to
percents with 4 decimal places.

i. Now add the word Continuously in A13 and 10000 in
B13. Then, in F13, enter this formula:
@EXP(.1*5)*B13.

Your worksheet is now complete. If you did everything
correctly, the future value of your investment should
increase from \$16,105.10 with annual compounding to
\$16,487.21 with continuous compounding. Save this file
as LB3EX4. This file will be used in Exercise 4-2 of
Chapter 4, so you should be sure you save it.

3-5 Find the NPV of this set of cash flows:

$CF_0 = -10,000; CF_1 = +5,000; CF_2 = 6,000; CF_3 = 7,000.$

The cost of capital is k = 12 percent. (Answer: NPV =
\$4,229.91) What would NPV be if k were 5 percent? 20
percent?

3-6 What is the IRR in exercise 3-5? (Answer: 33.9%)
What would the IRR be if CF_0 were -12,000? If it were
-15,000?

Chapter 4
Graphing Techniques

Table of Contents

Creating Graphs   123
        Line Charts   125
        Graph Options   127
Saving the Graph for Later Viewing   132
Naming the Graph and Using Named Graphs   132
Printing Graphs   135
Another Illustrative Graph   139
Summary   143
Summary of Commands   144

- -

A picture is often worth a thousand words, and this is
especially true in many types of financial analyses. 1-2-3
has excellent graphics capabilities, and in this chapter we
look at the different types of graphs you can make and
illustrate them with models developed in Chapter 3.

Creating Graphs

To get an idea of the types of graphs 1-2-3 can make, first
retrieve your future value worksheet, LB3X3, then slowly
type /G , looking at the control panel to see what each
keystroke does. The / opened the Main Command Menu, and by
typing G you selected <u>Graph</u> from the Main Menu. The Graph
menu is shown in Exhibit 4-1, and a complete listing of the
Graph commands, in tree diagram form, is given in Appendix
B. We will explain the commands as we move along.

==

Exhibit 4-1

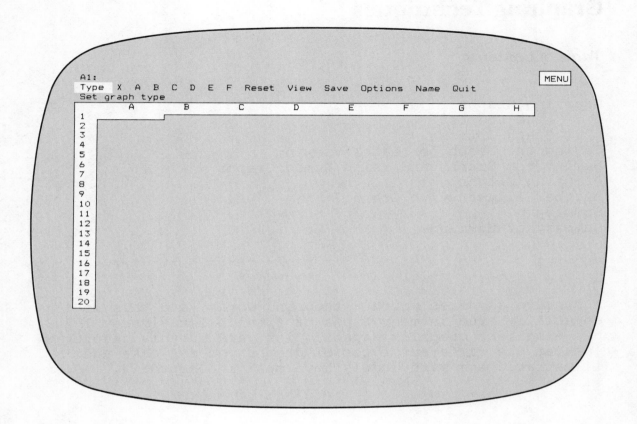

```
A1:                                                    ┌──────┐
Type  X  A  B  C  D  E  F  Reset  View  Save  Options  Name  Quit│ MENU │
Set graph type                                         └──────┘
          A         B         C         D         E         F         G         H
    1
    2
    3
    4
    5
    6
    7
    8
    9
   10
   11
   12
   13
   14
   15
   16
   17
   18
   19
   20
```

==

        The first entry in the graph menu, Type, is now
highlighted. Press RETURN , and the control panel will
show the types of graphs 1-2-3 will draw; they are as
follows:

1.   Line charts, as when time series data such as sales are
     plotted on the vertical axis against years on the
     horizontal axis. Line charts are often used to show
     how something grows over time.

124

2. Bar charts, as when current assets and fixed assets for
    different years are set as bars against one another.
    Bar charts are often used to show the relative sizes of
    different items, and how those relative sizes change
    over time.

3. XY, or "Scatter Diagram", charts, as when housing
    starts are plotted on the vertical axis against
    marriages on the horizontal axis. Scatter diagrams are
    used to show how changes in one item, such as mar-
    riages, affect another item, such as housing starts.

4. Stacked-bar charts, as when both total assets and in-
    ventories for different years are displayed in a bar
    chart.

5. Pie chart, as when the various types of assets are
    shown in the form of a pie. A pie chart can depict
    only one row or one column of values at a time.

We will use all of these graph types at one time or another,
but now we will develop a line chart to show you how the
1-2-3 graphing system works.

Line Charts

You should now have the Graph Type menu on your screen.
Type L or RETURN , and you will tell 1-2-3 that you want
to make a line graph. The main graph menu returns to the
control panel, and the highlighter returns to Type. Press
 X , and the prompt will ask you to specify the range of
values to be displayed on the X, or horizontal, axis. We
want to plot the periods (years) from Column A of File LB3X3
on the horizontal axis, so enter the range of those periods
by typing A4.A14 RETURN . The main graph menu returns,
with X still highlighted. Note that six letters follow the
X: A, B, C, D, E, and F. This indicates that we can plot
six items, or lines, on the graph--one for each of the
ranges A through F. (The only exception is the pie chart,
which can graph only one range at a time and which consequently has no X-range.) Now type A , and at the prompt
for the first data range type B4.B14 RETURN to indicate

that you want to plot the future value of $1 at 1 percent on
the Y-axis against Periods on the X-axis. Again, the main
graph menu returns to the control. We could specify up to
five more ranges, and thus get five more lines on our graph,
but let's not do that yet.
     To view the graph, your computer monitor must be
equipped with graphics capability; otherwise, you can create
and print graphs, but you cannot see the graph on the
screen. But if your monitor is equipped for graphics, you
can now type V for View to obtain a picture of how $1 will
grow if invested at 1 percent. You should see the graph
shown in Exhibit 4-2.

==

Exhibit 4-2

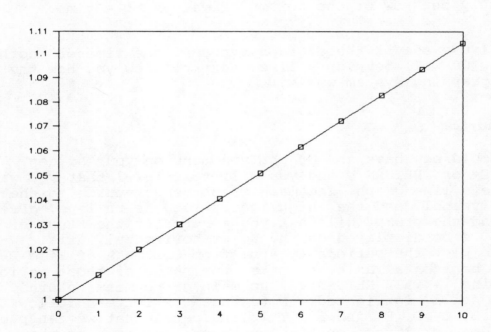

==

Note: If you have both a color graphics monitor and a black-and-white monitor, you will be able to view your graph on the graphics monitor and your worksheet on the black-and-white monitor at the same time. If you have only a graphics monitor, the graph will replace the worksheet on the screen. Press any key to return the worksheet to the screen.

At times, the X-axis labels will run together on the monitor; this would happen if the X range were specified as years, such as 1986, 1987, ..., 1996. We will see later how to solve this problem, and the solution will be to skip selected years in the display as, for example, if we displayed every fifth year. Also, note that 1-2-3 plotted the future value of $1 in hundredths. When you create graphs, 1-2-3 automatically determines a scale for the data points which allows the graph to fill as much of the screen and printed page as possible. In our example, 1-2-3 printed the Y-axis values in hundredths of a unit; however, if the Y-axis values had been large numbers, such as thousands, then 1-2-3 would have printed the Y-axis as thousands of units and added a label indicating this. There is a graph option available which allows you to specify the scale. It is generally preferable to let 1-2-3 choose the scale, but there are times, especially when you want the Y-axis to go to zero, that it is best to adjust the scale.
   Now let's add the amounts for 5 percent and 7 percent to our graph. First, if you have only one monitor, and you have not already cleared your computer screen, clear your graph from the screen by pressing any key. Next, we will plot the future value of $1 at 5 percent in the B range and the future value of $1 at 7 percent in the C range. Press
 B and then type F4.F14 RETURN , then C and type H4.H14 RETURN . View the graph again, by typing V , and you will see three curves plotted. The upper curve represents the 7 percent growth rate, the middle curve the 5 percent rate, and the lower one the 1 percent rate.

Graph Options

We need to add some information to our graph which will let others know what is being plotted. We will first <u>title</u> our

graph and axes, then add <u>legends</u> (or curve labels) to indicate what each curve represents.

To add titles, return to the main graph menu and type
O (for options) to get the Options menu. Then type T
(for titles). A menu with four items appears. It indicates
that we can add two lines of titles at the top of the graph,
First and Second, and a title for each axis. A title can
contain up to 39 characters. Type F (for first) then
enter the following title for the first title line:

COMPOUND VALUES

When you press the RETURN key, the Options menu reappears
on the screen. Now type TS and add a second title line:
Growth of $1 at Various Interest Rates . Press the
RETURN key. Type TX and then enter the word Periods
to label the X axis and type TY and then enter the words
Dollar Amount to label the Y axis.

With the Options menu still on the screen, type L to
select the Legend command; this, in effect, labels the lines
in your graph. The Legend options are the letters A through
F; you should enter a legend for each item plotted on your
graph. Try to keep your legend names short, as they must
all fit on one line at the bottom of the graph. The more
items you plot, the shorter your legends must be, because
the total number of characters for all legends can only be
19. Press A , and then enter the legend 1% for the A-range
by typing 1% RETURN . You will be returned to the Options
menu. Type L again, move the highlighter to B, and type
RETURN 5% RETURN . After returning again to the Options
menu, type L , move the highlighter to C, and type RETURN
7% RETURN . Your legends have now been established, and
1-2-3 returns you to the Options menu.

While still in the Options menu, type C for color and
then Q to quit the Options menu. You were returned to the
main graph menu, so you can now type V to view your modified graph. A printout of the graph (in black and white) is
shown in Exhibit 4-3. Your graph should now be in three
colors with each line distinguished by a different color and
symbol, and it should have legends and titles. Press any
key to return your screen from the graph to the worksheet.

Note: If your computer has a graphics card but you are using a monochrome monitor, you cannot get a color graph. On a monochrome monitor, 1-2-3 assigns a different symbol (instead of a different color) to each line. You can also go from color back to black and white by going to the Options menu and typing a B. Since most graphs are printed in black and white, it is useful to see what they look like in black and white.

Before leaving the Graph system, press T for Type. Now press S for Stacked-bar and then V for View. You should now see a stacked-bar chart. Experiment by typing, in sequence, (after pressing any key to return to the worksheet) the following commands. (Be sure to be in color if your monitor permits.)

TBV   Gives bar charts for the three sets of FVIFs. Press any key to return to your worksheet.

TXV   Gives a scatter diagram of each variable plotted against the X-axis variable, Periods. Since there is a precise mathematical fit, the scatter diagram is identical to the line graph you started with. That normally does not happen. Press any key to return to your worksheet.

TPV   Gives a pie chart of the 1 percent future value. This makes no sense, but it does show you what the pie chart looks like. (The first value adjacent to the slice at 1 o'clock is the X-axis value, and the number in parentheses is the percentage the first FVIF, 1.01, is of the sum of the values in Column B.) The pie chart would make a lot more sense if we used it to view the structure of a balance sheet. Press any key to return to your worksheet.

TLV   Gets you back to a line graph. Press any key to return to your worksheet.

We have now completed our graph. 1-2-3 has several
other graphics options--for example, you could put grid
lines on your graph--but we will not cover them now. For a
complete explanation of the other options available, see
pages 110-126 of the 1-2-3 Manual.

===

Exhibit 4-3

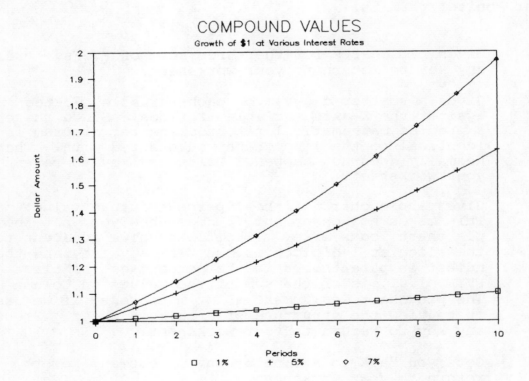

===

Exhibit 4-4 summarizes the steps for creating a line graph. Look it over, but keep your spreadsheet on the screen, as we will want to save the spreadsheet with the graph commands intact.

===

Exhibit 4-4
Creating a Line Graph

1.   /GTL ; this accesses the Line Graph subroutine.

2.   X (Range of cells to be used for horizontal axis)
      RETURN ; this specifies the X variable.

3.   A (Range of cells to be used for first Y variable)
      RETURN ; this specifies the Y variable. NOTE: If more
      than one set of variables is to be graphed on the same
      chart, continue with B (range) RETURN , C (range)
      RETURN , ... F (range) RETURN , for up to 6 Y
      variables on one graph.

4.   OTF (First title line) RETURN; TS (Second title line)
      RETURN; TX(X axis title) RETURN, TY(Y axis title)
      RETURN .

5.   LA (First legend name) RETURN, LB (Second legend name)
      RETURN . NOTE: Each set of Y variables should be
      matched with a legend name.

6.   C ; converts graph to color.

7.   Q ;   quits Options menu.

8.   V ; this lets you view the graph. (Remember, your
      computer must be properly equipped for you to view your
      graph on the screen.)

9. Press any key to return to the worksheet.

===

Saving the Graph for Later Viewing

Now return to READY mode by pressing Q and save the file,
using /FS . If you retrieved your File LB3X3, then after
pressing /FS 1-2-3 will prompt you to save the file under
that file name, which you accept by pressing RETURN .
1-2-3 now asks you if you really want to replace the old
File LB3X3. Type R to signify that you do. The graph
specifications will be saved along with the worksheet. Now,
whenever you press the function key F10 (the Graph function
key), the graph will appear on the screen--you do not need
to go into the Graph menu to produce it. Press any key to
return to your worksheet. If you make changes to the worksheet, the graph will automatically change to reflect the
new data, and the updated graph can be seen by pressing the
F10 key. This feature is not especially useful for our
present graph, because our worksheet is fixed. However,
later in the chapter we will use 1-2-3 graphs to examine the
loan amortization example we developed in the last chapter,
and you will see how useful graphs can be when analyzing
financial data.

Naming the Graph and Using Named Graphs

Later in the book, we will find it useful to develop several
graphs for a single worksheet--for example, we might have a
scatter diagram as a part of a regression analysis relating
inventories to sales and, separately, a line graph showing
how sales have grown over time. In these cases, we will
need to give each graph associated with the worksheet a
name. Here is the procedure for naming graphs:

1. From READY, with the modified file LB3X3 as the work-
    sheet on your screen, type /G to bring up the main
    Graph menu, from which you may view the graph you have
    created by pressing V . Alternatively, you can press
    the F10 key when in READY mode. Your graph should have
    three lines--for 1, 5, and 7 percent--and it should be
    in color, providing you do not have a monochrome

monitor. Now return to the main Graph menu by pressing any key.

2. On the Graph menu you will see the word Name; type N to bring up the Name menu, which appears as follows:

Use   Create   Delete   Reset

You would select "Use" if you had previously developed a number of graphs for the worksheet and wanted to view one of them. You would select "Delete" if you wanted to get rid of a previous graph. You would choose "Reset" if you wanted to get rid of all the graphs for the worksheet, and you would select "Create" if you wanted to name a newly created graph, as you do now. Therefore, press C for Create.

3. You will now be asked to name the graph you have created. If you have named some graphs previously, they will appear on the third line of the control panel. Since this is your first graph, no names should appear. (If you are using our diskette, however, you will see some graph names, and you will see some on your diskette shortly.) Graph names can include up to 14 characters. We normally give our graphs names which begin with the file name of our current worksheet plus some additional characters to distinguish them. Give this graph the name LB3X3_3LINESC , which indicates that it has three lines and is in color, by typing the name and entering it.

4. When you press RETURN , you will be returned to the main Graph menu. We need to make two more graphs--for later printing and also to show you how to use named graphs. First, let's make a graph with only one growth rate, like the one in Exhibit 4-2. To do so, proceed as follows:

   a. From the main Graph menu, press R for Reset.

   b. Move the pointer to B, and press RETURN , then move to C, and press RETURN again. Those two commands will cancel the B and C ranges as well as

their legends, and leave you with a graph for just
1 percent. Press Q and then V to make certain
that the 5 and 7 percent curves have been removed.
Press any key to return to the worksheet.

c. Now press O for Options, then B for Black and
White, and Q for Quit. Then press V again and
you will see that the graph is black and white,
which it should be when we print it. Note that
unless you have a color printer your graphs must be
in black and white for printing purposes.

d. Now let's name this new graph. Press any key to
return to the worksheet. Press N , then C , and
then enter this name: LB3X3_1LINEBW RETURN

e. You have been returned to the main Graph menu.
Type N and then U . You should see, on the
third line of the control panel, the names of the
two graphs you created. By moving the pointer and
pressing RETURN, you can make either of them the
current graph--the one that will be viewed when you
press the F10 or V keys and that you will change if
you do any resetting.

5. We need to make one more named graph: a three-lined
graph in black and white for printing. Make
LB3X3_3LINESC your current graph by moving the pointer
to it and pressing RETURN . After pressing any key to
return to the main Graph menu, proceed as follows:

a. Type O for Options, B to enter the Black and
White option, and Q to quit the Options menu.

b. Now type NC to tell 1-2-3 you want to create a
new named graph and give it this name:

LB3X3_3LINESBW RETURN

6. Type Q to quit the Graph menu, and then type /FS
LB3X3 RETURN R to save the file, with its named graph
settings, as LB3X3, which replaces your old LB3X3 file.

134

7. Now give yourself a test. Type /FR LB3X3 RETURN to
    retrieve the file. Then press the F10 key to see if
    you get a graph. Then press any key to get the work-
    sheet, and then type in /GNU to see if you have saved
    the three graphs. Make the different graphs current,
    and view them. Hopefully, you pass the test!

        Graphing can be important in research, as you can
    sometimes see relationships in graphs that are not apparent
    in a table full of numbers. Also--and more important--
    graphs are useful when you present your findings to others,
    in either written reports or oral presentations.

Printing Graphs

You can print your graphs, provided that you have the right
type of printer--graphs can generally be printed if you are
using a dot matrix printer but not if you have a letter-
quality printer. Here is the procedure for printing:

1. First, create and name your graph or graphs as we did
    above.

2. Next, you must save the graph on a picture file. Up to
    now, you have worked with only worksheet files, whose
    extensions in 1-2-3 are always .WK1. Now we turn to
    another type of file, whose extension is .PIC.

3. Go to the main Graph menu. You have now named your
    graphs as discussed above. Make LB3X3_1LINEBW the
    current graph by typing NU , highlighting it, and
    pressing RETURN .

4. Press any key to return to the main Graph menu, move
    the pointer to Save and press RETURN . You will be
    asked to enter a graph file name. File names are
    restricted to 9 characters plus an extension, which in
    this case will automatically be .PIC. Type LB3X3_1L
    for your file name and press RETURN ; that will save
    the graph specifications on a PrintGraph file.

135

5. Type NU and select LB3X3_3LINESBW to make it your
    current graph, press any key to return to the Main
    Graph menu, and then move the pointer to Save and press
     RETURN . Type LB3X3_3L RETURN to save this graph as
    a PrintGraph file.

6. Press Q to quit the Graph subroutine and return to
    READY, then save your worksheet again by typing /FS
    RETURN R .

7. Now type /QY to exit 1-2-3 and go to the Access menu.
    Select PrintGraph by typing P . If you are using a
    PC, a message will be displayed telling you to insert
    the PrintGraph disk in Drive A. Remove the System disk
    and put it away, then insert the PrintGraph disk and
    press any key. If you are using an XT on which the
    PrintGraph disk has been copied onto the hard disk, you
    will not get this message.

8. The PrintGraph main menu should be displayed on the
    screen, along with information on the PrintGraph con-
    figuration. Exhibit 4-5 shows our monitor screen after
    we have selected PrintGraph. The main menu items are

    Image-Select   Settings   Go   Align   Page   Exit

9. Press I , and you will see the graphs that you can
    make. You should see LB3X3_1L and LB3X3_3L.
        You can use the up and down arrows to highlight
    different graph files. If you press the space bar, the
    symbol # will appear to the left of the file name--that
    symbol tells 1-2-3 you want to print that graph. You
    can mark more than one graph--if you do, once one graph
    has been printed, the next one will automatically fol-
    low. If you change your mind and decide you do not
    want to print one of the graphs with a # by it, put the
    highlighter on the graph name and press the space bar
    again. The # will go away.
        If you press the F10 key, the highlighted entry
    will be graphed on your screen, though the labels may
    be blurry. You can use that feature to see if you have
    selected the right graph. Select LB3X3_3L by putting
    the # by it.
        You press the RETURN key to finalize the selec-
    tion of graphs and to return to the PrintGraph menu.

===

Exhibit 4-5

```
Copyright 1985 Lotus Development Corp.  All Rights Reserved.  Release 2   | MENU |

Select graphs for printing
| Image-Select |  Settings  Go  Align  Page  Exit
────────────────────────────────────────────────────────────────────
    GRAPH        IMAGE OPTIONS
    IMAGES       Size                  Range Colors      HARDWARE SETUP
    SELECTED       Top       .395      X Black           Graphs Directory:
                   Left      .750      A Black             B:\
                   Width    6.500      B Black           Fonts Directory:
                   Height   4.691      C Black             C:\1232
                   Rotate    .000      D Black           Interface:
                                       E Black             Parallel 1
                   Font                F Black           Printer Type:
                   1  BLOCK1                                IBM/Lo
                   2  BLOCK1                             Paper Size
                                                           Width      8.500
                                                           Length    11.000

                                                         ACTION OPTIONS
                                                           Pause: No    Eject: No
```

===

10. If you are using a computer in a computer center, or if
     you have used your computer to make graphs previously,
     your computer should already have the proper settings.
     In that case, skip to Paragraph 11. Otherwise, after
     you have selected the graph or graphs to print, move
     the pointer to Settings, press RETURN and move the

pointer to Hardware and press RETURN . Then proceed
as follows:

a. Select Graphs-Directory , and type in the directory where your graphs are stored. Normally, they
   will be on a floppy diskette in Drive B, so type
   B:\ RETURN . If you have the graphs stored on a
   hard disk, type its directory name.

b. Now select Fonts-Directory , and then type in the
   directory where the Lotus diskette is stored. For
   a PC, that would be Drive A, so you would type
   A:\ . On an XT where the Lotus disks are stored
   on the hard disk, enter that directory. Ours is
   C:\1232 , but yours might be different.

c. Now select Interface . Most people have parallel
   printers, and would enter 1 to show this.

d. Next, select Printer , type in the name of your
   printer, press the space bar to activate the #
   symbol, and then press the RETURN key.

e. Choose Size-Paper . We use 8 1/2 x 11 , so we
   would enter those dimensions typing L and
   entering the length of the paper and W and
   entering the width of the paper, then press Q ,
   and then Q again.

f. Set the Action options. We use No for both.
   Press Q to get out of the Action options.

g. Now move the pointer to Save and press RETURN to
   save the settings you just selected. The setting
   will be saved, and you will be returned to the main
   PrintGraph menu.

11. Now move the pointer to Align, and press RETURN to
    tell 1-2-3 that your printer paper is aligned. Be sure
    your printer is on and has paper.

12. Now move the pointer to Go, and press RETURN . The
    mode indicator will blink WAIT, and the graph or graphs
    will start printing. Printing takes several minutes,
    depending on the complexity of the graph.

13. When printing has been completed, the mode indicator
    will return to MENU. You can now type EY , then 1 ,
    to return to a blank 1-2-3 worksheet.

Another Illustrative Graph

We can also construct an interesting graph using the loan
amortization data in the file LB3X9. Retrieve this file,
put the pointer on Cell B4, and then type in .02 , or 2
percent interest per month, rather than .01. The monthly
payment jumps from $332.14 to $392.33, and the interest and
principal components of the payment also change. You could
examine the revised spreadsheet to see the effects of the
change in interest rates, but we can construct a graph that
gives a more vivid picture of what is happening. Here are
the steps required:

/GTS	This tells 1-2-3 that we want to make a stacked-bar graph.
X A11.A46 RETURN	This notes that we want periods 1 to 36 on our X-axis.
A C11.C46 RETURN	This tells 1-2-3 that we want the monthly interest component of the total payment to be our A range, that is, one of the items for which bars will be constructed.
B D11.D46 RETURN	This tells 1-2-3 that we also want bars drawn for the principal repayment component.
OLA	This tells 1-2-3 that we want to provide a legend for the A range, interest.
Interest RETURN	This enters the legend.
LB	This gives the prompt for the B range legend.

Principal RETURN	This enters the B range legend.
C	This tells 1-2-3 that we want the graph to be in color.
TF	This tells 1-2-3 that we want to enter the first title.
Loan Amorti- zation RETURN	This enters our first title. (We will use only one title line.)
TX	This tells 1-2-3 that we want to label the X-axis.
Period RETURN	This enters the X-axis label.
SYFC0 RETURN	This command, Scale Y-axis, Format Currency with 0 decimal places, tells 1-2-3 that we want to scale the Y-axis, formatting to dollars with no cents shown.
Q	This takes us back to the Options menu.
SS4 RETURN	This command, Scale Skip 4, tells 1-2-3 that we want to skip every fourth X-axis entry. If we did not do this, every month would be listed, and these would overlap and make it impossible to read X-axis entries.
Q	This takes us back to the main Graph menu.
V	This lets us view the graph. Yours should look like our Exhibit 4-6, except be in color. (Note that Lotus changed the number of items listed on the vertical axis, giving $50 increments, when printing out the graph.) If something is wrong with your graph, review the steps set forth above. Press any key to return to the worksheet.

Q	Once your graph is correct, type Q to return to READY mode.
/FS RETURN R	This saves the worksheet with the related Graph commands.

==

Exhibit 4-6

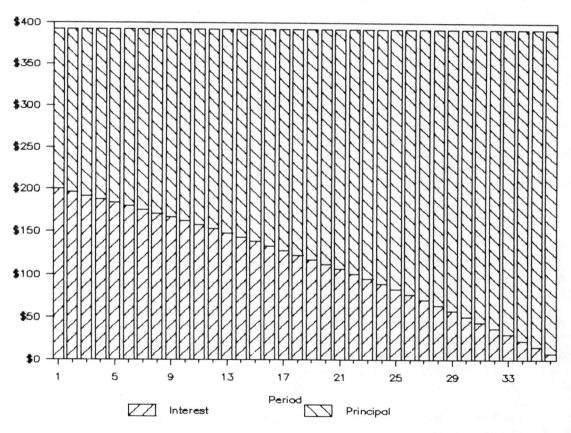

Loan Amortization

You now have a set of specifications which graph the key elements of your worksheet saved as part of your worksheet file on your storage diskette.

Let's experiment a bit with the worksheet and graph specifications. First, with the amortization table worksheet on the screen, press the F10 function key, which is 1-2-3's graph key; your graph should instantly appear. Press any key to return to the worksheet. Then go through these steps:

1. Put the pointer on Cell B4. Type and enter .01 if you do not already have it (or 1.00%) there. Then press the F10 key, and observe that the total payment (interest plus principal) is about $332, that the first month's interest is $100, and that the interest component declines while the principal component increases over time.

2. Go back to the worksheet, and type and enter .02 , or 2 percent per month, in B4. Press the F10 key. Notice (1) that the total payment increased from $332 to almost $400 and (2) that the first month's interest rose from $100 to $200. Also, the red (or pink) area now represents a greater proportion of the total area, indicating that interest now makes up a greater percentage of the total payments.

Now let's change our assumption--let's assume that the loan is for $100,000; that the periods are years, not months; and that the interest rate is 10 percent per year. Return to your worksheet. Type and enter 100000 in B3, .1 in B4, and per year in C4. Now press the F10 function key. Instantly you will see that in the early years the vast majority of the payment represents interest, and only a small part of the payment goes to reduce the outstanding balance. Toward the end of the 36 years, this situation is reversed. Note that the Y-axis is automatically converted to thousands--when we had a $10,000 loan and the payments were under $1,000, no scaling was done, but when our loan was increased to $100,000 and the payments went above $1,000, 1-2-3 automatically scaled in thousands.

Now go back to the worksheet, change the interest rate to zero (0) and then press the F10 key. With a zero interest rate, each payment goes entirely to repay the principal. Now change the interest rate to .02, .05 .1, .2, and .3, pressing F10 each time you change the interest rate, and observe the dramatic differences in the graphs. Of course, the worksheets provide exactly the same information, but if you were making a presentation and had created a series of graphs, you could display them side by side and make some points more quickly and with greater emphasis. In the following chapter, we will give you further points on using 1-2-3 to improve the quality of any presentations you might have to make.

Summary

The goal of this chapter was to show you how to create, save, and print graphs. We illustrated these techniques using models developed in Chapter 3. In the chapters that follow, we will create graphs where they are appropriate and in the process help you improve your graphing skills.

Chapter 4
Summary of Commands

Command	Function	Page
Graphics:		
/GTL	Access line graph subroutine	125
X(Range) RETURN	Specify X variable	125
A(Range) RETURN B(Range) RETURN ...	Specify Y variables	125
O	Option command	128
FGL	Format for all ranges lines between data points	127
FGS	Format for all ranges symbols between data points	127
FGB	Format for all ranges both lines and symbols between data points	127
FGQ	Quit format option	127
TF(Title) RETURN TS(2nd title) RETURN	Add titles	128
TX(X-axis title) RETURN TY(Y-axis title) RETURN	Add axis titles	128
LA(Legend name) RETURN LB (Legend name) RETURN ...	Add legends	128
C	Add color	128
SY	Scale Y axis	127
SX	Scale X axis	127
Q	Quit options	128

144

Command	Function	Page
V	View graph	128
/GTB	Access bar graph subroutine	129
/GTX	Access scatter diagram subroutine	129
/GTP	Access pie chart subroutine	129
Printing a graph:		
P	Select PrintGraph from main menu.	136
I	Permits user to select graphs for printing	136
	Select file(s) for print by moving highlighter to graph name and pressing space bar after each selection.	136
RETURN		
AG		138
Saving a graph:	Must be in graph subroutine	
S(Graph name) RETURN	Save graph for printing	135
NC(Graph name) RETURN	Save graph to update worksheet	133
Q	Quit graph subroutine	132
R	Reset all or some graph settings	133
RG	Resets all graph settings	133
RX	Cancels X range	133
RA ... RF	Cancels various Y ranges	133
RQ	Returns user to main graph menu	134
/FS(File name) RETURN R	Save worksheet	132
/QY	Quit 1-2-3	136

145

Chapter 4 Exercises

4-1 (Line Graph) Retrieve File LB3X9, the amortization schedule, and create a line graph which shows the remaining balance at the end of each period. Begin by typing /GRG to clear the graph settings you had previously made. (Note: When you save the file for this exercise, <u>do not</u> save it under file name LB3X9, for to do so would cause you to lose the original graph settings. We will save the exercise under file name LB4EX1.) The X-range should be set at A10.A46, and the A-range should be E10.E46. Clean up the appearance of your graph with these steps:

1. Use the Option Scale Skip command (OSS 12) to instruct 1-2-3 to display only every 12th period on the X-axis.

2. Enter the first title line Loan Amortization Remaining Balance and the second title line At the End of Each Month .

3. Title the X-axis Period and the Y-axis Dollars .

4. Format the A range to draw the line only (no symbols) by typing (from the Option menu) FALQ .

Name this graph LB4EX1, and save it as LB4EX1. Then, save the file as LB4EX1. If you have a graphics printer, print the graph.

4-2 (Bar Graph--Note that you can work this problem only if you saved the model created in Exercise 3-4 in Chapter 3.) Retrieve File LB3EX4, and modify it as follows:

1. Enter the labels ^Increase over in Cell G4, ^Annual Compounding in G5, and \- in G6.

2. Increase Column G width to 18.

3. Enter the formula +F7-$F$7 in Cell G7. Copy this formula in G8.G13 to calculate the increase in the

future value of $10,000 at 10 percent from compounding more frequently than once a year.

Now create a bar graph which shows the increase in value from more frequent compounding. (Note: Our graph does not show the continuous compounding bar because the graph would be too crowded.) The X-range should be A8.A12, and the A-range should be G8.G12. Clean up the appearance of your graph by:

1. Enter the first line title Change in the FV of $10,000 at 10% and the second line title from Annual to Non-Annual Compounding .

2. Title the X-axis Compounding Periods and the Y-axis Dollars .

3. Go to your worksheet. In Column A do the following editing:

   a. Change Semiannual to S. Ann.
   b. Change Quarterly to Qtrly.

4. Now view your edited graph.

Name this graph LB4EX2, and save it as LB4EX2. Also, save the file as LB4EX2. Print the graph, if possible.

4-3 Retrieve File LB3X2 which shows the interest earned on a $100 deposit at 10% interest. Change the model as follows to calculate the annual interest earned on the deposit at 10, 15, and 20 percent.

   a. Do a file extract of cell Range A1.C14 and save this as File LB4EX3. Retrieve File LB4EX3.

   b. Reset column widths to the following: A=8, B=10, C=10, D=10, E=10, F=10, G=10.

   c. Copy the headings Beginning Amount in Bank and Interest Earned into Columns D and E and then into Columns F and G.

   d. Add the following formulas in these cells:

147

```
         Cell D3     +B3+.05
         Cell F3     +D3+.05
```

e. Copy Cells B9.C14 into the range D9.E14 and then
    into F9.G14.

f. Change the heading from LB3X2 to LB4EX3.

g. Create a line graph which shows the amount of
    interest earned during each of the 6 years, 1986-
    1991, at the 3 different interest levels. (Hint:
     /GTLX A9.A14 RETURN A C9.C14 RETURN B E9.E14
    RETURN C G9.G14 RETURN O LA 10% RETURN LB 15%
    RETURN LC 20% RETURN TF INTEREST EARNED RETURN TS
    At Varying Interest Rates RETURN TX Years RETURN TY
    Interest Earned RETURN CQV . Press any key to
    return to worksheet. To save graph for printing,
    type S LB4EX3 RETURN Q . To save graph specifica-
    tions on file, type /FS LB4EX3 RETURN R .)

h. Print the line graph created in Step g.

Chapter 5
Statistical Functions, IF Statements, and Data Base Operations

Table of Contents

Statistical Functions	150
Average	154
Maximum and Minimum	154
Standard Deviation	154
Count	155
Lookup Function	155
IF Statements	159
"And" and "Or" in IF Statements	161
Embedded, or Nested, IF Statements	163
Move Command	164
Data Commands	166
Data Sort Command	166
Data Fill Command	168
Data Table 1	169
Data Table 2	175
Data Table 1 with Two Output Variables	177
Graphing Data Table Results	178
Other Data Commands	178
File Commands	179
File Xtract	179
File Combine	180
Summary	184
Summary of Commands	186

- -

We have covered many of Lotus 1-2-3's commands in the first four chapters, and we have introduced a number of finance functions. This chapter covers several additional--and important--functions and commands.

Statistical Functions

Lotus 1-2-3 <u>functions</u> always begin with the symbol @.
Earlier, we used the @SUM, @NPV, and several other financial
functions. The complete set of 1-2-3 functions (over 50 of
them) is given in the 1-2-3 Manual, Pages 228-234, but in
this section we discuss the following statistical functions:

@AVG(List)   Calculates the <u>average</u> of the values in
                        the list.

@MAX(List)   Determines the <u>maximum</u> value in the
                        list.

@MIN(List)   Determines the <u>minimum</u> value in the
                        list.

@VAR(List)   Determines the <u>variance</u> of the values in
                        the list.

@STD(List)   Determines the <u>standard deviation</u> of the
                        values in the list.

@SQRT(X)   Determines the positive <u>square root</u> of
                        X.

@COUNT(List)   <u>Counts</u> the number of cells in the list.

@VLOOKUP(X, range,   <u>Looks up values</u> that meet some specified
   column number)   criteria within a given data range, for
                        example, grades that exceed 80.

@IF(test condition,   Compares the value within a cell to a
   action if true,   specified test condition, then takes one
   action if false)   action if the specified condition is met
                        (true) and another action if the
                        condition is not met (false).

Note that many of these functions accept lists as arguments.
A <u>list</u> is defined as one or more single values or ranges. A

list can contain both single values and ranges. For example, the argument list in the function @MAX(A1,B3.B9,C3.C9) is a valid one. In this example, 1-2-3 would determine the single largest value from the argument list.

We illustrate each of these functions with the data in Exhibit 5-1, so you need to create a spreadsheet by typing in the data and labels as shown in the exhibit. First, before entering anything, format the worksheet globally to one decimal place with this command: /WGFF1 RETURN . Also, note that your blank worksheet began with 8 columns all set at 9 characters. If you are using Release 2 and you change any column's width using the /WC command, then the width you set will appear in square brackets on the top line of the control panel whenever the cell pointer is on any cell in that column; widths of columns left at the default width (9) or set by the Global command are not indicated in the control panel. We like to adjust our column widths so that all the columns in the worksheet can be seen on the screen or printed on the page; that is not always possible, but it is convenient. With this in mind, before entering any data or labels, change these column widths in your worksheet: B = 7; C = 8; D = 7; F = 7; and I = 7. This will give you 9 columns (A through I) that total 72 characters, the screen's capacity, rather than the 8 columns that the default width would produce. Generally, we set column widths as we develop a worksheet, but in this case it will save you time if you set them at the outset at the widths noted above.

Now start entering data and labels. Be sure to list the student names beginning in Cell A5, to begin the midterm grades in Cell B5, and to begin the final exam grades in Cell C5. We used the Range Label command to center the column labels in the ranges A2.F3 and G3.I4. To enter grades in Column H, type an apostrophe and press the space bar four times before entering the grade. (Note that by doing this, when we later enter the VLOOKUP function in that column, the grades will be centered in Column E.) Also, note that we used the PrintScreen, or PrtSc, key to print out Exhibit 5-1. With the printer turned on, you simultaneously press the uppercase (or Shift) key and PrtSc, which is the top half of the * key on the numeric pad part of the keyboard, and everything shown on the screen will be printed out. We did this in order to display the row number and column letters and thus to help you set up your worksheet so that it conforms with ours.

We will modify the worksheet later to make it resemble
Exhibit 5-2, with Baker listed before Ball. However, at
this point set your worksheet up exactly as we have it in
Exhibit 5-1 and save it as File LB5X1, because we want to
revise it later in the chapter.

==

Exhibit 5-1

```
A1: 'FIN 4414, Section 1   Fall 1985   (LB5X1)                    READY

           A        B        C        D        E      F       G          H        I
 1   FIN 4414, Section 1   Fall 1985    (LB5X1)                    Grade Table
 2                     Final  Overall                 Grade  ------------------------
 3     Name    Midterm  Exam  Average  Grade  Points  Average              Grade
 4                                                    at Least:  Grade     Points
 5   Adams      72.0   83.0                              0.0      F          0.0
 6   Ball       94.0   92.0                             60.0      D          1.0
 7   Baker      48.0   62.0                             70.0      C          2.0
 8   Fox        93.0   89.0                             80.0      B          3.0
 9   Lee        51.0   95.0                             90.0      A          4.0
10   Nye        86.0   94.0
11   Ricks      87.0   72.0
12   Smith      78.0   97.0
13   Toda       81.0   62.0
14   Wade       65.0   58.0
15
16   Average
17   Maximum
18   Minimum
19   Std. Dev.
20   Count
```

==

152

==

Exhibit 5-2

```
 A1: 'FIN 4414, Section 1    Fall 1985  (LB5X2)                    READY

         A        B      C       D       E      F       G        H      I
   1  FIN 4414, Section 1     Fall 1985   (LB5X2)             Grade Table
   2                  Final   Overall            Grade  ---------------------
   3     Name    Midterm  Exam  Average   Grade  Points  Average          Grade
   4                                             at Least:  Grade  Points
   5  Adams      72.0    83.0    78.6      C      2.0       0.0     F      0.0
   6  Baker      48.0    62.0    56.4      F      0.0      60.0     D      1.0
   7  Ball       94.0    92.0    92.8      A      4.0      70.0     C      2.0
   8  Fox        93.0    89.0    90.6      A      4.0      80.0     B      3.0
   9  Lee        51.0    95.0    77.4      C      2.0      90.0     A      4.0
  10  Nye        86.0    94.0    90.8      A      4.0
  11  Ricks      87.0    72.0    78.0      C      2.0
  12  Smith      78.0    97.0    89.4      B      3.0
  13  Toda       81.0    62.0    69.6      D      1.0
  14  Wade       65.0    58.0    60.8      D      1.0
  15             ---------------------------------------
  16  Average    75.5    80.4    78.4             2.3
  17  Maximum    94.0    97.0    92.8             4.0
  18  Minimum    48.0    58.0    56.4             0.0
  19  Std. Dev.  15.5    14.6    12.3             1.3
  20  Count      10.0
```

==

    We want to base final grades on a weighted average
which gives 40 percent of the weight to the midterm and 60
percent to the final. Therefore, with the pointer on Cell
D5, type

                    .4*B5+.6*C5 RETURN

and then copy it into D6.D14.

Average

The <u>average</u> of a range of data is found by using the @AVG(List) function. To find our overall class average, put the pointer on D16 and type

@AVG(D5.D14) RETURN

Then copy this formula into Cells B16.C16 to get the average grades for the midterm and the final.

It is important to note that if a blank appears within the range, 1-2-3 ignores it. Thus, if Smith had not taken the midterm and a blank had appeared by his name, then Smith would have been ignored when calculating the midterm average.

Note: Make sure that all blank cells are really empty. A blank cell that has a label prefix entered in it will be treated as a zero value and will <u>not</u> be ignored in the average calculation.

Maximum and Minimum

The functions @MAX(List) and @MIN(List) determine the <u>maximum</u> and <u>minimum</u> values. Enter @MAX(B5.B14) in B17 and @MIN(B5.B14) in B18 to get the high and low scores on the midterm, and copy into C17.D18 to get the maximum and minimum scores for the final and overall grade. To do this copy, put the pointer on B17 and type /C B17.B18 RETURN C17.D18 RETURN . Again, if a blank had been included in the range, it would have been ignored.

Standard Deviation

To obtain the <u>standard deviation</u>, enter @STD(B5.B14) in Cell B19 and then copy the formula into C19.D19. Note: This is a <u>population</u> standard deviation calculated with n in the denominator rather than n - 1, the value used for a sample standard deviation. To compute the sample standard deviation, you would enter

@SQRT(@COUNT(B5.B14)/(@COUNT(B5.B14) - 1))*@STD(B5.B14)

If you are calculating the standard deviation for class grades, as here, the population standard deviation is correct. However, if you are dealing with stock market returns for a given period as estimators of future returns, you should consider your data to be a sample and thus you should use the sample standard deviation. Most financial calculators have the sample standard deviation as a built-in function. If you compare a Lotus 1-2-3 result with a calculator result, you must allow for this distinction.

Count

In some of our classes, we have hundreds of students. The registrar gives us a count of the number of students enrolled in the course. We can have 1-2-3 count the names on our spreadsheet class roll to make sure we have not omitted anyone. To obtain the count, put the pointer on B20 and then enter @COUNT(B5.B14) .
 You should note that blanks within a range are counted. Thus, if several students had missed the midterm and therefore had blanks rather than grades, a count of the midterm grade range (B5.B14) would still produce the answer 10. If you plan on stopping here, remember to change the filename in the worksheet heading to LB5X2 and save this file as LB5X2. We will be making additional changes to this worksheet later in the chapter.

Lookup Function

In constructing worksheets, we occasionally need to take values from a data set located in part of the worksheet and use these values in some other part. For example, we might be constructing projected income statements for a corporation for the period 1986 through 1996 under different assumptions about sales and costs. In a good year, taxable income, and hence tax rates, would be high, while rates would be low in bad years. This situation could be handled as follows:

1. Put a tax table, which shows tax rates for different income brackets, in some area of the worksheet:

Taxable Income	Tax Rate
Under $25,000	0.15
$25,000-$50,000	0.17
.	.
.	.
.	.

2. Develop income statements in some other part of the worksheet.

3. After calculating pre-tax income for a particular year, have Lotus 1-2-3 use the @VLOOKUP function to determine the applicable tax rate from the tax table.

4. Use the tax rate that was looked up to calculate taxes, and then go on to complete the income statement.

Rather than developing a new example to demonstrate how to use @VLOOKUP, we can use our course grade record. If you do not have File LB5X2 on your screen, retrieve this file. First, note that we have set up a "Grade Table" in the range G5.I9 (the labels are not counted as being in the range). For 90 or higher, we give A = 4.0; from 80 to 89.9, we give B = 3.0; from 70 to 79.9, we give C = 2.0; for 60 to 69.9, we give D = 1.0; and for below 60, we give F = 0.0. Note that there are actually two lookup functions, @VLOOKUP and @HLOOKUP, where the V and H designate vertical and horizontal. We used the vertical version in our example because we set up our grade table vertically, with columns rather than rows. Had we reversed this procedure, we would have used @HLOOKUP. We want to assign grades depending on the overall averages shown in Column D, beginning with the grade in D5,

156

and to place those grades in Column E, beginning in Cell E5. Therefore, put the pointer on E5 and enter the following statement, whose arguments are defined in the following paragraphs:

@VLOOKUP(D5,G$5.I$9,1)

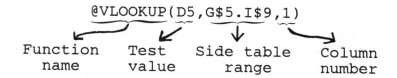

Function name   Test value   Side table range   Column number

<u>Function Name</u>. @VLOOKUP is the function's name.

<u>Test Value</u>. The first term within the parentheses, D5, is the "test value." Lotus 1-2-3 will look up this value in the first column of our "side table" and then assign the value in an adjacent column to the cell on which the pointer is located (E5). Note that in our example the assigned value is a label. This is permissible in Release 2, but Releases 1 and 1A require the assigned value to be a numeric value.

<u>Range</u>. The second term within the parentheses, G$5.I$9, is the range of the "side table." Labels are not included in the range. In a moment we will copy the VLOOKUP function down the E column, and then the $ signs will be needed to keep the row numbers absolute. Otherwise, with the pointer on D6, the VLOOKUP range would change to G6.I10, and similar errors would be encountered as we moved on down Column E.

The first column in the side table range is called the <u>comparison column</u>. It must be designated in the same units as the test value (averages, in this case), and it must be set up in <u>ascending</u>, or <u>increasing</u>, order; otherwise, you will get an ERR message.

The second column in our side table is called the <u>result column</u>. Lotus 1-2-3 looks up the test value (D5) in the comparison column (G5.G9), starting at the top and moving down until it finds a comparison value which <u>exceeds</u> the test value. 1-2-3 then assigns the <u>preceding</u> value in the results column to the cell where the pointer is located. In our example, the test value for Adams is 78.6. 1-2-3 looks down the "Average at Least" column (G5.G9) until it finds the first comparison value which exceeds 78.6; that value is 80. Then it backs up one row and assigns the grade C, which it finds in the adjacent column on that row, to Cell E5. Thus, since Adams has an average between 70 and 80, he is given a C.

Column Number. The third term in the VLOOKUP function, 1, is the column number--it tells 1-2-3 how many columns over from the first (or comparison) column to go to pick up the result, in this case the grade. (Again, note that in Releases 1 and 1A the result must be a numeric value.) The comparison column is assigned the number zero (0). There-fore, the third term can also be interpreted to mean the number of columns to the right of the comparison column.

You should now have the grade C in Cell E5, indicating that Adams received a C. Now copy E5 into the range E6.E14 to assign grades to other students.

We also want to assign grade points and to calculate the class GPA. We do this by using the third column in the side table. Write this function in Cell F5:

@VLOOKUP(D5,G$5.I$9,2)

Now 1-2-3 will assign a value two columns over from the comparison column and place it in Cell F5. Copy the formula into F6.F14. You can complete the worksheet by copying the formulas in Cells D16.D19 into F16.F19.

In closing, here are two rules to remember when using the @VLOOKUP function:

1. The values in the first column of the side table must be listed in ascending order, that is, with the smallest numbers at the top.

2. No duplicate numbers can appear in the first column.

IF Statements

Lotus 1-2-3's function for IF statements is extremely useful--indeed, it is essential in many types of worksheets. The @IF function examines a test statement, takes a designated action if the statement is true, and takes another designated action if the statement is false. Thus, the @IF function is like a decision tree:

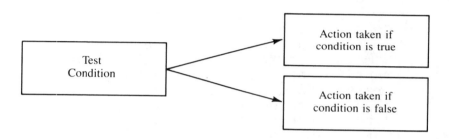

We can illustrate the @IF statement with our class grade record. Suppose we had 750 students, and we were asked, "How many students received a B or better?" We could physically count the A and B grades, but we could also do this:

1. Put the pointer on J5--the worksheet shifts when we do this--and then enter this statement:

    @IF(F5>=3,1,0)

    A zero will appear in J5, indicating that Adams did not receive a B or better.

159

2. Copy the statement into J6.J14 to determine the other students' status, and format the range J5.J16 to be fixed with zero decimal places. Here is an interpretation, using the 1-2-3 Manual's nomenclature. First, the general @IF statement is:

$$@IF(Cond,x,y)$$

where

   @IF = Function name.

   Cond = Condition, or test statement. It must be set up as equal to, greater than, or less than some designated value. In our example, we want to test the value in F5 to see if it is greater than or equal to 3, so for the condition we write F5>=3. You <u>must</u> specify "greater than or equal to" as >=; Lotus will not accept =>. If you enter =>, 1-2-3 will beep and switch to EDIT mode, thus telling you that your statement is incorrect and prompting you to correct it.

   x = Value that 1-2-3 assigns if the condition, or test statement, is true. In our example, if F5 is greater than or equal to 3, then 1-2-3 puts a 1 in Cell J5. 1 indicates B or better.

   y = Value that 1-2-3 assigns if the test statement is false. In our example, 1-2-3 puts a 0 in Cell J5 if F5 is less than 3. This indicates that the student received a grade lower than B.

3. Put the pointer on J16 and enter @SUM(J5.J14) , which in effect counts the number of students with an A or B.

4. Add the column heading " B or in Cell J3 and "Better? in Cell J4 to label the column.

"And" and "Or" in IF Statements

You can also use "and" and "or" in IF statements. For
example, suppose you wanted to identify all students who
either made an A in the course <u>or</u> made 90 or more on the
final. This statement would do it:

@IF(F5=4#OR#C5>=90,1,0)

Similarly, if we wanted to identify students who made both
an A in the course <u>and</u> 90 or more on the final, we would
write:

@IF(F5=4#AND#C5>=90,1,0)

The test condition in an IF statement must be numeric, but
the x and y arguments can be numeric, "string" values, or
cell addresses in Release 2. (In Releases 1 and 1A, the x
and y arguments must be numeric values or cell addresses.)
For example, suppose we had a class with 750 students, and
we wanted to "flag" all those who were failing at the midterm. Here's how we could get that information:

1. Put the pointer on Cell K5, and enter this:

@IF(B5<59.999," FAILING",K$1)

The cell K1 has a zero value. Adams passed the midterm, so the word "FAILING" does not appear; rather,
0.0 appears.

2. Copy the IF statement in Cell K5 into the range K6.K14.
Two fail warnings are given, along with some zeros.

3. The zeros are not useful. Move the pointer to Cell K1 and press the space bar, then the RETURN key. The zeros go away--a blank label has replaced the value zero in K1. (We could have used /WGZY to get rid of these zeros, but that would have eliminated some other zeros we wanted to keep.)

4. Note that if a string (which generally means a label) is included in the IF statement, it must be enclosed in quotes; thus, we had to put quotation marks around "FAILING".

5. Add the column headings 'Failed in Cell K3 and 'Midterm? in Cell K4 to label the column.

6. If you are planning on stopping here, make sure you save this file as LB5X2.

We could also have used formulas in the arguments of the IF statement. For example, suppose we had noted that the average score for the class as shown in D16 was below 80, and we wanted to curve the grades in our class so that the average was 80. If we decided to make this adjustment, we would add a column to the worksheet for an adjusted grade and enter the following statement:

$$@IF(D\$16<80,D5+(80-D\$16),D5)$$

Lotus 1-2-3 would (1) note that D16 is less than 80, then add the difference between 80 and D16 to the score shown in D5. This adjusted grade would be shown in the cell pointer's location. We would then copy this IF statement to adjust all the grades.

Embedded, or Nested, IF Statements

Embedded, or nested, IF statements can also be used.
Schematically, we would have something like this:

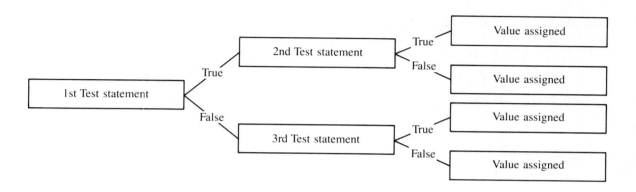

We use nested IFs in some of the models later in the book,
but here is a generic example:

$$@IF(E5>=3,@IF(D5>90,2,1),0)$$

The statement says:

1. If the value in E5 >= 3, examine Cell D5.

    a. If D5 > 90, assign a 2 to the cell on which the
        pointer is located.

    b. If D5 <= 90, assign a 1.

2. If the value in E5 < 3, assign a 0 to the pointer
    location cell.

We will use @IF statements later in this chapter, and exten-
sively in the later model chapters.

Move Command

In constructing worksheets, we often find it necessary to
move a block of material from one position to another.
Lotus' <u>Move</u> command makes this easy. To illustrate, suppose
we notice that for proper alphabetical listing Baker should
come before Ball on our grade record--we goofed when we set
it up. We can correct the error as follows:

1. Put the pointer on A6, and then type

                              /M

    The slash opens the main command menu, and the M tells
    1-2-3 that you want to move something.

2. You want to move the material in the range A6.F6 down
    one row and the material in A7.F7 up one row. However,
    if you move A6.F6 to A7.F7, you will overlay (and thus
    lose) the data now in A7.F7. So, let's move A6.F6 to
    temporary storage in A22.F22, which is empty. Here's
    what we do:

    a. In response to the prompt now on the screen, asking
        you what you want to move, type A6.F6 RETURN , or
        press the right arrow 5 times and then press
         RETURN .

    b. You will get a new prompt, asking where you want to
        move the items. Type A22 or, alternatively, use
        the down arrow to put the pointer on Cell A22, and
        then press RETURN . Page down to see that the
        move was executed, then page back up. Note that
        you must specify in full the FROM range, but you
        need only specify the left corner of the TO range.

    c. Now type /MA7.F7 RETURN followed by A6 RETURN ,
        or, alternatively, put the pointer on A7, type
         /M , 5 right arrows, and RETURN , and then move

the pointer to A6 and press RETURN . Either set
of commands will move Baker's record up to the
correct position.

d. Now type /MA22.F22 RETURN A7 RETURN to bring Ball
    out of temporary storage and put her record in its
    proper alphabetical order. Again, you could also
    use pointer commands to effect the move.

3. Now, look at your worksheet. Cells J6.K7 do not match
    with Cells A6.F7. We moved part of the worksheet but
    we need to move J7.K7 to J6.K6 and vice versa.
    Remember that our Grade Table in Columns G, H, and I is
    correct, so we do not want to move it. Here are the
    commands to move Cells J6.K7.

    a. Type /M J6.K6 RETURN J22 RETURN . This moves the
        information in Row 6 to Row 22, so Row 7 can be
        moved to Row 6.

    b. Type /M J7.K7 RETURN J6 RETURN . This moves Row 7
        to Row 6.

    c. Type /M J22.K22 RETURN J7 RETURN . This series of
        commands completes the move.

Here we moved only one row at a time, but we could have
moved large blocks, or ranges, such as A1.F15. (Remember,
if we did this we would have to move Cells J1.K15 too.) The
entire FROM range must be specified, but only the upper left
cell of the TO range is required. The biggest danger when
moving things around is putting something on top of something else you need. It is vital to execute moves slowly,
and to be sure of what you are doing. If you are moving a
large block of data on a worksheet that is too large to
allow you to see all the entries at once, you should note on
a separate piece of paper the FROM and TO ranges, and make
sure there is nothing in the TO range. (If you are stopping
here, remember to save your worksheet as LB5X2.)

Data Commands

Database management is an important part of business operations, and 1-2-3 has a data base management system built
into it. In this section we discuss some, but not all, of
1-2-3's data commands.

Data Sort Command

You are probably tired of our class grade record by now, but
bear with us as we use it to illustrate another useful
command, Data Sort. To begin, let's define a few terms:

Database. A database is simply a designated range of
cells containing one or more columns and at least two
rows.

Field. Each column of the database is defined as a field.

Field name. The first row, at the top of the database,
contains a set of labels called field names.

Record. Each subsequent row in the database is defined as
a record.

You could think of the range A3.F14 of Exhibit 5-2 as a
database, with Columns A through F as the fields, with Row 3
designating the field names, and with Rows 5 through 14 as
the records. Thus, "Adams" is the first record, and "Midterm" is the name of the second field. (In some database
operations, we would have to delete the blank row--Row 4--so
that the first row in the database would consist of field
name labels and the second row would be the first record.)
    Now let's use the Data Sort command to sort the Overall
Average column so as to rank the students in descending
order, with the person having the highest overall average at
the top. Here are the keystrokes necessary to do the sort:

/DS	The slash (/) opens the main command menu; D, for Data, opens the Data menu; and S indicates that we want to sort.
D	This second D tells 1-2-3 that we want to specify a <u>data range</u>. This range must be specified before a sort can be performed.
A5.F14 RETURN	We want to sort the records contained in the range A5.F14, so in response to the prompt we enter A5.F14. Here are two rules to follow when specifying data ranges:

1. <u>Do not</u> include headings in the range.

2. The column on which the sort will be made, or on which the rank is based, is called the <u>primary key</u>; it must be included in the data range. In our example, Column D will be the primary key. As noted below, you can also specify a <u>secondary key</u> for use as a "tie breaker."

P	The P asks for the <u>primary key</u>, or the value upon which the sort is to be made.
D5 RETURN	We want to sort based on Column D, so we enter D5. D6, D7, ..., D14 would have done just as well--only the D is essential.
D RETURN	We want the highest grades on top, so we enter D, which means <u>descending</u> order.
S	As noted above, we can specify a secondary key which serves as a "tie breaker" if two scores in the primary key column are identical.
A5 RETURN A RETURN	We elected to use names to break ties, so we enter A5. If two students have identical scores, we want them listed alphabetically, so we enter A for <u>ascending</u>. 1-2-3 regards going from A toward Z as ascending.

167

G	G is for "Go," and it tells 1-2-3 to go ahead and execute the sort. The sort will not be performed unless a data range and a primary key have been specified.

If you did not make any errors, your worksheet, after a short "WAIT," will show students rank-ordered by their overall averages, with Ball on top and Baker at the bottom.

In actual use, we would print out our ranked worksheet to get a paper record, then return our list to alphabetical order with these commands:

/DSDA5.F14 RETURN PA5 RETURN A RETURN SD5 RETURN D RETURN G

Use this command to get your grade record back in alphabetical order. Now save this file as LB5X2.

Data Fill Command

A second useful database command is <u>Data Fill</u>, which fills a range of cells with sequential numbers. Be sure you saved LB5X2, then type /WEY to get a blank worksheet on your screen. With the pointer on A1, type

/DF A1.Z1 RETURN	This tells 1-2-3 you want to fill the range A1.Z1 with data.
1985 RETURN	1-2-3 asks you what number you want to start the range with, that is, the A1 value, and suggests 0. You reject this prompt by entering 1985.
RETURN	1-2-3 asks you by how much you want to change the entry in each cell. You accept the prompt of 1 by pressing the RETURN key.

RETURN   The Data Fill command will go either to
                          the end of the specified range or to the
                          default stop point, 8191. Press RETURN.
                          The fill will stop at Z1, filling in the
                          years 1985-2010 in Row 1. Press the End
                          and right-arrow keys to see that this is
                          so. You could have specified a column of
                          years by making your range A1.A26.

We will use the Data Fill command in the next section.

Data Table 1

A third database command is <u>Data Table</u>, which is useful in
sensitivity, or "what-if", analysis. Whereas the Data Sort
command rearranges an existing database, the Data Table
command creates new data by changing a selected input variable in a systematic way and then showing how a key output
variable changes with changes in the input variable.
    We will explain how to construct and use data tables
with the data in Exhibit 5-3, which gives projected cash
flows for a project. Management thinks that unit sales
could be above or below the forecasted level (100 units) by
as much as 50 percent, and you have been asked to show how
the NPV would vary at higher or lower sales levels. Proceed
as follows.
    First, either retrieve file LB5X3 from the diskette
supplied to you or else recreate the worksheet shown in
Exhibit 5-3. If you recreate the worksheet, first type in
the labels just as we show them, then note the following
points:

1.   Project Cost is in Cell A6; 1985 is in B4; Column A
     has a column width of 16; and k = , NPV = , and IRR
     = are all right-aligned.

2.   Enter .1 in B2; 10000 in B6; 100 in C8; 50 in
     C9; +C8*C9 in C11; .35*C11 in C12; 2000 in C13;
     +C12+C13 in C15; +C11-C15 in C17; .46*C17 in C19;
     +C17-C19 in C21; +C13 in C22; and +C21+C22 in
     C24.

3.   Enter -B6 in B24.

169

4. Enter underlines as shown in Exhibit 5-3 in Columns B and C.

5. Copy C8.C25 to D8.G25.

6. Change D8 to +C8 , and copy to E8.G8.

7. In B27, enter +B24+@NPV(B2,C24.G24) .

==

Exhibit 5-3

```
A1: [W16] 'Initial Set-Up to Explain the DATA TABLE Command (LB5X3)        READY

          A          B        C        D        E        F        G
 1  Initial Set-Up to Explain the DATA TABLE Command (LB5X3)
 2            k =    10.00%
 3
 4                   1985     1986     1987     1988     1989     1990
 5                          ---------------------------------------------
 6  Project cost    $10,000
 7
 8  Unit sales                 100      100      100      100      100
 9  Sales price                $50      $50      $50      $50      $50
10
11  Revenues                $5,000   $5,000   $5,000   $5,000   $5,000
12    Op. costs             1,750    1,750    1,750    1,750    1,750
13    Depreciation          2,000    2,000    2,000    2,000    2,000
14                          ---------------------------------------------
15    Total costs           $3,750   $3,750   $3,750   $3,750   $3,750
16                          ---------------------------------------------
17  Taxable income          $1,250   $1,250   $1,250   $1,250   $1,250
18
19    Taxes (46%)             575      575      575      575      575
20                          ---------------------------------------------
21  Net income               $675     $675     $675     $675     $675
22  Depreciation           2,000    2,000    2,000    2,000    2,000
23                          ---------------------------------------------
24  Cash flow     ($10,000) $2,675   $2,675   $2,675   $2,675   $2,675
25                          =============================================
26
27          NPV =    $140              IRR =   10.55%
```

==

8. In E27, enter @IRR(.1,B24.G24) . (If at the start of recreating this worksheet you used a Global Worksheet Format command with a fixed decimal place of zero, this cell will appear as zero until you format it as a percent.)

9. Format as necessary to complete the replication of Exhibit 5-3.

At this point, you should have a worksheet on your screen that is identical to Exhibit 5-3, and, just as important, that was constructed in exactly the same way. If you plan on stopping here, make sure you save this worksheet as LB5X3.

Now take a look at Exhibit 5-4, which extends Exhibit 5-3 by adding two "data tables." In a moment, we will show you how to create Data Table 1 and Data Table 2 as shown in the lower part of Exhibit 5-4. First, though, let's make clear what we are trying to accomplish. A data table is constructed to show how one variable changes in response to changes in another variable. Thus, Data Table 1 shows how the NPV changes as the level of annual sales varies--if sales turn out to be as low as 50 units, the NPV will be -$3,186, but the NPV will be +$3,467 if sales are as high as 150 units.

Data Table 2 shows how the NPV is affected by two variables, unit sales and the cost of capital (k). The output variable (NPV) is shown in the interior cells, the first input variable (unit sales) is shown in the left column, and the second input variable (cost of capital) is shown across the top of the table. Notice that the value in Cell E46, 140, is the NPV when the cost of capital, k, is 10% and sales are 100 units; this is the NPV reported in Cell B24 above. Notice also that the middle output column, the column headed by 10 percent, is identical to the upper data table--the middle column shows how the NPV varies with sales when the cost of capital is held constant at 10 percent, the value used to construct Data Table 1.

===

Exhibit 5-4

Example of DATA TABLE Command (LB5X4)
k =   10.00%

	1985	1986	1987	1988	1989	1990
Project cost	$10,000					
Unit sales		100	100	100	100	100
Sales price		$50	$50	$50	$50	$50
Revenues		$5,000	$5,000	$5,000	$5,000	$5,000
Op. costs		1,750	1,750	1,750	1,750	1,750
Depreciation		2,000	2,000	2,000	2,000	2,000
Total costs		$3,750	$3,750	$3,750	$3,750	$3,750
Taxable income		$1,250	$1,250	$1,250	$1,250	$1,250
Taxes (46%)		575	575	575	575	575
Net income		$675	$675	$675	$675	$675
Depreciation		2,000	2,000	2,000	2,000	2,000
Cash flow	($10,000)	$2,675	$2,675	$2,675	$2,675	$2,675

NPV = $140   IRR =   10.55%

DATA TABLE 1:

Unit Sales	NPV
	+B27
50	($3,186)
75	(1,523)
100	140
125	1,804
150	3,467

DATA TABLE 2:

Unit Sales	Cost of Capital				
+B27	0%	5%	10%	15%	20%
50	(1,013)	(2,218)	(3,186)	(3,975)	(4,624)
75	1,181	(318)	(1,523)	(2,504)	(3,312)
100	3,375	1,581	140	(1,033)	(2,000)
125	5,569	3,481	1,804	438	(688)
150	7,763	5,380	3,467	1,909	624

===

Now that you understand what data tables do, let's actually construct one at the bottom of your file worksheet. Here are the steps necessary to construct Data Table 1, a one-variable table:

1. Enter "Unit "Sales in Cells B29 and B30. This is the <u>input label</u>, because unit sales is the item we will vary.

2. Leave B31 blank. The cell between the input label and the first variable value must always be blank.

3. Enter 50 , 75 , 100 , 125 , and 150 in Cells B32.B36. This is the <u>input data</u>; we will see what happens as sales vary from 50 to 150 units. (We could use Data Fill, starting with 50 and using 25 as the step, to do this. Data Fill is especially useful for large data tables.)

4. Enter "NPV in C30. This is the <u>output label</u>, and NPV is the output we want to examine.

5. Enter +B27 in Cell C31. This is the <u>formula</u> for NPV as specified in Cell B27. Note, though, that when you enter +B27, the screen shows the value 140.3546. (It may show 140 if you formatted your LB5X3 worksheet using the Global Worksheet command with a fixed decimal place of zero.) To make the cell read +B27, execute this command: /RFT RETURN . That command invokes 1-2-3's TEXT format, which causes formulas rather than the values created by formulas to appear on the screen.

    Note: You could have typed the formula given in Cell B27, rather than the cell reference +B27, into Cell C31; this procedure is useful if you are creating a data table that does not rely on formulas used elsewhere in the worksheet.

6. Type in the following steps to cause 1-2-3 to fill the output column of your data table. You can leave the cell pointer on C31, but it does not matter where the pointer is located.

/DT1	The slash opens the main command menu; the D tells 1-2-3 you want to use a Data command; the T says you want to make a Table; and the 1 says you will use just one input variable. So, you are using the "Data Table 1" command. We will look at Data Table 2 shortly.
B31.C36 RETURN	At the prompt asking for the range of your data table, you type B31.C36. <u>The range (1) must not include labels; (2) must include the formula cell (Cell C31, which shows +B27); and (3) must include both the input data column and the soon-to-be-filled output column.</u> The blank cell under the input label must also be included in the range.
C8 RETURN	After you enter the range, you get a prompt asking you to enter Input cell 1: You must specify here the cell in your cash flow statement where the input variable is first used. Look back over the worksheet, and you will see that unit sales first appears in Cell C8. Therefore, enter C8 as Input Cell 1.

If you did everything correctly, the mode indicator will flash WAIT for a moment, and then the NPVs associated with the various sales levels will appear in your data table. Lotus 1-2-3 substituted each of the values in your data table input column into Cell C8, then recalculated the full worksheet five times to generate the set of five NPVs, and finally wrote those NPVs in the output column of your worksheet. You should now add the DATA TABLE 1 : headline in Cell A29 and format as necessary to replicate Data Table 1 as it appears in Exhibit 5-4. We will be adding a second data table to this exhibit, but you should go ahead and save your file now as LB5X4 (remember to change LB5X3 in the title to LB5X4), so this work will not be lost if the power should go off.

Data Table 2

1-2-3's <u>Data Table 2</u> command shows the joint effects of two input variables, such as unit sales and the cost of capital, on an output variable such as NPV. Look at our Exhibit 5-4, and then type in on your worksheet Data Table 2's labels in the range A41.G42. Then proceed as follows:

1. In Cell B43, execute these keystrokes:

    +B27 RETURN

    The output variable we are interested in is NPV. The formula for NPV is found in Cell B27 in your main worksheet. We must enter the output formula in the proper Data Table 2 location, which is B43. As we shall see shortly, B43 is the upper left corner of the Data Table Range (labels are not included in the range). To convert from a value to a formula, leave the pointer on B43 and type

    /RFT RETURN

2. Now type in the unit sales in the column range B44.B48, as shown on Exhibit 5-4. The input variable given in this column is known as <u>Input 1</u>.

3. Now use the Data Fill command to enter cost of capital values. With the pointer on Cell C43, type

    /DF C43.G43 RETURN

    Then accept the start prompt, 0, by pressing the RETURN key. At the step prompt, type .05 RETURN , and then press RETURN again to accept 8191 as the stop (recognizing that the actual stop will be much earlier). Format the range C43.G43 to percents with

175

zero decimal places. Thus, we will find NPVs at five costs of capital. The input variable given in the row across the top of the table is <u>Input 2</u>. (Note: We could have made a larger table by adding more columns for additional percentages and more rows for additional sales. The decision to restrict the data table input values was ours, not a limitation of 1-2-3.)

4. Now we are ready for the Data command; type

/DT2

This tells 1-2-3 that you want to make a two-input-variable data table. You will now receive a prompt asking for the range of the data table you are constructing. The correct range is B43.G48. Notice that the range is the rectangle which includes the row containing the output formula cell address and values for Input Variable 2, the column containing the output formula and the values for Input Variable 1, and the cells where the NPVs will be put. Therefore, type

B43.G48 RETURN

5. You will now receive a prompt asking you to enter the worksheet cell address of Input Cell 1. Input 1 is the unit sales, which first enters the worksheet at C8, so type C8 RETURN . Next, you will receive a prompt asking for Input Cell 2. Input 2 is the cost of capital. It first appears in Cell B2, so type

B2 RETURN

6. The mode indicator will flash WAIT for a moment, and then 1-2-3 will complete Data Table 2, giving you NPVs for the specified combinations of unit sales and capital costs. Format as necessary to replicate Exhibit 5-4 and save your complete worksheet as LB5X4.

Data Table 1 with Two Output Variables

Go back up to your Data Table 1. Suppose your boss asked
you to conduct a similar analysis using IRRs as well as
NPVs. Although we do not show it in our exhibit, it would
be easy to add, proceeding as follows:

1. Put the heading IRR right aligned, in D30.

2. Put +E27 , the formula for IRR, in D31. Format it as
    text: /RFTD31 RETURN .

3. Format the range D32.D36 to percentages with two deci-
    mals: /RFP RETURN D32.D36 RETURN .

4. Type /DT1 to tell 1-2-3 that you want to make (in
    this case, add to) a table.

5. In response to the prompt, enter the range B31.D36
    RETURN .

6. In response to the prompt, enter C8 . After a brief
    WAIT, 1-2-3 will expand your Data Table 1 to include
    IRRs. We do not show this in our exhibit, but you
    should have it on your screen. You do not need to save
    this. However, if you do save this as LB5X4, your file
    will differ slightly from ours. This is fine, but you
    should keep in mind that the files are different, so
    that when we use LB5X4 in Chapter 6 you will not be
    confused.

Note that a Data Table 1 always uses one input variable unit
sales in our example), but it can show the effects of
changes in that variable on two or more output variables. A
Data Table 2, on the other hand, uses two input variables,
and it shows the effects of changes in those variables on
one output variable.

177

Graphing Data Table Results

We use data tables primarily for sensitivity analysis--to
see how a change in an input variable like sales or cost of
capital will affect an output variable like NPV. Graphs are
useful in interpreting sensitivity results, and with 1-2-3
it is easy to graph data table results. For example, these
commands will give you a picture of how Exhibit 5-4 project's NPV will vary with changes in the cost of capital--
that is, the commands will draw the project's net present
value profile:

/GTLX C43.G43 RETURN A C45.G45 RETURN B C46.G46 RETURN

C C47.G47 RETURN OCQV

These keystrokes produce NPV profiles at sales levels of 75,
100, and 125 units. You could go on to add titles and
legends to your graph and then save your worksheet. Then,
whenever you retrieved File LB5X4, you could view the graph
merely by pressing the F10 function key. If you have our
diskette, press the F10 key to see our graph. (Remember
that if you would like to print the graph, you must do both
a graph save and a file save.)
  If you make any changes to your worksheet--for example,
increase the sales price to $60--they will not be reflected
in your data table; you will have to execute the Data Table
commands again. That's relatively easy, though, as 1-2-3
remembers the data table's range and input cell addresses.
You can make the necessary changes and then press F10 to see
the new graph.

Other Data Commands

Lotus has three other Data commands which you should be
aware of so that if you need them in the future, you can
refer to the Lotus Manual for their use. Briefly, these are
as follows:

1. <u>Data Distribution</u>. This command finds all the records that meet a specified criterion and then sorts on that criterion. For example, we could use Data Distribution with the grade spreadsheet to group, and thus construct a frequency distribution of, all students with grades of A, B, C, D, and F.

2. <u>Data Matrix</u>. This command multiplies and inverts square matrices.

3. <u>Data Query</u>. This is a <u>major</u> set of commands which can be used to screen records in a database. For example, each record could relate to a customer, and then Data Query could be used to draw out those customers who tended to pay late, to sort accounts by size of annual sales in order to send them Christmas cards, and so on. Security analysts could have information on a large set of companies and then use Data Query to select companies that meet specified criteria, such as dividend yields of at least 6 percent, debt ratios of less than 40 percent, and so forth.

If you work with databases, you will want to study the Lotus 1-2-3 manual and learn how to use these other Data commands.

File Commands

We discussed how to save files (/FS) and how to retrieve them (/FR) back in Chapter 2. Now we take up two new File commands, <u>File Xtract</u> and <u>File Combine</u>.

File Xtract

The <u>file extract</u> command is used to extract and save part of a worksheet for use in a worksheet in some other file. To begin, retrieve file LB5X3, the partially completed capital budgeting worksheet, by typing /FRLB5X3 RETURN . Then type as follows:

/FX	This tells 1-2-3 you want to extract part of the current file and save it on another file.
F	1-2-3 permits you to save either whole formulas or just the numerical values created by them. In our example we want to save formulas, so we press F.
LB5X5 RETURN	After pressing F, 1-2-3 asks us to specify a file name under which to save the extracted material. We can use an existing file name, but if we do, we will lose everything in the old file. Therefore, we want to use a new file name. Thus far in this chapter we have set up four files, so this will be the fifth. Therefore, enter LB5X5.
A8.A24 RETURN	For the purpose at hand, all we want are some of the labels in Column A. Therefore, enter A8.A24. WAIT flashes a few times, and then the mode indicator reads READY.
/FR LB5X5 RETURN	We now have a new file whose name is LB5X5 as shown in Exhibit 5-5. Retrieve it to see that it exists and that the extracted material is placed on the new worksheet starting in the upper left corner. This placement always occurs to conserve space.

File Combine

It is often useful to combine files, and to do so we use 1-2-3's File Combine command. To illustrate the process, we will take some income statement data from LB5X4 and combine it with our own newly extracted file, LB5X5. We will first set up a named range in LB5X4 and then combine it with LB5X5.

```
=================================================================
```

Exhibit 5-5
Illustration of File Xtract Command

Unit sales
Sales price

Revenues
    Op. costs
    Depreciation

    Total costs

Taxable income

    Taxes (46%)

Net income
Depreciation

Cash flow


```
=================================================================
```

/FR LB5X4
RETURN   These keystrokes retrieve file LB5X4.

/RNC   This command tells 1-2-3 that you want to work
                with a <u>Range</u>, and specifically that you want to
                <u>Name</u> a range. The C indicates that you want to
                <u>Create</u> a named range. (You can also use pre-
                viously created named ranges.)

DATA RETURN   1-2-3 asks you to enter a name for the range.
               Use DATA.

C8.C25
RETURN   We want to pick up the income statement data
               for 1986, so we enter the range containing that
               data.

/FS LB5X4
RETURN R   The step just above gave the range C8.C25 the
               name DATA. You must now save the file LB5X4 as
               modified to include this new information. The
               indicated keystrokes make this save. Note that
               when you save a file under the name of a file
               that has already been saved, 1-2-3 asks you if
               you want to replace the old file. In this case
               you do, so press R.

At this point, file LB5X4 has a named range. We can ask
1-2-3 to extract that named range and combine it with information on another file; we show you how in the next series
of steps.

/FR LB5X5
RETURN   We want to use our labels-only file, LB5X5, as
               the base file in the File Combine. When you
               combine files you take information from one and
               put it on another (which we call the base
               file). You must start the File Combine command
               with the base file on the screen, which is what
               we just did.

Highlighter   With LB5X5 on the screen and the mode indicator
to B1   at READY, move the highlighter, or cell pointer,
               to B1. This must be done at this point to
               indicate to 1-2-3 where you want to place the
               named range that is to be added. If you left
               the pointer on A1, the combine would not work
               because 1-2-3 would overlay two sets of infor-
               mation on one range, destroying the original
               information in the process.

182

/FCCN	Now type the indicated command. The /F opens the File Command menu; the first C says you want to combine files; the second C says you want to copy; and the N says you want to add a named range rather than an entire file.
DATA RETURN	You named the range that you want to extract DATA, so in response to the prompt, type DATA.
LB5X4 RETURN	You will receive a prompt asking you what file you want to combine with the one on the screen. Since you want to pick up the named range from LB5X4, enter that file name. WAIT will flash for a moment in the mode indicator, and then the named range will appear on the screen.

To complete the worksheet, insert four rows at the top
(/WIR B1.B4 RETURN), and then provide a title and a year
label as we show in Exhibit 5-6. Also, save the file under
the file name LB5X6.

One example of how the File Combine command could be
used in a realistic situation is to produce consolidated
financial statements for a firm with a number of divisions.
For example, visualize the data in Column B of Exhibit 5-6
as the 1986 income statement for one store of a fast-food
chain. Data for other stores could be extracted from their
separate files and combined on one file, which could then be
summed across the rows to produce the corporation's consolidated statements. Of course, you could keep the records of
all the stores on one large worksheet in the first place,
and thus avoid having to combine files, but there are two
good reasons for not doing so: (1) it would probably be
more convenient to have each store's data on a separate file
for ease of updating, and (2) when you updated one store's
records, the entire worksheet would go through the recalculation process, and for that reason you might be sitting
there watching the WAIT mode indicator blink for inordi-
nately long periods of time. Both of these reasons often
make it desirable to break worksheets down into more
manageable components, and when you do, the File Xtract/File
Combine commands can be most useful.

If you do much work with 1-2-3, you will doubtless find
many uses for File Combine yourself.

```
================================================================

                      Exhibit 5-6


Completed Illustration of the File Combine Command   (LB5X6)

                          1986
                          ----------
Unit sales                 100
Sales price                $50

Revenues                 $5,000
   Op. costs              1,750
   Depreciation           2,000
                          ----------
   Total costs           $3,750
                          ----------
Taxable income           $1,250

   Taxes (46%)             575
                          ----------
Net income                $675
Depreciation             2,000
                          ----------
Cash flow                $2,675
                          ==========

================================================================
```

Summary

In this chapter we have covered some additional Lotus 1-2-3
functions and commands; you will need them when you begin

modifying our financial management models later in the book and writing your own models. IF statements are used in many of our models, and you will use the Move command often as you construct various models. The Data Table commands are especially helpful for performing "what-if", or sensitivity, analyses, and the File Xtract and File Combine commands will be useful in manipulating worksheet files.

Chapter 5
Summary of Commands

Command	Function	Page

Data Fill:

/DF(Enter range to
fill with data) RETURN
(Enter value you want
to start with) RETURN
(Enter amount by which
you want values to
be increased)
RETURN RETURN · · · · · · · · · · · · · · · Fills a range with increasing values · · · 168

Data Sort:

/DSD(Enter range to
sort) RETURN
P(Enter value sort
based on) RETURN

D(Sort in descending
order, A for ascending
order) RETURN

S(Enter cell which
breaks "tie breakers")
RETURN
A(Ascending order,
D for descending
order) RETURN
G · Sorts a data set according to a · · · · · · 167
                                                   specified criterion.

Data Table 1:

/DT1(Enter range of
data table) RETURN
(Enter input cell)
RETURN · · · · · · · · · · · · · · · · · · · Creates data table with 1 input variable · · 174

186

Command	Function	Page

Data Table 2:

```
/DT2(Enter Range of
Data Table) RETURN
(Enter Input Cell 1)
RETURN
(Enter Input Cell 2)
RETURN                    Creates data table with 2 input variables 176
```

File Combine:

```
/FR(File name) RETURN
/RNC(Enter range name) RETURN
(Enter data range) RETURN
/FS(File name) RETURN R
/FR(File name) RETURN
Move cell pointer to place
where named
range is to be added
/FCCN(Enter range name)
RETURN
(Enter file name)
RETURN                    Combines information from 2 files into 1 181
                          file
```

File Xtract:

```
/FXF(File name) RETURN
(Enter range to be
extracted) RETURN
/FR(File name) RETURN     Extracts information from one file and    180
                          puts that information in another file
```

Functions:

@AVG(List)	Calculates average of values in the list	150,154
@MAX(List)	Determines maximum value in the list	150,154
@MIN(List)	Determines minimum value in the list	150,154
@VAR(List)	Determines variance of values in the list	150

Command	Function	Page
@STD(List)	Determines the standard deviation of values in the list	150,154
@SQRT(X)	Determines the positive square root of X	150
@COUNT(List)	Counts the number of cells in the list	150,154
@VLOOKUP(X,range, column number) @HLOOKUP(X,range, row number)	Looks up values that meet some specified criteria within a given data range	150,157
@IF(test condition, action if true, action if false)	Compares the value within a cell to a specified test condition, then takes one action if the condition is met and another if it is not met	150,159

Move:

/M(Range to move from) RETURN (Range to move to) RETURN	Moves cells from one position to another	164

Chapter 5 Exercises

5-1   Set up a worksheet like the one shown below. Use the
      global column width adjustment (/WGC) to set columns 12
      characters wide, and then give Column B a width of 5.
      Format as shown.

```
           A        B        C          D          E          F
 1   Accounts Receivable Record
 2
 3   Customer Name:                              Maximum
 4   ------------------                Amount     Credit
 5      Last     Init.    City          Due       Allowed    Overdrawn?
 6   ----------------------------------------------------------------
 7   Porter      B      Columbia        3000      20000
 8   Smith       P      Augusta        16000      10000
 9   Brown       T      Atlanta         2000       5000
10   Carter      J      Plains          6000      20000
11   Allen       M      Atlanta         5000       8000
12   Dooley      V      Athens             0      10000
13   Carter      B      Plains         11000      10000
14
15
16
17
18
19
20
```

a.   (Data sort) Arrange alphabetically. (Hint:
     /DSDA7.F13 RETURN P A7 RETURN A RETURN S B7 RETURN
     A RETURN G)

b.   (Data sort) Now arrange in order of maximum credit
     allowed (highest listed first). Use alphabetical
     order for "tie breakers."

c.   (IF statement) Write a formula that will put the
     word YES in Column F if the amount due exceeds the
     allowed credit. If you are using Release 1 or 1A,
     substitute 1 for YES. (Hint: Put the pointer on
     Cell F1 and press the space bar once, then move the
     pointer to Cell F7 and write this formula:

              @IF (D7>E7,"YES",+F$1)

     Then copy this formula into F8.F13.)

     (1) Why did we press the space bar in F1?
     (2) Why did we use the quotes around YES?
     (3) Why did we use the dollar sign in the formula?

189

d. (IF statement) Add the word Badly , centered, in Cell F4, and then change the formula in Column F to print YES if the account is overdrawn by $10,000 or more, (Hint: Use the Edit key, and add to the formula in F7 these items:

#AND#D7-E7>10000   )

e. (Data sort) Resort the worksheet back into alphabetical order.

f. (Move command) Reverse Columns D and E. Now look at your IF statement (by putting the pointer on F7); when the move was executed, was the IF statement adjusted?

g. (Statistics) Use 1-2-3 to find the average allowed credit, the standard deviation of the amounts due, and the number of customers (1) who have credit lines and (2) who owe money. (Hint: For Part (2) you will need to set up an additional column as we did in LB5X2, the grade example, in Chapter 5.) Also, find the maximums and minimums of Columns D and E. Write the appropriate formulas in Column D and then copy them into Column E.
You should have had a zero (0) for Dooley in the amount due column. Use /RE to make that cell blank. What effect does having a blank rather than a zero have on the values you just calculated?

5-2 (Data Table 1) Retrieve file LB5X4, the one with data tables. Set up a Data Table 1 which shows the effect of sales prices of $40, $45, $50, $55, and $60 on both NPV and IRR.

5-3 (Data Table 2) Retrieve file LB5X4. Set up a Data Table 2 which shows the effects of sales prices at the levels indicated in Exercise 5-2 and the costs of capital at the rates given in LB5X4.

Chapter 6
Regression Analysis and Other Topics

Table of Contents

Regression Analysis   191
Word Processing with 1-2-3   197
Small (Compressed) Print Option   201
Solving Complex Equations   204
Alternative Recalculation Procedures   209
Protection Features   211
      Protecting Cells   211
      Protecting Files   213
Summary   214
Summary of Commands   215

- -

In this chapter, we first discuss 1-2-3's regression analysis capabilities, and then we look at some other useful features, including word processing, the small print option, how 1-2-3 can be used to solve equations, recalculation procedures, and 1-2-3's cell and file protection capabilities. Several of these procedures apply only to Release 2; we have noted this where applicable.

Regression Analysis

Lotus 1-2-3, Release 2, has an excellent, easy to use multiple regression routine. This procedure is found only in Release 2, so if your use of 1-2-3 is restricted to Release 1 or 1A, you may want to skip this section. The regression routine allows you to do simple (one dependent and one independent variable) regression and multiple regression with up to 16 independent variables. Although only linear regression is employed, the variables can be transformed to logs, exponents, reciprocals, and products of one another to investigate nonlinear relationships. Further, the intercept term can either be calculated or forced to zero. You can also use the derived equation to obtain predicted values, and you can plot the data to get a visual picture of the relationships. The standard error of the estimate, the R^2, the degrees of freedom, and the standard errors of the coefficients, along with the estimated regression equation, are given as standard output, and you can easily obtain t-statistics.

One typical application of regression analysis is to analyze a set of historic data (such as sales over the past 10 years) to establish a trend, which is then used as the basis for forecasting sales when constructing a set of forecasted financial statements. Multiple regression would bring other factors that might affect sales such as interest rate levels, Gross National Product, and the like, into the analysis. We will apply 1-2-3's regression routine to historic data to develop relationships for use in forecasting models in a later chapter. Now, though, we will explain how to use the regression routine with a relatively simple example. First, retrieve File LB5X2, the completed class grade record from Chapter 5. We will add the students' overall grade point averages and SAT scores, placing them in the range L5.M14, and then run a regression using as the dependent variable the course grade and the overall GPA and SAT scores as the independent variables. Our purpose is to find out if grades in this course are consistent with the students' abilities as measured by their SAT scores and overall GPAs.

The relevant section of our spreadsheet is shown in Exhibit 6-1. Recognize that the information in Exhibit 6-1 is an addition to our grade spreadsheet as developed in File LB5X2--we used the Print Screen command to print out the relevant section. Here are the steps you must go through to add the new data, run the regression, and interpret the results:

1. Get your version of LB5X2 on your screen, put the pointer on F3, and type /WTV to freeze Columns A through E. Press the left arrow. You will get a beep, which shows that the columns are frozen.

2. Press the right arrow until Column L is adjacent to
   Column E. Then, looking at our Exhibit 6-1, add to
   your worksheet column head labels in L2.M3 and data in
   L5.M14. Format as necessary for consistency with
   Exhibit 6-1.

3. Type /DR , the Data Regression command, to tell 1-2-3
   that you want to run a regression.

4. Press X , then enter the range L5.M14 RETURN . This
   establishes overall GPAs and SAT scores as your X, or
   independent, variables.

5. Now press Y , for Y-range, and enter the range D5.D14
   RETURN to establish the overall average as the Y, or
   dependent, variable.

6. You normally would want to calculate the intercept
   term, so move the highlighter to Intercept , press
    RETURN , and then press RETURN again.

7. Now you must specify the output range, or the location
   on your worksheet where 1-2-3 will report the regression output. The range must be at least nine rows
   long, and it must be the greater of four columns or two
   columns plus the number of independent variables wide.
   Thus, our output range in this example must be at least
   nine rows by four columns. Only the upper left corner
   of the range must be specified. In our case, L16 is a
   good corner point, as we currently have nothing in the
   range L16.O24. (Any data in the output range given
   would be overlaid and lost.) Therefore, move the
   pointer to Output-Range , press RETURN , and then
   press L16 RETURN .

8. Press G , and 1-2-3 will generate your regression
   output and return the mode indicator to READY.

9. Type /WTC to clear the titles and use the arrow keys
   to get the full output range, L16.O24, on your screen.

10. Format Cells O23 and O24 to five decimals as follows:
    /RFF5 RETURN O23.O24 RETURN . This is necessary in
    order to read the SAT coefficient and its standard
    error.

```
==================================================================

                        Exhibit 6-1
                    Regression Analysis



┌─────────────────────────────────────────────────────────────────┐
│ L1:                                                      │READY│ │
│                                                                   │
│  ┌──────────────────────────────────────────────────────────┐    │
│  │       L        M       N        O       P       Q      R  │    │
│ 1 └───┐                                                       │    │
│ 2     │ Overall          Predicted                           │    │
│ 3     │  GPA      SAT    Average                              │    │
│ 4     │                                                       │    │
│ 5     │  2.8     1065     76.9                                │    │
│ 6     │  1.7      650     57.7                                │    │
│ 7     │  4.0     1450     96.7                                │    │
│ 8     │  3.6     1305     89.8                                │    │
│ 9     │  2.4     1030     71.9                                │    │
│10     │  3.8     1325     92.3                                │    │
│11     │  2.9     1050     77.7                                │    │
│12     │  3.2     1195     83.5                                │    │
│13     │  2.6     1010     73.8                                │    │
│14     │  1.8      945     63.9                                │    │
│15     │                                                       │    │
│16     │       Regression Output:                             │    │
│17     │ Constant                      27.8                   │    │
│18     │ Std Err of Y Est               4.0                   │    │
│19     │ R Squared                      0.9                   │    │
│20     │ No. of Observations           10.0                   │    │
│21     │ Degrees of Freedom             7.0                   │    │
│22     │                     GPA      SAT                     │    │
│23     │ X Coefficient(s)    10.9     0.01745                 │    │
│24     │ Std Err of Coef.     5.5     0.01887                 │    │
│25     │ t statistic          2.0     0.92                    │    │
└───────┴──────────────────────────────────────────────────────────┘
```

==

11. The coefficients of the independent variables are shown, in order, on Row 23. Since the first X-variable was GPA, we know that its regression coefficient is 10.9 and its standard error is 5.5. The corresponding values for SAT scores are 0.01745 and 0.01887. Add GPA and SAT as labels in Cells N22 and O22, respectively. The R^2 value is 0.9. We added the t-statistics as shown on Line 25, using the equation t-statistic = Regression coefficient/Standard error--that was not part of the regular regression output. Put the formula +N23/N24 in Cell N25 and copy it to Cell O25 to obtain the t-statistics. Format Cell O25 to 2 decimal places. Here is the equation as we would write it in a report:

Overall average = 27.8 + 10.9(GPA) + 0.01745(SAT)

$R^2 = 0.9$

There is clearly a relationship between grades in this course and students' GPAs and SAT scores, but other factors also have a bearing.

12. When running a multiple regression, you need to be sure that the independent variables are not highly corre-lated with one another. You can test for multi-collinearity, or correlation among independent variables, by running a simple regression on each pair of independent variables. If two independent variables are highly correlated with each other, only one of them should be included in the multiple regression.

13. We often find it useful to go a bit further with our regression results before writing up a report. One easy but useful step is to graph the results, proceeding as follows:

a. Enter the labels Predicted in N2 and Average in N3.

b. To calculate the first student's predicted grade, enter this formula in N5:

+O$17+L5*N$23+M5*O$23 RETURN

We are picking up the constant as reported in O17, the regression coefficients as reported in N23 and O23, and the first student's GPA and SAT to predict his overall average in our course. The predicted value as shown in N5 is 76.9.

c. Copy the formula in N5 into the range N6.N14 to predict scores for the other students.

d. We will now construct a scatter diagram, or XY graph, so type /GTX .

e. We will use the horizontal, or X, axis for the predicted values, so type XN5.N14 RETURN .

f. We want to have actual values on the vertical, or Y, axis, so assign the actual values to the A range by typing AD5.D14 RETURN .

g. Type OFASQ . You just formatted the line that will represent the A range--the actual values--so that only the symbols will appear. Type C to get a colored graph and then Q to go back to the main Graph menu. Type V to view your graph to this point. You should see some squares with a general upward slope.

h. Now we will "draw" the least squares regression line on the graph. First, press any key to return to the Graph menu and type BN5.N14 RETURN to enter predicted values as the B range, which will be a second set of points on the graph. Then type OFBL to tell 1-2-3 that you want the B range formatted to have lines drawn between each point in that range. Then type QQV to view the graph. Now you should see a straight line, which depicts the predicted values, connected by lines to produce the line on your screen.

i. Press any key, then type OLA Actual RETURN and LB Predicted RETURN to provide legends.

j. While still in the Options menu, type TF Class
    Grades RETURN and TS Overall Average = f(GPA,SAT)
    RETURN TX Predicted Grades RETURN and TY Actual
    Grades RETURN to label the axes.

k. Type Q to quit the Options menu, then press V
    to view your graph. You can print the graph if you
    want to (however, you must first do a graph save),
    and if you now save the worksheet, the graph speci-
    fications will also be saved. Remember to change
    the file name in the heading to LB6X1 and save this
    file as LB6X1 on your diskette.

Word Processing with 1-2-3

Word processing software packages exist which can do all
sorts of neat things necessary to produce letters, reports,
and even books. Word processors can underline, set things
in boldface, put in exponents and subscripts, number pages
automatically, and even check your spelling. Lotus 1-2-3
was not designed as a word processor, so its capabilities in
that area are limited, but we do often find it convenient to
use it as such, especially to add explanatory notes to
worksheets. We do this by employing the LABEL mode and
recognizing the following points:

1. Labels can be up to 240 characters long.

2. If a label is too long to be displayed in a cell, 1-2-3
    displays as much of it as it can. If blank cells are
    to the right of the label's cell, 1-2-3 will borrow
    space from them to display the label.

3. A column consisting of several rows of "long labels"
    can be used to write a paragraph.

4. The screen can display 72 characters, and regular
    printers normally print a maximum of 80 characters
    (wide printers can normally print 140 characters).

5. Let's suppose you want to add an explanatory note at the top of your completed Data Table worksheet from Chapter 5, (saved as LB5X4). We have added such a note, as shown at the top of Exhibit 6-2. You could proceed as follows:

   a. Retrieve file LB5X4.

   b. Put the pointer on A2, and then type

      /WIRA2.A8 RETURN

      to add seven blank rows.

   c. Move the pointer to A3, and type the first line of the paragraph in Exhibit 6-2. Use the space bar to indent. Then complete the note, line by line, typing each line starting in the A column.

6. Now suppose you show your boss your analysis. She likes it, but she asks you to change the beginning of your note on Line 3 from "This worksheet" to "The worksheet shown below."

7. To make this change, go to A3, press the Edit key, F2 , and go into EDIT mode. Then press Home to move the cursor back to the left end, and use the right arrow to place the cursor under the i in "This". Press the Delete key twice, type an e , and then use the arrow key to move the cursor to the i in "is". Finally, type the phrase shown below and press the RETURN key to get the statement your boss wants.

8. Now you have a problem--the label in Cell A3 is too long for the screen, and it will not print out on 8 1/2 x 11 paper.

```
================================================================================

                              Exhibit 6-2


     Example of DATA TABLE Command (LB6X2)

          This worksheet is designed to demonstrate the use of the /DATA
     TABLE command. We begin with a capital budgeting worksheet, below
     which we add two data tables, one showing the sensitivity of NPV to
     unit sales and the other showing NPV's sensitivity to both sales and
     the cost of capital.

               k =     10.00%

                       1985     1986     1987     1988     1989     1990
                       ----------------------------------------------------
     Project cost     $10,000

     Unit sales                  100      100      100      100      100
     Sales price                 $50      $50      $50      $50      $50

     Revenues                 $5,000   $5,000   $5,000   $5,000   $5,000
        Op. costs              1,750    1,750    1,750    1,750    1,750
        Depreciation           2,000    2,000    2,000    2,000    2,000
                       ----------------------------------------------------
        Total costs            3,750    3,750    3,750    3,750    3,750
                       ----------------------------------------------------
     Taxable income          $1,250   $1,250   $1,250   $1,250   $1,250

        Taxes (46%)             575      575      575      575      575
                       ----------------------------------------------------
     Net income               $675     $675     $675     $675     $675
     Depreciation            2,000    2,000    2,000    2,000    2,000
                       ----------------------------------------------------
     Cash flow      ($10,000) $2,675   $2,675   $2,675   $2,675   $2,675
                       ====================================================

          NPV =     $140              IRR =     10.55%

     DATA TABLE 1:   Unit
                     Sales    NPV
                              +B34
                        50   (3,186)
                        75   (1,523)
                       100      140
                       125    1,804
                       150    3,467




     DATA TABLE 2:   Unit                    Cost of Capital
                     Sales   ----------------------------------------------------
                     +B34        0%       5%      10%      15%      20%
                        50   (1,013)  (2,218)  (3,186)  (3,975)  (4,624)
                        75    1,181     (318)  (1,523)  (2,504)  (3,312)
                       100    3,375    1,581      140   (1,033)  (2,000)
                       125    5,569    3,481    1,804      438     (688)
                       150    7,763    5,380    3,467    1,909      624




================================================================================


                                    199
```

9. You could retype the whole statement, but Lotus 1-2-3 has a command that will solve the problem much more quickly--the Range Justify command. This command reformats and puts all the words where you can see them. To use Range Justify, type these keystrokes:

/RJ   This tells 1-2-3 you want to "justify," which means even out the length of lines in a range of words typed as a column of labels. 1-2-3 then prompts you to specify the range.

A3.G8 The mode indicator flashes WAIT for a few
RETURN moments, and then your reformatted note appears.

/FSLB6X2 Change the title at the top to LB6X2, and
RETURN then save the file.

  You should observe these rules when you use the Range Justify command:

Rule 1. You must include enough blank lines below the text that is to be reformatted to accommodate the reformatted material. Further, you must include these blank lines in your range. In our example, we had only two words that needed to be brought into the visible range, so we really did not need to worry about this; however, on long notes, we often do not know how much extra space will be required. At those times we make a guess, being sure to guess too high, and then insert several blank rows below the text for inclusion in the range. After reformatting, we delete any extra rows.

Rule 2. You can reformat only one paragraph (or note) at a time. First, if you tried to reformat two paragraphs at once, the process would actually merge them. Second, if you had a blank line between paragraphs (or even within a paragraph), 1-2-3 would simply stop after reformatting down to the blank line. This would occur even though you specified the full range to be justified. You simply have to reformat each paragraph separately.

<u>Rule 3</u>. If you add notes to a worksheet, avoid indenting
except at the start of paragraphs, because if you do, blanks
will appear if you later change your notes and use /RJ.
Some people number notes in a list format and indent everything except the item numbers. This is not a good procedure, as it makes it difficult to use the Range Justify
command.

Small (Compressed) Print Option

Printers designed for 8 1/2 x 11 paper can normally handle
only 80 characters. Thus, if you had a wide worksheet--say,
one with 10 columns by 10 characters wide--you would have to
print it in two passes. However, 1-2-3 offers a <u>small print</u>
<u>option</u>, which compresses the type and thus permits you to
get more data on a single page.
　　　To explain how the compressed print option works, first
retrieve LB5X3. Then move the pointer to Cell G4, and type
this:

/CG4.G25 RETURN

H4.I25 RETURN

This adds columns for 1991 and 1992 by copying the range
G4.G25 to H4.I25. With data from 1985 to 1992, you have too
many characters to print on 8 1/2 x 11 paper using normal
printing, but with 1-2-3's small print option, we can make
it fit. First, note the range of data you want to print:
It is A1.I27. Also, edit Cells B27 and E27, changing the Gs
to Is to correct the NPV and IRR for the additional years.
(NPV increases to $3,023 and IRR to 18.69%.) Then do the
following to obtain a printout using the small print option:

/PPR　　　　　　This tells 1-2-3 you want to print to the
A1.I27 RETURN　printer (rather than to a file), and 1-2-3
　　　　　　　　asks for the range to be printed. Since you
　　　　　　　　want the entire worksheet, enter A1.I27.

OS	After the RETURN, 1-2-3 waits for you to tell it what else you want it to do. OS tells it you want to use a print option called Setup.
	Now 1-2-3 asks you to enter a "setup string," which is a series of commands to your printer (which must be a dot matrix or some other flexible printer in order to get a different type size). Each printer requires its own unique set of commands to activate the compressed print option. Here are the steps to determine the setup string:
	1. Look in your printer's Operation Guide (or User's Manual) index for a section on printer control codes or ASCII codes, and determine the ASCII code that will compress the character print. (In a computer lab, ask an operator about this.) On an Epson printer, the ASCII code is 015. The Prowriter codes are 027 and 081, used together.
\015 RETURN	2. To use the compressed print option on an Epson, type, in response to the prompt, Enter Setup Print String: \015 RETURN. On a Prowriter, type \027\081 RETURN. Other printers require still other setups. (In a computer lab, the operators should be able to give you this information.)
MR130 RETURN	After typing the RETURN in the setup string, you are returned to the Options menu. By typing MR130 RETURN, you extend the right margin so that the printer will print 130 rather than 76 characters per line.
Q	This takes you out of the Options menu.
A	This aligns the paper.
G	This sends the worksheet to the printer, which prints it in compressed pitch, as shown in Exhibit 6-3.

===

Exhibit 6-3

Initial Set-Up to Explain the DATA TABLE Command (LB6X3)
            k =   10.00%

	1985	1986	1987	1988	1989	1990	1991	1992
Project cost	$10,000							
Unit sales		100	100	100	100	100	100	100
Sales price		$50	$50	$50	$50	$50	$50	$50
Revenues		$5,000	$5,000	$5,000	$5,000	$5,000	$5,000	$5,000
Op. costs		1,750	1,750	1,750	1,750	1,750	1,750	1,750
Depreciation		2,000	2,000	2,000	2,000	2,000	2,000	2,000
Total costs		$3,750	$3,750	$3,750	$3,750	$3,750	$3,750	$3,750
Taxable income		$1,250	$1,250	$1,250	$1,250	$1,250	$1,250	$1,250
Taxes (46%)		575	575	575	575	575	575	575
Net income		$675	$675	$675	$675	$675	$675	$675
Depreciation		2,000	2,000	2,000	2,000	2,000	2,000	2,000
Cash flow	($10,000)	$2,675	$2,675	$2,675	$2,675	$2,675	$2,675	$2,675

===

        NPV = $3,023   IRR =   18.69%

===

Once you have completed the small print option, you may want to save your worksheet as LB6X3, which will save your Print options. If you need to print this worksheet again, you will not have to enter your setup string. However, you may also want to reset the string to regular print on your

printer. We normally use 12 characters per inch. On an
Epson printer, to reset the Print option you would use this
string: \018. On a Prowriter, you would use this string:
\027\078. If you do not reset the Print option, the next
worksheet you print will be printed in small print. Alternatively, you can return the print to regular type by typing
\PPCFQ, which resets the setup string to the global default
setting.

> Note: On many printers, the most recent setup string
> sent to the printer remains in effect until the printer
> is turned off. This means that if you print a new
> file, the second file also will be printed in com-
> pressed print. Therefore, you should turn the printer
> off and back on after printing a file using a setup
> string to clear the printer's memory.

Solving Complex Equations

Lotus 1-2-3 can be used to solve complex equations where an
iterative process must be used to solve for an unknown.
This iterative process can be accomplished through trial and
error or by using the 1-2-3 IF statements along with the
automatic recalculation feature. We will explain how each
method is used with the data in Exhibit 6-4, which determines the expected rate of return on a nonconstant growth
stock, in this case one expected to grow at a rate of 20
percent for four years (D_0, not shown, was $1.67) and at 6
percent thereafter. The input data section shows the initial stock price, P_0, the projected dividends in the four
years of supernormal growth, and the long-run projected
growth rate, g, after four years. These inputs are used to
solve for k in the following valuation equation:

$$P_0 = \frac{D_1}{1+k} + \frac{D_2}{(1+k)^2} + \frac{D_3}{(1+k)^3} + \frac{D_4}{(1+k)^4} + \left(\frac{D_4(1+g)}{k-g}\right)\left(\frac{1}{1+k}\right)^4$$

$$24 = \frac{2.00}{1+k} + \frac{2.40}{(1+k)^2} + \frac{2.88}{(1+k)^3} + \frac{3.46}{(1+k)^4} + \left(\frac{3.46(1.06)}{k-0.06}\right)\left(\frac{1}{1+k}\right)^4$$

204

This is the valuation equation for a nonconstant growth stock, where g is variable from Years 1 through 4, but it stabilizes at 6 percent after Year 4. The last term in the equation evaluates the stock as a constant growth stock at t = 4, and finds the PV of P_4.

===

Exhibit 6-4

Determining k for a Nonconstant Growth Stock (LB6X4)

1. Manual Iterative Solution Technique:

Instructions: Begin with a guess as to the rate of return, inputted as a decimal in cell C20. Compare the value in G19 with Po in C12. Make changes in C20 until the value in G19 is approximately equal to the stock price, Po. If G19>C12, increase C20, and lower it if G19<C12.

INPUTS:			OUTPUT:	
Stock price	= Po	$24.00	PV D1	$1.70
Year 1 div.	= D1	2.00	PV D2	1.74
Year 2 div.	= D2	2.40	PV D3	1.78
Year 3 div.	= D3	2.88	PV D4	1.82
Year 4 div.	= D4	3.46	Sum PV D1-D4	7.05
Long run div.			Est. of P4	32.20
growth	= g	6.00%	PV of P4	16.96
			Est. of Price, Po	$24.00
K GUESS		17.39%		

2. Using @IF statements to automate the iterative process.

Instructions: Input the necessary data into C30.C36.

INPUTS		OUTPUT	
-------------		---------	
Po	$24.00	PV D1	$1.70
D1	2.00	PV D2	1.74
D2	2.40	PV D3	1.77
D3	2.88	PV D4	1.81
D4	3.46	Sum PV D1-D4	7.02
		Est. of Po	23.58
G	6.00%	k est.	0.173333
K GUESS	17.58%		

===

205

The top half of Exhibit 6-4 shows how to solve for k using the trial-and-error method. Follow these steps to set up your worksheet:

1. Type in the labels as given on Exhibit 6-4. Then input the data on P_0, D_1 to D_4, and g, the long-run growth rate, in Column C, Cells C12.C18. Also, make a guess as to the rate of return, and input it as a decimal in C20. We often start with 10 percent, input as .10 and formatted as a percentage, but $(D_1/P_0) + g$ is also a good starting point. Note that g should be input in Cell C18 as 0.06 and formatted to a percentage.

2. In the output section, we find the PV of the first four dividends and the PV of the price at t = 4, when the stock is a constant growth stock. In finding these PVs, we use the discount rate given in Cell C20 for K GUESS. Here are the formulas used in the output cells:

Labels in Column E	Cell in which Formula Is Placed	Formula
PV D1	G12	+C13/(1+$C$20)
PV D2	G13	+C14/((1+$C$20)^2)
PV D3	G14	+C15/((1+$C$20)^3)
PV D4	G15	+C16/((1+$C$20)^4)
Sum PV D1-D4	G16	@SUM(G12.G15)
Est. of P4	G17	(C16*(1+C18))/(C20-C18)
PV of P4	G18	+G17/(1+C20)^4
Est. of Price, P_0	G19	+G16+G18

3. The values calculated in Step 2 are all "first approximations" based on the discount rate that was input as K GUESS. Unless by some freak chance K GUESS started out as the correct value, it will change, and so will the values in Column G, in the iterative process. (Note that Part 1 of Exhibit 6-4 shows the final guess along with the associated calculations.)

4. To begin the iterations, we compare the value in Cell G19, which is an estimate of P_0 based on the discount rate in C20, with the actual price as input in C12. If G19>C12, our guess about the discount rate was too low, so we must raise it. Conversely, if G19<C12, we must lower the discount rate.

5. Put the pointer on C20 and type in a new guess, observe the new price estimate in G19, and continue changing C20 until G19 is approximately equal to C12. Convergence occurs with K GUESS = 17.39 percent. Type in your guesses as decimals, not as percentages.

The manual approach set forth above is probably the easiest procedure if you need to evaluate only one equation. However, if you needed to find the rates of return for many stocks, it would be more efficient to automate the process. See the lower section of Exhibit 6-4. Here are the steps we used to develop and then use the model:

1. Input the labels, initial price, dividends, and long-run growth rate as was done above.

2. Use the following formulas to find K GUESS and the PV of the dividends and P_4. Enter the formula for K GUESS in Cell C38 first, and wait to enter the other formulas until we tell you to do so, in Step 4 below.

Label	Cell for Formula	Formula
K GUESS	C38	@IF(G36>0,G36,+C31/C30+ C36)
PV D1	G30	+C31/(1+$C$38)
PV D2	G31	+C32/((1+$C$38)^2)
PV D3	G32	+C33/((1+$C$38)^3)
PV D4	G33	+C34/((1+$C$38)^4)
Sum PV D1-D4	G34	@SUM(G30.G33)
Est. of P_0	G35	+G34+((C34*(1+C36)/(C38-C36))*(1/((1+C38)^4)))
k Est.	G36	@IF(C30=G35,C38,@IF(C30< G35,C38+.0025,C38-.0025))

207

3. Look closely now at the formula in C38 for K GUESS. It tells 1-2-3 to compare the value in G36 with 0. If G36>0, then substitute the value in G36 into C38; but if G36 is not greater than zero--which will be the case when the model starts--then place in C38 the value for $(D_1/P_0) + g$. Therefore, this value will be the initial K GUESS, but it will change each time the model is recalculated. This initial value is 14.33 percent.

4. Now enter the other formulas in Column G. When you finish, circularity will exist in the model--the formula in G36 will depend on the value in C38, but the value in C38 will also depend on G36. What we will have, in effect, is a system of simultaneous equations. 1-2-3 will notify us of this situation by a highlighted CIRC at the bottom of the screen.

5. Now look closely at the formula in G36 for k est. It is a nested, or embedded, IF statement which asks 1-2-3 to compare the value in C30, the known price, with the estimated price that was calculated in G35 and, if the two are equal, to give k est. the value of K GUESS. However, if the value in C30 is less than that in G35, this means that the value of K GUESS was too low, so 1-2-3 is told to increase K GUESS by .0025, or .25 percent, and try again. If C30 is greater than G35, 1-2-3 is told to lower K GUESS by .0025 and try again.

6. 1-2-3 recalculates each time a change is made to a worksheet. We can tell 1-2-3 to recalculate manually by pressing the F9 function key, the one at the extreme lower left corner of the keyboard. Every time you press F9, 1-2-3 recalculates the worksheet. (We discuss recalculation in more detail in the next section.) When we initially keyed in this problem, G36 had a value of zero, so K GUESS was set at $(D_1/P_0) + g$ = 2/24 + .06 = .14333. That value was too low, so Est. of $P_0 > P_0$. When we pressed the F9 key, 1-2-3 added .0025 to .14333, got .14583, and calculated a new value for Est. of P_0, which was still too large. Successive iterations by pressing the F9 key caused the discount rate to rise and the estimate of P_0 to get closer and closer to the actual P_0.

7. However, since K GUESS changes in increments of .0025, we can never get to the exact value; rather, we oscillate around the exact value. Hence, with this model we can never (or rarely) get an exact solution to the rate of return. When we see the Est. of P_0 in G35 oscillating between \$24.13 and @23.58, and k est. oscillating between 17.33 and 17.58 percent, we know we are as close as we can get with this model. You may save this file as LB6X4.

8. We could edit the formula in G36 and use an adjustment factor of .0001 rather than .0025 to get a closer estimate--with .0001, we would be within 1/100 of 1 percent. We could use a tolerance adjustment of .00001 and get even closer. Note, however, that the smaller we set the adjustment factor, the greater the number of iterations required to get a solution. So we face a trade-off between accuracy and calculating speed.

More elaborate and efficient models could be written which would lead to an accurate solution in fewer iterations. For example, Newton's method for solving polynomials could be used. Given the level of accuracy of most stock market data, such as forecasted dividends and growth rates, we usually do not worry about small errors.

Alternative Recalculation Procedures

In the preceding section, we discussed Lotus 1-2-3's recalculation procedures. Actually, 1-2-3 gives you several choices, all of which are worth discussing. To begin, type /WGR to call up the menu which lists the recalculation options:

Natural. By using the /WGRN option (which is the default option), whenever you change an input value in a 1-2-3 worksheet, 1-2-3 recalculates all relevant cell values to adjust them to the new input. The change "ripples" through the worksheet in what Lotus calls "natural" order, meaning that the values in all cells that are used in other cells are calculated first. For example, if the value in B2 is used in A1, then B2 is recalculated before A1. As noted, 1-2-3's default procedure is Natural.

Column-Wise or Row-Wise. You can ask 1-2-3 to recalculate down columns (/WGRC) or across rows (/WGRR). We have never used this option.

Automatic. /WGRA is, like Natural, a default setting, and it simply means that when you change an input, 1-2-3 automatically recalculates the worksheet. If you have 50 inputs and want to change each of them, 50 recalculations will occur.

Manual. If you have a large worksheet and want to change a number of inputs, then it will pay you to use the Manual recalculation option. If you type /WGRM, no recalculation will occur when you change an input (unless you have a circular reference, in which case recalculations will occur even if recalculation is set on Manual). Rather, when you change the input, the highlighted word CALC will appear at the bottom of your screen. Now you must press the Calc key, F9, before 1-2-3 will do the recalculation. As noted above, this is a useful feature when you have a large worksheet and want to change a number of inputs before doing the recalculation. If you made the changes with recalculations set on Automatic, the recalculation would occur after each input change, and you would have to wait for each recalculation before making each data change. Using Manual recalculation, you would simply change all the inputs, then press the F9 key to get one recalculation, and save time. You can go back to Automatic simply by typing /WGRA.

Iterations. As we saw in our discussion of the lower model in Exhibit 6-4, if you have a circular reference you must have the model go through a number of recalculations to reach an approximate solution. We simply pressed the F9, or Calc, key until we got as close as we could get with our model. Alternatively, we could have told 1-2-3 the number of recalculations we wanted it to perform when we press the

F9 key. If you typed /WGRI, you would get a prompt asking how many iterations you wanted. You could select from 1 to 50. Then, when you pressed the Calc key (F9), 1-2-3 would automatically go through the requested number of iterations. Note, though, that 1-2-3 will recalculate the indicated number of iterations whenever a change is made to the worksheet, which can be time consuming if you are making a number of changes. This is another reason for setting the worksheet on Manual recalculation whenever you use the Iteration feature and change several inputs.

Before leaving this section, press the ESC key four times to get back to READY mode and type /WGRN and /WGRM to insure that you have your recalculation settings on both natural and manual.

Protection Features

1-2-3 offers two protection features. One protects cells in a worksheet against inadvertent errors such as erasing them or entering data on top of data already in the cell. The other protection feature keeps people from retrieving a file you do not want them to have access to, such as a file with employees' salaries.

Protecting Cells

It is often useful to set up a worksheet with two types of cells, protected and unprotected. For example, in Chapter 8 we will set up a spreadsheet wherein you enter balance sheet and income statement data, after which the spreadsheet model generates common-size statements and a set of ratios. You may use the model to analyze different companies by erasing the data for one company and then inserting new data for the next company.
    When changes are to be made to a worksheet by erasing certain cells, there is a danger that a cell which should be retained will be erased, or one whose data should not change will be changed in error. To guard against those possibilities, 1-2-3 permits you to protect selected cells. For

example, retrieve file LB6X4 (if it is not already on your screen), where you found the rate of return on a nonconstant growth stock. Suppose you want to give that worksheet to someone and have him or her find rates of return on different stocks. Normally, the person would simply change the data in Cells C12.C20 (or in C30.38) and get a new rate of return. But if you are afraid they might inadvertently change some other part of the worksheet and thus "mess it up," you can guard against that possibility by protecting all cells except those in the range C12.C20; then, only the cells in that range can be changed. Here are the keystrokes required:

    /   Main command menu
    W   Worksheet
    G   Global
    P   Protection
    E   Enable

If you just typed /WGPE, then no cell in the worksheet can be changed. If you try to write something in a blank cell, or to change one of the filled cells, you will get a "beep" and an error message. After typing these keystrokes you will be in READY mode. Then put the pointer on Cell C12, and type

                    /RU C12.C20 RETURN

Those keystrokes unprotect cells in the range C12.C20, making it possible to change those cells but no others.
        You may have noticed a change in the entries in your unprotected cells--items in unprotected cells are distinguished to differentiate them. You may have to use the brightness knob on your monitor (the one that is half black and half white) to help you see better which ones are protected. Turn the brightness down low, and the unprotected cells will stand out brightly. (On a color monitor, the unprotected cells will generally appear green and the protected cells white.) The cell pointer should be on some other cell to enable you to see the contrast in the unprotected cell.

                            212

If you wanted to make other changes in the worksheet--say, add a note at the bottom--you would temporarily disable the global protect feature with this command:

/WGPD

Then, once the changes were made, you could reprotect by typing

/WGPE

Protecting Files

If you are using 1-2-3 Release 2, you can restrict access to one or more files on your storage diskette or hard disk. Suppose a company's treasurer wants to restrict access to salary data, yet wants to have diskettes (or a hard disk) available to a selected group of employees who must work with that data. Here's how the file could be protected:

1. Retrieve the file to be protected and have it on the screen.

2. Type /FS .

3. Type in the name of the file--for example, Salaries --press the space bar , type a P , and then press RETURN .

4. 1-2-3 will then ask you to enter a password, which can be up to 15 characters long. For this exercise, use xyz . When you type xyz, three little boxes will appear on the screen.

5. Press RETURN , and you will be asked to verify the password. Type xyz again, and enter it.

6. Once the protected file has been saved, you cannot retrieve it unless you know the password, <u>so never save a file with a password without being sure you can remember it</u>.

7. To retrieve the file, type /FR (file name) . You will be asked to enter the password. Type xyz RETURN , and your file will be retrieved.

8. To change the password, or to unprotect the file, do the following. First, type /FS , then press ESC . If you press RETURN now, the file will be saved unprotected under the name (file name). If you want to change the password--say, to abc--after ESC, press the space bar , type P , and press RETURN . Then enter abc , and proceed as before.

Summary

This chapter dealt with 1-2-3's regression analysis procedure, and it also introduced several additional topics, including word processing, the compressed print option, iterative procedures for solving equations, recalculation procedures, and 1-2-3's protection features. We will use all of these procedures when we go on to the financial models in Part II.

Chapter 6
Summary of Commands

Command	Function	Page
Alternative Recalculation Procedures:		
/WGRN	Recalculations made in "natural" order (Default option)	209
/WGRC	Recalculations made down columns	210
/WGRR	Recalculations made across rows	210
/WGRA	Recalculates automatically with any changes made (default option)	210
/WGRM	No recalculation made until F9 key is pressed	210
/WGRI(Select # of iterations) RETURN	Requests number of calculation iterations	210
Compressed print: /PPR(Enter range to be printed) RETURN OS(Enter setup string for your printer) RETURN MR130 RETURN QAG	Changes print from normal size to compressed print	201
Data Regression: /DR X(Enter X range) RETURN Y(Enter Y range) RETURN I RETURN O(Enter output range) RETURN G	Performs a linear regression analysis	193

Command	Function	Page
Protecting files: /FS(File name)(Press space bar)P RETURN (Enter password) RETURN (Verify password) RETURN	Protects a file	213
/FR(File name)(Enter password) RETURN	Retrieves a protected file	214
/FS(Press Escape key) RETURN	Unprotects a protected file	214
/FS(Press Escape key) (Press space bar) P RETURN (Enter new password) RETURN (Verify new password) RETURN	Changes passwords	214
Protecting/unprotecting cells: /WGPE	Global protect feature	212
/RU(Enter range to be unprotected) RETURN	Overrides Global Protect	212
/WGPD	Disables global protect feature	213
Range Justify: /RJ(Enter range) RETURN	Reformats paragraphs with changes	200

Chapter 6 Exercises

6-1 Annual sales and advertising expenditure data for the last 10 years for Landover Corporation are given below. Landover's managers would like to know what relation-ship exists between sales and advertising to help them plan the firm's future advertising expenditures. Enter the labels and data shown below into a 1-2-3 worksheet. Actual sales will be the dependent, or y, variable and advertising expenditures will be the independent, or x, variable. Use the Data Regression command to perform a regression analysis on the data and answer the following questions.

```
          A         B         C         D         E         F         G         H
1    Landover Corporation Regression Analysis (LB6EX1)
2
3    Sales and Advertising Expenditures are shown in millions.
4
5                        Advert.
6      Year    Sales    Expand.
7    ------------------------------------------
8      1976     3.3      0.23
9      1977     3.0      0.20
10     1978     3.7      0.29
11     1979     4.0      0.37
12     1980     3.1      0.33
13     1981     3.8      0.24
14     1982     4.2      0.38
15     1983     4.9      0.36
16     1984     4.5      0.40
17     1985     5.6      0.44
18
19
20
```

a. What is the equation of the least squares model? (Hint: Move pointer to Cell A20 and type the following: /DRX C8.C17 RETURN Y B8.B17 RETURN O A20 RETURN I RETURN G) Your equation should be of the form Sales = a + b (advertising expenditures), where a is the y-intercept (constant) value and b is the slope of the regression line.

217

b. Identify the values for the following:
1. R^2
2. Standard error of the y estimate
3. Standard error of the coefficient
4. Degrees of freedom

c. In Column D type the label headings ˆPredicted in Cell D5 and ˆSales in Cell D6. Then in Cell D8 type in the equation which will calculate predicted sales based on your regression model developed in Part 1. Remember to use absolute cell references for the intercept and slope ranges. Copy this equation into Cells D9.D17 and format Cells D8.D17 to 1 decimal place.

d. Create a scatter diagram of actual sales versus predicted sales. Plot the actual sales values as symbols and the predicted sales value as a line. Use title headings, legends, save your graph, and print it out. Save your file as LB6EX1. (Hint: Type the following:

/GTXX D8.D17 RETURN A B8.B17 RETURN OFASQCQ B D8.D17 RETURN OFBLQLA Actual RETURN LB Predicted RETURN TF Annual Sales RETURN TS as a Function of Advertising RETURN TX Predicted Sales RETURN TY Actual Sales RETURN Q .

Now, press V to view the graph and press any key to return to the worksheet. Remember to save the graph so you may print it out, and if you save the worksheet as LB6EX1, the graph specifications will be saved.)

6-2 Retrieve File LB6EX1. Go to Cell A1, insert 7 blank rows, and type the following text:

	A	B	C	D	E	F	G	H
1	This worksheet shows actual sales and advertising expenditures of							
2	Landover Corporation during the period from 1976-1985. A regression							
3	equation is developed and its output is shown below. Predicted sales							
4	are determined using the regression model developed using the Lotus							
5	Data Regression command.							
6								
7								

218

a. Change the text from "This worksheet shows" to "The worksheet shown below details". Notice that the first line of the text is too long. Use the Range Justify command to correct this problem.

b. Type the following text on the remainder of Line 5:

The data given below can be changed so that a new regression equation can be developed.

Obviously, the line will not all fit on Line 5. Use the Range Justify command to correct this problem. You may resave the file as LB6EX1.

6-3 Retrieve File LB6EX1. Before doing anything else to the file, change the automatic recalculation procedure to manual. Now, change the data in Cells B17.C26 as shown below. Then redo the Data Regression command by typing /DRG to develop a new regression model. (Note: You do not need to change the X or Y ranges that have been previously entered.) Once that has been done, press the F9 key so that the predicted sales values are recalculated. Check your scatter diagram to see how these changes look on your XY graph. If you wish to print this new graph you must save it--either with a new graph file name or as a replacement for the old graph file name.

Sales	Advertising Expenditures
15	0.72
18	0.74
24	0.92
22	1.10
25	0.98
29	1.12
30	1.43
32	1.33
35	1.31
38	1.52

Save the file as LB6EX3.

Chapter 7
Macros

Table of Contents

Basic Macros   222
Rules for Creating and Using Macros   223
An Illustrative Macro   227
Summary   231

- -

This chapter discusses <u>macros</u>, an important feature of
1-2-3. It also provides as an example a model which uses
macros to create interest factor tables.

Macros add a programming dimension to 1-2-3. In
essence, a "macro" is a typed list of keystrokes. Rather
than have 1-2-3 <u>execute</u> a set of commands as you type each
one, as we have done throughout the book up to this point,
you can save the commands in a "program" and then have the
program executed at a later date. To write a macro program,
you type the command keystrokes as a label into a cell or
group of cells. The cell or set of cells is given a name
which always consists of a backslash plus one letter, such
as \A. At that point, the cells containing the commands are
defined as a macro whose name is \A. Then, whenever you
simultaneously press the ALT key (located in the lower left
section of the keyboard) and the letter designator of your
macro, 1-2-3 will automatically execute the set of keystrokes. Note that 1-2-3 accepts both \A and \a as the name
of the macro; therefore, although we show the macro name as
\A, you may use either uppercase or lowercase letters to
name and execute macros.

The 1-2-3 Manual distinguishes between two different
types of macros: (1) <u>basic macros</u>, which are relatively
easy to use, and (2) <u>advanced macros</u>, which provide true
programming capabilities to Lotus 1-2-3. The Manual recom-
mends that people not attempt to work advanced macros unless
they are either experienced users of 1-2-3 basic macros or

experienced programmers. Therefore, we shall concentrate
our discussion on basic macros.

Basic Macros

To illustrate how basic macros work, get a blank worksheet
on your screen. Suppose you are setting up some reports for
your company, West Corporation, and you want the company's
name to appear in a number of places on the worksheet.
Here's what you could do:

1. Drop down to an out-of-sight location, say, B21.

2. Type in

             West Corporation~

   Notice that the word Corporation is immediately followed by a tilde (~), which on most keyboards is the
   uppercase character over the single left quote. Next,
   press the RETURN key. West Corporation~ will now
   appear in Cell B21.

3. With the pointer still on B21, type

               /RNC \A RETURN RETURN

   This creates a <u>named range</u> called \A in Cell B21; that
   is, it gives the single-cell range B21 the name \A.

You now have a macro named \A which will print the words
West Corporation in the cell where the pointer is located
each time you simultaneously press the ALT and the A keys.
Try it by going to Home and pressing, simultaneously, ALT
A . Then go to a few other cells, and you will see that
each time you press ALT A, the words West Corporation
appear.

Rules for Creating and Using Macros

In this section we provide some general rules pertaining to macros. After that, we provide an illustration of how macros are used.

1. When making a macro, always go through the keystrokes once (either in your mind or, better yet, both on a piece of paper and on the computer) to establish the exact sequence of keystrokes you want in your macro.

2. The tilde (~) is the macro symbol for RETURN. Thus, in our macro which wrote the words West Corporation, the tilde told 1-2-3 to enter the label West Corporation. Without the tilde, nothing would have happened--it would have been like typing the words West Corporation and then forgetting to press the RETURN key.

3. Note that a macro is a label. By construction, a macro must be a label. Thus, if you want to write a macro that would logically start out with a symbol that 1-2-3 would read as a number or a formula, such as @ or 1, you must use the apostrophe (') prefix. Also, if your macro uses a command which requires accessing the main menu, the slash must be preceded by an apostrophe as well. For example, a macro that tells 1-2-3 to display all numbers in a worksheet as integers would be written as '/WGFF0~; without the apostrophe, 1-2-3 would see the / as the command menu designator, and the command would be executed immediately rather than being stored as a macro to be executed later as a part of a macro program.

4. Macros are typed in some out-of-the-way place; this is called their location. For example, the location for our illustrative macro was Cell B21, which was off the screen.

5. Most keystrokes can be entered into a macro merely by typing the appropriate key; however, certain keys must

be indicated, or designated, as shown in Exhibit 7-1.
A number of other key indicators are discussed in the
1-2-3 Manual, but we omit a discussion of them here,
because we rarely use them.

===

Exhibit 7-1
Macro Key Indicators

Macro Key Indicator	What It Does	Macro Key Indicator	What It Does
~	RETURN	{esc}	Escape
{down}	Move down 1 row	{graph}	Graph (F10 key)
{up}	Move up 1 row		
{left}	Move left 1 column	{end}	End key
{right}	Move right 1 column	{bs}	Backspace
{pgdn}	Move down 1 page	{name}	F3 key
{pgup}	Move up 1 page	{abs}	F4 key
{bigleft}	Move left one screen	{window}	F6 key
{bigright}	Move right one screen	{query}	F7 key
{home}	Go to Cell A1	{table}	F8 key
{del}	Delete	{calc}	Recalculate spreadsheet (F9 key)
{edit}	Edit (F2 key)		
{goto}	Go to (F5 key)		
{?}	Pause for manual input until user presses RETURN	{beep}	Causes the computer to beep

Note: A repetition factor can be inserted to produce con-
secutive uses of the key within braces; for example, {right
3} moves the cell pointer three spaces to the right, while
{calc 5} causes five recalculations.

===

Whenever you type one of these indicators, 1-2-3
performs the indicated operation when it comes to it in
a macro. For example, if 1-2-3 finds the term {up 2}
when executing a macro, the same thing happens as if

you press the up arrow key (↑) twice--the pointer moves up two cells. Note from Exhibit 7-1 that all indicators except the tilde must always be placed in braces; also, the brace is interpreted as a label, so a macro beginning with a brace does not need an apostrophe.

6. Each macro must be (1) in a single cell or (2) in a column of adjacent cells. We generally put simple macros in a single cell, but we write long, complex macros into a column of cells, generally with one logical step in each cell. For example, if we wanted to write a macro that caused the pointer to go to Cell A2, then to double the contents of Cell A1, and then write the result in A2, we would type it into two cells as follows:

{goto}A2~

'+A1*2~

7. <u>Ending the macro</u>. There must be a blank cell or a non-label cell at the end of the macro--this tells 1-2-3 that you have completed the macro. If the cell just below the last cell in a macro is a label, 1-2-3 will assume that it is part of the original macro, even if it is meant to be a second one, and will execute it along with the first macro. So we always leave the cell below each macro blank.

8. <u>Naming the macro and specifying its location</u>. Once you have typed in your macro, you must specify its range and give it a name. You specify the range with these commands:

/RNC   This tells 1-2-3 you want to create a named range.

\A RETURN   This names the range \A, or "backslash A". All macro names must contain the backslash plus one letter; therefore, the maximum number of macros per worksheet is 26, that is, \A, ... \Z.

B21 RETURN   Assuming you have located the macro in Cells
                    B21.B22, this tells 1-2-3 that the macro \A is
                    located in the range that begins in B21. When
                    naming macro ranges, it is necessary to
                    specify only the beginning cell.

   We generally write macros in one column, put their
names (that is, \A, \B, and so forth) in the column
just to the left, and then insert comments in a column
to the right of the macro column if that would be
useful.
        If you have several macros in a big worksheet,
1-2-3 will give you a list of the macros and their
locations. Move to a blank cell which has enough blank
space below it to accommodate a list of the macros, and
type this command:

                    /RNT RETURN

   A table listing the macros' names and the first cell of
each of their ranges will instantly be created.

9.   Executing the macro. Once a macro has been created and
     named, it will be invoked, or executed, whenever you
     simultaneously press the ALT key and the macro's letter
     designator. (The backslash is not typed when invoking
     the macro.) The execution command can be given from
     any location. For example, if the pointer is on X10
     and you press ALT A , the macro {goto}A2~'+A1*2~
     will cause 1-2-3 to immediately go to A2 and put
     therein the contents of A1, doubled, and then leave the
     pointer at A2, just as if you had typed the keystrokes
     in the macro. However, if we leave off the {goto}A2~
     part of the macro, then A1*2 will have been entered in
     the cell with the pointer at the time the macro command
     [Alt] A was executed.
          As a macro is executed, the pointer literally
     moves about the screen, and the operations called for
     by the keystrokes are literally performed. However,
     the execution is generally too fast for you to follow
     what is happening. To help you follow the macro's
     steps, you can, before you execute the macro, press the

226

ALT key and, with ALT still depressed, press the F2 key to put 1-2-3 into STEP mode. The word STEP will appear at the bottom of the screen. Then, when you execute the macro by pressing ALT A (or whatever other letter designates your macro), it will proceed one keystroke at a time, and you can cause each keystroke to be executed by pressing the RETURN key repeatedly. This will let you see exactly what the macro is doing, and it can be helpful in debugging complex macros. You can leave STEP mode and go back to regular execution by pressing ALT F2 again.

An Illustrative Macro

In Chapter 3 you created a table which calculated the future value of $1 for 10 periods and 7 interest rates. You then modified that model to create interest factor tables for the present value of $1, and also the future and present values of an annuity of $1 per period. You followed these steps to create the additional tables from the first one:

1. You changed the title of the spreadsheet.

2. You changed the formula for 1 percent, 0 periods.

3. You copied the new formula down the 1 percent column.

4. You copied the 1 percent column across the remaining columns.

It was necessary to go through those four steps each time you wanted to create a different interest factor table. It was also necessary to save each table as a separate model if you wanted to be able to use it in the future.

Now we will show you how to create these tables with only one spreadsheet using macros. You will retrieve the future value interest factor table, LB3X3, and add four easy macros to it. These macros will convert the model to any of the four interest factor tables simply by typing ALT and the letter attached to the macro. The required steps are listed below. Remember, if you make a typing error, you can press the F2 function key, go into EDIT mode, and correct the error. You can do this either before or after you enter the statement.

1. Retrieve file LB3X3 from your storage diskette or from our diskette.

2. Type \WIR A1.A6 RETURN to add 6 blank lines at the top. Then type INTEREST FACTOR TABLE MODEL (LB7X2) in Cell A1, and type the note shown in Exhibit 7-2 in Cells A3.A5. This step is not necessary for the macro to work, but you should get in the habit of adding notes to your models so you will not forget what you have done and also so other people can use them.

3. Move to Cell B22 and enter the following:

    {goto}a7~Future Value of $1 at the end of n periods~

    This tells 1-2-3 to move the pointer to Cell A7 and to enter the label "Future Value of $1 at the end of n periods" into that cell.

4. Move to Cell B23 and enter this:

    {goto}b10~(1+b$9)^$a10~

    This puts the pointer on Cell B10 and enters the future value formula there.

5. Go to Cell B24 and enter this:

    '/cb10~b11.b20~

    This tells 1-2-3 to copy the future value formula contained in B10 down the 1 percent column. Make sure you type the label prefix ' ; otherwise, the Copy command will be executed immediately.

6.   Go to B25, and enter

        '/cb10.b20~c10.h20~

     to copy the 1 percent column formulas into the other
     columns.

7.   Move back to Cell B22, and name this cell \A by typing

                /RNC\A RETURN RETURN

8.   Move to Cell A22, and enter '\A to enter the label
     \A. This is to remind you of the name of the macro
     which starts in B22.

9.   Now go to Home , and then press the ALT and the A
     keys simultaneously. Your macro should execute. If
     something looks wrong, check your typing.

     You have now created a macro which will convert the
spreadsheet into a future value interest factor table when
the ALT and A keys are pressed simultaneously. You could
go through similar steps to make the other three tables.
Instead, retrieve our file LB7X2, which is shown in Exhibit
7-2, and take a look at our macros. The macro to create a
present value table begins in Cell B27 and is named \B; the
future value annuity macro starts in B32 and is named \C;
and the present value annuity macro starts in B37 and is
named \D. The four macros are very similar. The first line
of each macro gives a title to the interest factor table the
macro makes, the second line enters the correct formula in
Cell B10, and Lines 3 and 4 of the macro copy that formula.
When we wrote these macros, we actually copied the four
lines of the first one into each of the other macro ranges
and then edited the first two lines by going into EDIT mode
with the F2 function key. The third and fourth lines of
each macro are identical.

==

Exhibit 7-2

INTEREST FACTOR TABLE MODEL (LB7X2)

You can use this model to create interest factor tables. Press ALT A
to create a future value table, ALT B for a present value table,
ALT C for a fv annuity table, and ALT D for a pv annuity table.

FUTURE VALUE OF $1 AT THE END OF N PERIODS

PERIODS	1.00%	2.00%	3.00%	4.00%	5.00%	6.00%	7.00%
0	1.0000	1.0000	1.0000	1.0000	1.0000	1.0000	1.0000
1	1.0100	1.0200	1.0300	1.0400	1.0500	1.0600	1.0700
2	1.0201	1.0404	1.0609	1.0816	1.1025	1.1236	1.1449
3	1.0303	1.0612	1.0927	1.1249	1.1576	1.1910	1.2250
4	1.0406	1.0824	1.1255	1.1699	1.2155	1.2625	1.3108
5	1.0510	1.1041	1.1593	1.2167	1.2763	1.3382	1.4026
6	1.0615	1.1262	1.1941	1.2653	1.3401	1.4185	1.5007
7	1.0721	1.1487	1.2299	1.3159	1.4071	1.5036	1.6058
8	1.0829	1.1717	1.2668	1.3686	1.4775	1.5938	1.7182
9	1.0937	1.1951	1.3048	1.4233	1.5513	1.6895	1.8385
10	1.1046	1.2190	1.3439	1.4802	1.6289	1.7908	1.9672

```
\A        {goto}a7~Future value of $1 at the end of n periods~
          {goto}b10~(1+b$9)^$a10~
          /cb10~b11.b20~
          /cb10.b20~c10.h20~

\B        {goto}a7~Present value of $1 at the end of n periods~
          {goto}b10~1/((1+b$9)^$a10)~
          /cb10~b11.b20~
          /cb10.b20~c10.h20~

\C        {goto}a7~Future value of $1 per period for n periods~
          {goto}b10~@FV(1,b$9,$a10)~
          /cb10~b11.b20~
          /cb10.b20~c10.h20~

\D        {goto}a7~Present value of $1 per period for n periods~
          {goto}b10~@PV(1,b$9,$a10)~
          /cb10~b11.b20~
          /cb10.b20~c10.h20~
```

==

Although we do not do it here, we often use the Global Protect command to keep people from messing up our models. When we have the protection enabled, we must begin the macro with /WGPD to disable the global protection feature and allow the macro to modify the model; otherwise, the various cells could not be changed. We then end the macro with /WGPE to reactivate the protect feature. This is illustrated in our two Chapter 15 models, which call for new input data to be entered into an option pricing model and a bond duration model, for a macro to then cause output data to be generated, and finally to return the models to the point where they are ready for new input.

Summary

The purpose of this chapter was to introduce you to 1-2-3's macros, which are "programs within a program." Normally, as you enter instructions through the keyboard, 1-2-3 executes the various steps as you type them in. However, 1-2-3's macro system permits you to enter instructions and have them stored for later execution--the set of stored instructions is defined as a macro.

At this point you should be able to recognize the usefulness of macros, and you may even be able to create some simple macros yourself. In many of the chapters which follow, we use macros (1) to call up graphs, (2) to print the worksheet using different Print options for different ranges, and (3) to use one model with multiple scenarios. You should be able to look at these macros and to understand what they are doing.

Chapter 7 Exercises

7-1 Retrieve File LB7X2 on the diskette that came with the Lotus book. Page down your worksheet so that Cell A21 is in the left-hand corner of your computer screen and all 4 macros are displayed on the screen as well. Now, do the following:

a. Press the ALT key and A simultaneously to run the first macro which creates the Future Value Table. Print the Future Value Table.

b. Do Step 1 for each of the remaining macros, making sure that you follow how each macro works so you will be able to do Exercises 7-2 and 7-3.

7-2 Retrieve File LB5X4. In LB5X4 we have set up 2 Data Tables. If we wanted to change data in the model, we would have to go through the keystrokes again to update the data table.

a. Write a macro which would update Table 1 if data in the model were changed. Make sure you type and enter the macro in a blank cell. (Hint: '/DT1 B31.C36~C8~). Remember to name the macro range \A, so that your macro can be executed by pressing the ALT key and A simultaneously. Try executing your macro to make sure it works.

   1. Change unit sales and sales price in the model. Use your macro to update Data Table 1.

b. Write a macro which would update Data Table 2, if data in the model were changed. Make sure you type and enter the macro in a blank cell. (Hint: '/DT2 B43.G48~C8~B2~). Remember to name the macro range \B, so that your macro can be executed by pressing the ALT key and B simultaneously. Try executing your macro to make sure it works.

   1. Change unit sales and sales price in the model. Use your macro to update Data Table 2. Save your file as LB7EX2.

7-3 Retrieve File LB5X4. Extract the cell range A1.G27 and
     set up a new file named LB7EX3. Retrieve File LB7EX3.

     (Note: This problem requires the student to write two
     long, but easy macros. The macros will enter the
     labels and command keystrokes necessary to create the
     specified data tables.)

     a. Write a macro which will create Data Table 1,
         complete with headings. (Hint: Set up your macro
         with the same keystrokes given in Chapter 5, pages
         169-174.) Remember to name the macro range \A.
         Press the ALT key and A simultaneously to see
         if your macro works. If your macro does not work,
         press the ALT and F2 keys simultaneously, then
         press ALT and A to run your macro in STEP mode
         to debug it.

     b. Write a macro which will create Data Table 2,
         complete with headings. (Hint: Set up your macro
         by following the keystrokes given in Chapter 5,
         pages 175-176.) Remember to name the macro range
         \B. Press the ALT and B keys simultaneously to
         see if your macro works. If your macro does not
         work, press the ALT and F2 keys simultaneously,
         then press ALT and B to run your macro in STEP
         mode to debug it. Save your file as LB7EX3.

Part II
Financial Analysis Models

Part II consists of eight chapters containing nine financial applications models. We begin with Chapter 8; it contains information pertinent to all the model chapters, so you should read it before using any of the models. Chapter 8 also provides a model for analyzing financial statements, while Chapter 9 gives a model for forecasting financial statements. Chapter 10 deals with cash budgeting, and Chapter 11 presents a model for analyzing lease versus buy decisions. Chapter 12 develops a fairly complex model for analyzing capital structure decisions, and Chapter 13 builds a model for facilitating capital budgeting analysis. Chapter 14 provides a bond refunding model, and Chapter 15 contains two models which solve two complicated financial equations--the Black-Scholes option pricing model and the bond duration equation.

Except for Chapter 8, which should be read first because it covers generic material which applies to all the model chapters, the Part II chapters can be covered in any order. Each follows a similar format: (1) The first table, or computer screen, describes the contents of the model file; (2) the second table shows the model's principal inputs; (3) then one or more output tables display the results of the analysis; and (4) if appropriate, we perform a sensitivity analysis to show the effects of changes in input assumptions on the key output items. You can use these models to help solve your own business or case problems--just substitute your own data in place of our illustrative data, and the models will generate your required output. We use 1-2-3's global protection feature to protect all the spreadsheet cells except those in which data should be entered; the unprotected data entry cells show up highlighted on the monitor. On occasion, you may find it necessary to modify our models (other than for data inputs) to fit the specifications of your problem; if so, you may turn off the global protection feature while making the modifications.

235

In developing models such as the ones in Chapters 8 through 15, this question always arises: Just how general should the models be? It is always easier to develop a model for a specific problem, and the more one attempts to expand the ability of the model to handle diverse cases, the more complex it becomes. Thus, generalized models are harder to write, harder to use, and harder to modify than simple ones, but there is obviously an advantage in having a model that can deal with more than one set of conditions. We debated just how far to go toward generalized models. Hopefully, we went far enough to accommodate most of the situations you will encounter. However, given the variety of things that can occur in practice, that is not likely-- you will almost certainly run into situations where our models accommodate 25 years of data but you need 30, or we assume monthly payments but your case calls for quarterly payments, or our model is set up for end-of-period payments but you have beginning-of-period payments.

If modifications are required, this should present no problem. First, think through the modifications, and list the sections of our model where changes must be made. Then, read our model into memory and start changing it, but save the modified model frequently (under a new file name, so our original model is left intact in case you need to go back to it). As you make individual changes, be sure that they do what they are supposed to do, then save before going on to the next change. Then, if ERR messages suddenly pop up, go back to the last saved file and look again at the change that produced the ERRs (or incorrect numbers). If you approach the modification process slowly and carefully, you should have no difficulties.

Chapter 8
Analysis of Financial Statements

We set up a simplified balance sheet back in Chapter 2. Now we will construct a more elaborate one, add an income statement, and then use these two statements to develop a sources and uses of funds statement, common-size statements, and a set of financial ratios. Our analysis uses data from Firestone Tire & Rubber Company, but the models are set up so data can be inserted for any company and used to generate a set of output data.

Layout of the Spreadsheet

Figure 8-1 gives a schematic diagram of the layout of the spreadsheet used in this chapter, and Table 8-1 gives a listing of the file contents and instructions for its use. Then, Tables 8-2 through 8-7 provide printouts of the major sections of the spreadsheet model with base case data.

Our model is straightforward. You type your balance sheet and income statement data into Tables 8-2 and 8-5, and when you press the F9 function key (the Calc key), the computer does the arithmetic necessary to generate Tables 8-3, 8-4, 8-6, and 8-7. We will discuss the various statements as we go through the chapter, but it is useful to note several points that will be of help when you build your own models:

1. <u>The layout itself</u>. If you set up a complex, multi-section worksheet, it can be confusing to you, and especially so to others, to keep track of where different things are done. To avoid that problem, we recommend the use of a schematic diagram such as that shown in Figure 8-1.

==

Figure 8-1
Layout of Spreadsheet

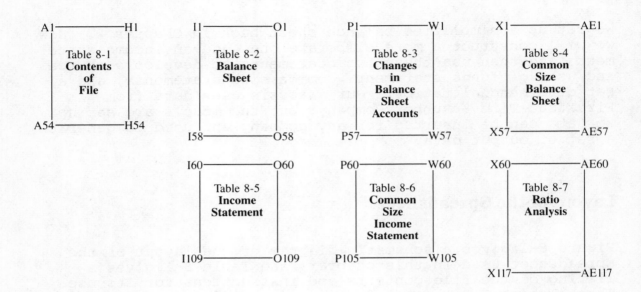

==

2. <u>Conserving disk space</u>. When we first developed the
    spreadsheet LB8X1, we had both a completed model and,
    separately, a number of "template" models. (A <u>template</u>
    is a model which has labels and formulas but leaves the
    data fields blank for others to fill in.) We later
    decided that it would be better to show you how to
    convert our models to templates than to provide them.
    Also, we experimented with running the various
    submodels both vertically and horizontally down the
    worksheet, and we used the Move command to shift things
    around.

==

Table 8-1

Table 8-1. Contents of File LB8X1 and Directions for Its Use (A1.H54)

    I. To position a table on the screen:

        1. Press function key F5, the "GoTo" key.
        2. Type the first cell shown in the range in the directory
           shown below, starting on line 34.
        3. Press the RETURN key.
        4. To return to the directory, press the F5 key and go to A34.

   II. The ranges for the tables will fit on a printed page. Thus, when
     you construct a table, you can print it by specifying the given
     range as the print range.

 III. The tables now have illustrative data. By using the Range Erase
     command on the data in Tables 8-2 and 8-5, you can convert the
     tables to template models. Then, when you complete the income
     statement and balance sheet with data for your own company, the
     other tables will be completed automatically. Note that all cells
     except input data cells in Tables 8-2 and 8-5 are protected.
     If you need to modify the model, you may disconnect the protect
     feature with this command: /WGPD. If you attempt to write in a
     protected cell, you will hear a beep and receive an error
     message. Press ESC to return to READY mode.

  IV. Note that unless you disconnect the protect feature, only the
     data cells can be changed--all formulas are protected. Thus, you
     cannot erase the entire balance sheet or income statement at one
     pass; you can erase only the ranges above the subtotals, which
     are formulas, hence protected. Also, note that once you erase
     the data in the worksheet, zeros and ERRs appear throughout.
     When you enter new data, the ERRs will disappear.

   V. Here are the tables and their addresses:

Cell Range	Number	Description of Table
A1.H54	8-1	Contents of file LB8X1
I1.O58	8-2	Balance sheet
P1.W57	8-3	Changes in balance sheet accounts
X1.AE57	8-4	Common-size balance sheet
I60.O109	8-5	Income statement
P60.W105	8-6	Common-size income statement
X60.AE117	8-7	Ratio analysis

  VI. Here are the macros used in the worksheet:

    /GNULB8X1A~Q~   Press ALT A to view the stacked bar
                           chart for current assets. Press any
                           key to return to READY mode.

    /GNULB8X1L~Q~   Press ALT B to view the stacked bar
                           chart for current liabilities. Press
                           any key to return to READY mode.

==

Once a cell has been used in the worksheet, it will remain in the worksheet's memory range, even if you move or erase its contents. Thus, if you go down 300 rows and across to Column CM, as we did, then the end point in the worksheet matrix will be CM300, and the matrix will contain 300 X (26+26+13) = 19,500 cells. (The model actually has as its endpoint AE117, so it includes only 31 X 117 = 3,627 cells.) Further, the more cells the matrix contains, other things the same, the greater the disk space occupied. Sometimes disk space usage does not matter, but sometimes it does. For example, in this book we wanted to get everything on one disk in order to hold down the production costs and price of the book.

As we were setting up our worksheet, we developed a schematic diagram like Figure 8-1, and we used it to see how much blank space was in the spreadsheet. Then we moved sections around once more to reduce blank space. However, while our models were consolidated, the spreadsheet's memory still contained a matrix defined by the longest row and column that we had ever used. To eliminate this, we used the File Xtract command as follows (see Chapter 5 for details):

/FXF
Asks 1-2-3 to do a file extract, saving formulas.

LB8X1 RETURN
Saves the extracted material under the file name LB8X1.

A1.AE117 RETURN
Specifies the range of the current file (also LB8X1) that we want to extract and place in the new file LB8X1. Thus, we replaced the old, large file LB8X1 with a new, more compact version.

3. Using the GoTo function key. We have not stressed the use of the GoTo function key, F5, up to now. However, in the remainder of the book we will set up spreadsheets in a manner similar to the one described in Figure 8-1. You can then move quickly to various parts

of the spreadsheet by pressing the F5 function key, then the upper-left cell address, and RETURN. For example, to see the set of ratios, press F5 , then X60 , and then RETURN ; Table 8-7 will appear on your screen.

Note that when you use the GoTo function key, if you go to a cell that is currently on the screen, the matrix shown on the screen will not change--only the pointer will move. However, if you <u>GoTo</u> a cell not shown on the current screen, that cell will be positioned in the upper left corner of the screen. This feature is especially nice in worksheets like our present one, because it positions the tables properly on the screen.

Note also that we set things up so (1) that you can use BigRight (Ctrl right-arrow) and BigLeft (Ctrl left-arrow) to move from one statement to another, and (2) each lower statement begins on Row 60, which facilitates the use of PgUp and PgDn. You should strive to build convenience into your worksheets.

4. <u>Printing</u>. We set up Tables 8-2 through 8-7 so that they can be printed out on 8 1/2 X 11 paper. To print the ratio analysis table, for example, type /PPRX60.AE117 RETURN AG . If you expect to print your worksheet output, keep the size of the worksheet's components in mind while you are setting it up. We have also used the command Worksheet Page (/WP) in our worksheet File LB8X1; this command inserts a code on the line where it is entered to tell 1-2-3 to end the page on that line when the worksheet is printed. We typed /WP in Cell A59. (Note that when we entered the Page command an extra row was inserted; we immediately deleted this extra row.) Then we specified our print range as A1.AE117 and each of our tables printed neatly with Table 8-1 on the first page, 8-2 on the next page, and so on.

5. <u>Protection</u>. We designed the spreadsheet on the assumption that you will use our model simply by changing the balance sheet and income statement data. On that assumption, we used 1-2-3's protection feature to set things up so that only the basic balance sheet and income statement data can be changed. This will minimize the chances that a formula will be erased or that

something else will be done to mess up the models. To
enable 1-2-3's protection feature, after completing the
worksheet, we typed

                        /WGPE

This invoked the Global Protection command, meaning
that no cells can be changed. (If we tried at this
point to fill a blank cell, to move a cell, or to
change anything in a cell, we would get a "beep" and an
error message. Pressing the ESC key would put us back
in READY mode.)
        Next, we "freed" those cells in which we wanted
you to be able to make data changes. For example, we
wanted you to be able to change the company's name from
Firestone to something else, so we wanted to unprotect
Cell K3, and we did this by placing the pointer on K3
and typing

                    /RU RETURN

In addition, we wanted you to be able to input data
into the range N7.O14, so we typed

                  /RU N7.O14 RETURN

We had formulas in N16 and O16, so we left those cells
protected. Similar unprotects were made in other
ranges of Columns N and O. Note that we typed the
company name in Cell K3 only, and we entered the cell
reference +K3 wherever we wanted the company name to
appear; thus, the cells in which the company names
appear, other than K3, were left protected.
        On a color monitor, the unprotected cells will
appear green and the protected cells white. On a
monochrome monitor, the protected cells will appear
brighter if you turn the contrast knob on the monitor
(the one with a half-moon) to the left.

If you want to make other changes, you can use these keystrokes to turn off, or disable, the protection feature:

/WGPD

This permits you to change any cell in any way you choose. We recommend, however, that you reprotect the worksheet after you make changes. (Note that it is not necessary to disable the model's Global Protection feature if you are making changes only to the unprotected data cells in the balance sheet and income statement.)

6. <u>Macros</u>. Two macros are used in this spreadsheet; both produce graphs, and both are discussed later in the chapter.

7. <u>Manual recalculation</u>. Our worksheet is fairly complicated, and it takes several seconds for any data change to ripple through all parts of the worksheet. If 1-2-3 were set on Automatic, then recalculations would be done every time an item of data was entered. That would slow things down greatly when entering data for a new company. Therefore, we used the Manual recalculation procedure:

/WGRM

That means that whenever you finish changing data in the balance sheet or income statement, you must then press the F9 function key (CALC) to cause calculations to be made.

The Balance Sheet

The balance sheet is presented in Table 8-2; it is developed
in the range I1.O58 of the spreadsheet. Like most balance
sheets, ours is divided into five sections:

1. Current assets
2. Fixed assets

3. Current liabilities
4. Long term debt
5. Stockholders' equity

We entered data in each section, then used the @SUM(Range)
function to add up the accounts and complete the balance
sheet.
    Put the balance sheet on your screen by retrieving from
our diskette the file LB8X1 (/FR LB8X1 RETURN) and pressing
the F5 (GoTo) key and typing I1 (or look at Table 8-2
if you do not have a computer). The highlighted cells are
unprotected. The data are from Firestone's 1984 Annual
Report. If you put the pointer in Column N (or O) and move
down the column, you will see that numbers appear in the
upper left corner of the control panel for the highlighted
cells, but formulas appear for the unhighlighted cells.
Also, the symbols PR and U appear in the control panel to
designate protected and unprotected cells.
    Using the down-arrow or PgDn key, look at Cell N58.
Here we repeat N25, Total assets, to facilitate a comparison
with total claims and thus to check that the balance sheet
balances.

Table 8-2
Balance Sheet

Table 8-2. Balance Sheet (I1.058)

Company Name: Firestone Tire & Rubber Company

	($ Millions)	
Assets	1984	1983
Current Assets		
1. Cash and cash items	$94	$77
2. Short-term investments	32	289
3. Accounts and notes receivable, net	526	660
4. Inventories	554	455
5. Prepaid expenses and deferred taxes	82	80
Total Current Assets	$1,288	$1,561
Fixed Assets		
1. Property, plant, & equipment, net	$1,131	$1,053
2. Investments, at cost or equity	39	35
3. Other assets	113	80
4.		
5.		
Total Assets	$2,571	$2,729
Liabilities & Stockholders' Equity		
Current Liabilities		
1. Short-term loans	$56	$24
2. Accounts payable	301	286
3. Accruals	394	410
4. Domestic and foreign taxes	130	110
5. Long-term debt due within one year	53	63
Total Current Liabilities	$934	$893
Long-term Debt		
1. Long-term debt and capital leases	$240	$381
2. Deferred income taxes	113	110
3. Minority interests in subsidiaries	48	54
Total Long-term Debt	$401	$545
Preferred Stockholders' Equity	$0	$0
Common Stockholders' Equity		
1. Common stock (without par value)	$63	$63
2. Additional paid-in capital	187	190
3. Ret.Erns. less foreign curr. adj.	1,265	1,229
4. Treasury stock	(279)	(191)
Total Common Stockholders' Equity	$1,236	$1,291
Total Liabilities & Equity	$2,571	$2,729
T.A. (check)	$2,571	$2,729

Using the Balance Sheet Model as a Template

We set up Firestone balance sheets for 1983 and 1984. We
examined Firestone's balance sheets, as presented in the
annual report, while we wrote the model. The accounts used
by Firestone are similar to those used by most companies.
Still, one can expect to find variations occasionally, and
when they occur, you must adapt the model. We would begin
by simply typing in a new company name in K3 and changing
the dates if necessary in N7 and O7. Then we would erase
these ranges as follows:

```
/RE N10.O14 RETURN
/RE N19.O23 RETURN
/RE N31.O35 RETURN
/RE N40.O42 RETURN
/RE N46.O46 RETURN
/RE N49.O52 RETURN
```

That creates a blank, or template, balance sheet model. The
formulas produce zeros for all summations, but as soon as
you insert data for your company, the zeros will disappear
and your company's totals will appear. (As we discuss later
in the chapter, you could write a macro that would do all of
those Range Erase steps with two keystrokes. If you planned
to use the model to analyze a number of companies, it would
pay to do this.)
    If your company does not use some of the accounts
Firestone uses, just leave them blank. If it has additional
accounts, you can either add lines or consolidate accounts.
Adding lines is somewhat dangerous, because you may then
have to change other parts of the worksheet. For that
reason, we generally prefer to consolidate accounts. Remember that to add lines to the model, you would have to disable the model's Global Protection feature first.

Changes in Balance Sheet Accounts

Table 8-3 shows changes in balance sheet accounts, with each
change classified as either a source or a use of the

corporation's liquid resources. An increase in an asset is a use, since it tends to draw funds from alternative uses. Conversely, a decrease in an asset is a source of funds, as resources are provided for other uses. Increases in liabilities or equity capital are sources of funds, while decreases in these accounts constitute uses.

Table 8-3 is loaded with @IF formulas similar to those we discussed in Chapter 5. For example, move the pointer to Cell U12, and look at the formula for this cell:

Cell U12   @IF(N12<O12,O12-N12,0)

Cell N12 is the most recent year's value for Accounts receivable, while the previous year's value is in Cell O12. The change is a negative $134 million, and this is a source of funds since it comes from a decrease in an asset. The IF statement asks if it is true that the most recent value is less than the previous value--in other words, did the asset decrease? If the statement is true, then Cell U12 will show O12-N12 because this difference is a source of funds. On the other hand, if the statement is false--the asset either did not change or increased in size--then Cell U12 will display a value of zero. Cell W12 is similar to U12, except the formula uses > rather than < and reverses the two cell addresses of the next equation in the IF statement. Other cells in Table 8-3 were developed similarly.

Sources and uses must be equal over any time period. This equality provides you with a check on the accuracy of the statement of changes. By studying the statement of changes in balance sheet accounts, analysts gain a better idea of which assets are being built up and where the company is getting the financing for these activities. We could have extended Table 8-3 to bring it closer to a full-blown sources and uses of funds statement. For example, we could have added net income as a source and dividends paid as a use, and we could have brought in depreciation as a source and increases in gross plant (rather than net plant) as a use. However, to construct a true sources and uses statement, we would need information on plant retirements, treasury stock repurchases, and so on. Therefore, we simply constructed the "rough-and-ready" sources and uses statement shown in Table 8-3.

Table 8-3

Table 8-3. Changes in Balance Sheet Accounts (P1.W57)

Company Name: Firestone Tire & Rubber Company

		Changes	
Assets		Source	Use
Current			
1.	Cash and cash items	$0	$17
2.	Short-term investments	257	0
3.	Accounts and notes receivable, net	134	0
4.	Inventories	0	99
5.	Prepaid expenses and deferred taxes	0	2
Total Current Assets			
Fixed Assets			
1.	Property, plant, & equipment, net	0	78
2.	Investments, at cost or equity	0	4
3.	Other assets	0	33
4.		0	0
5.		0	0
Total Assets			
Liabilities & Stockholders' Equity			
Current Liabilities			
1.	Short-term loans	32	0
2.	Accounts payable	15	0
3.	Accruals	0	16
4.	Domestic and foreign taxes	20	0
5.	Long-term debt due within one year	0	10
Total Current Liabilities			
Long-term Debt			
1.	Long-term debt and capital leases	0	141
2.	Deferred income taxes	3	0
3.	Minority interests in subsidiaries	0	6
Total Long-term Debt			
Preferred Stockholders' Equity		0	0
Stockholders' Equity			
1.	Common stock (without par value)	0	0
2.	Additional paid-in capital	0	3
3.	RE less foreign curr. adj.	36	0
4.	Treasury stock	0	88
Total sources and uses		$497	$497

248

Common-Size Balance Sheet

Table 8-4, which begins in Cell X1, presents a common-size balance sheet, which is simply a balance sheet in which each item is expressed as a percentage of total assets. This statement is useful for comparing a single firm across time or a group of firms at a given point in time.

Once you enter data into Table 8-2, the basic balance sheet, and press the CALC function key, F9, Tables 8-3 and 8-4 will be constructed automatically. Notice that to construct Table 8-4, we merely divided each account by total assets. First, we wrote this formula in Cell AC10:

$$+N10/\$N\$25$$

Then we copied it into the range AC11.AC56. We used the Range Erase (/RE) command to blank out cells that should be blank; we entered sum functions in the cells where subtotals should occur; and we used \- and \= to add underlines and double underlines. We used the command /RFP RETURN AC10.AC56 RETURN to format to percentages. The formulas in Column D were input in a similar manner.

Note that if you erase the data from the balance sheet in Table 8-2 to convert it to a template, then all cells in Table 8-4 will show the term ERR. This is an error message telling you that you are dividing by zero--total assets are now zero. However, as soon as you make data entries in Table 8-2, the ERRs will be replaced by percentages (some of which may be zero).

Table 8-4

Table 8-4. Common-Size Balance Sheet (X1.AE57)

Company Name: Firestone Tire & Rubber Company

	Percent of Total Assets	
Assets	1984	1983
Current		
1. Cash and cash items	3.66%	2.82%
2. Short-term investments	1.24%	10.59%
3. Accounts and notes receivable, net	20.46%	24.18%
4. Inventories	21.55%	16.67%
5. Prepaid expenses and deferred taxes	3.19%	2.93%
Total Current Assets	50.10%	57.20%
Fixed Assets		
1. Property, plant, & equipment, net	43.99%	38.59%
2. Investments, at cost or equity	1.52%	1.28%
3. Other assets	4.40%	2.93%
4.	0.00%	0.00%
5.	0.00%	0.00%
Total Assets	100.00%	100.00%
Liabilities & Stockholders' Equity		
Current Liabilities		
1. Short-term loans	2.18%	0.88%
2. Accounts payable	11.71%	10.48%
3. Accruals	15.32%	15.02%
4. Domestic and foreign taxes	5.06%	4.03%
5. Long-term debt due within one year	2.06%	2.31%
Total Current Liabilities	36.33%	32.72%
Long-term Debt		
1. Long-term debt and capital leases	9.33%	13.96%
2. Deferred income taxes	4.40%	4.03%
3. Minority interests in subsidiaries	1.87%	1.98%
Total Long-term Debt	15.60%	19.97%
Preferred Stockholders' Equity	0.00%	0.00%
Stockholders' Equity		
1. Common stock (without par value)	2.45%	2.31%
2. Additional paid-in capital	7.27%	6.96%
3. RE less foreign curr. adj.	49.20%	45.03%
4. Treasury stock	-10.85%	-7.00%
Total Stockholders' Equity	48.07%	47.31%
Total Liabilities & Equity	100.00%	100.00%

Income Statement

Our income statement is given in Table 8-5, range I60.O109. The income statement is set up like the balance sheet--data items are unprotected, formulas are protected. You can use the Range Erase command to clear the Firestone data, or you can simply overwrite the Firestone data with data for your company. As with the balance sheet, you may have to consolidate some income statement items or else modify our statement to accommodate your company's income statement data.

Notice that the number of shares outstanding is given on Line 107; this value is divided into income available to common stockholders to obtain earnings per share, EPS. Should you desire, you can add data on total dividends and dividends per share. Again, the cells for EPS will show ERRs if you erase the number of shares, but the error messages will go away when you refill the cells having information on the number of shares.

Common-Size Income Statement

Our common-size income statement, Table 8-6, begins in Cell P60 and is set up like the common-size balance sheet. It too will be filled with ERRs when the basic income statement is blank, but the ERRs will be replaced with percentages as soon as you complete the income statement.

Table 8-5

Table 8-5. Income Statement (I60.0109)

Company Name: Firestone Tire & Rubber Company

	($ Millions)	
	1984	1983
Net Sales	$4,001	$3,669
Cost and expenses:		
1. Cost of sales	3,187	2,839
2. Selling, admin. & general expenses	728	667
3. Provision for phase-outs & realign.	0	0
4. Foreign currency (gains) losses	15	1
5. Other income, net	(47)	(32)
6.		
Total costs and expenses	$3,883	$3,475
Net operating income, earnings before interest and taxes (EBIT)	$118	$194
Less interest expense:		
1. Interest expense	$43	$66
2. Interest income	(29)	(23)
3.		
Total interest expense	$14	$43
Earnings before taxes	$104	$151
Income taxes	41	63
Net income before extraordinary gains/losses	$63	$88
Extraordinary gains/losses, after-tax	13	11
Other after-tax gains or (losses):		
1. Discontinued operations	26	12
2.		
Dividends to preferred stockholders	0	0
Net income available to common stockholders	$102	$111
Number of common shares outstanding	46,387,000	49,024,000
Earnings per share of common stock	$2.20	$2.26

252

```
================================================================
```

Table 8-6

Table 8-6. Common-Size Income Statement (P60.W105)

Company Name: Firestone Tire & Rubber Company

	Percentage of Net Sales	
	1984	1983
Net Sales	100.00%	100.00%
Cost and expenses:		
1. Cost of sales	79.66%	77.38%
2. Selling, admin. & general expenses	18.20%	18.18%
3. Provision for phase-outs & realign.	0.00%	0.00%
4. Foreign currency (gains) losses	0.37%	0.03%
5. Other income, net	-1.17%	-0.87%
6.	0.00%	0.00%
Total costs and expenses	97.05%	94.71%
Net operating income, earnings before interest and taxes (EBIT)	2.95%	5.29%
Less interest expense:		
1. Interest expense	1.07%	1.80%
2. Interest income	-0.72%	-0.63%
3.	0.00%	0.00%
Total interest expense	0.35%	1.17%
Earnings before taxes	2.60%	4.12%
Income taxes	1.02%	1.72%
Net income before extraordinary gains/losses	1.57%	2.40%
Extraordinary gains/losses, after-tax	0.32%	0.30%
Other after-tax gains or (losses):		
1. Discontinued operations	0.65%	0.33%
2.	0.00%	0.00%
Dividends to preferred stockholders	0.00%	0.00%
Net income available to common stockholders	2.55%	3.03%

```
================================================================
```

253

Ratio Analysis

The spreadsheet model in Table 8-7, which begins in Cell X60, calculates 12 standard financial ratios. We could construct other ratios and add them to the table. We also would add industry average data; we could have done so except for the fact that every industry has a somewhat different set of averages, so for template purposes we would have a problem. Again, note that Table 8-7 will be filled with error messages until the basic balance sheet and income statement have been completed.

Graphs of Financial Data

To paraphrase Confucius, a picture is worth a thousand numbers. Indeed, graphs of financial data are extremely useful to corporate managers, security analysts, and bank loan officers to help detect trends and other basic relationships. Since we have only two years of data, time series graphs, such as line graphs of ROE over time, are not suitable for our model, but we do use a stacked-bar graph to illustrate how to build graphs with Lotus 1-2-3. You should follow our steps except for the last one. Since that last step replaces our model, make it only if you are sure you did everything correctly or if you have a backup copy of our model.

==

Table 8-7

Table 8-7. Ratio Analysis (X60.AE117)

Ratio	1984	1983
1. Current ratio		
current assets/current liabilities	1.38	1.75
2. Quick (acid test) ratio		
current assets less inventories, divided by current liabilities	0.79	1.24
3. Inventory turnover ratio		
net sales/inventory	7.22	8.06
4. Average collection period		
average sales per day	11.11	10.19 $ million
receivables/avg sales per day	47.33	64.76 days
5. Fixed assets utilization (fixed assets turnover)		
net sales/net fixed assets	3.12	3.14
6. Total assets utilization		
net sales/total assets	1.56	1.34
7. Total debt to total assets		
total liabilities/total assets	51.9%	52.7%
8. Times interest earned		
EBIT/interest charges	8.43	4.51
9. Profit margin on sales		
net income/net sales	2.55%	3.03%
10. Basic earning power ratio		
EBIT/total assets	4.59%	7.11%
11. Return on total assets (ROA)		
net income/total assets	3.97%	4.07%
12. Return on common equity (ROE)		
net income available to common divided by common equity	8.25%	8.60%

==

    We began the construction of the graphs by positioning
Table 8-2 on the screen; use F5 (GoTo) I1 RETURN to
get in position. We then graphed the current assets in 1983
versus 1984. Here are the keystrokes we used:

/GTS   This told 1-2-3 that we wanted to make
                            a stacked-bar graph.

X N7.O7 RETURN   This told 1-2-3 that the range in-
                            cluded the years 1984 and 1983 and
                            that these values should appear on the
                            X-axis.

A N14.O14 RETURN   This specified the first data range.

B N13.O13 RETURN   This specified the second data range.

C N12.O12 RETURN   This specified the third data range.

D N11.O11 RETURN   This specified the fourth data range.

E N10.O10 RETURN   This specified the fifth data range.

OTF   This told 1-2-3 that we wanted to set
                            the first title.

CURRENT ASSETS
RETURN   This established the first title line.

TS   This told 1-2-3 that we wanted to set
                            the second title.

Firestone Tire
RETURN   This established the second title
                            line.

LA Prepd RETURN
LB Inv RETURN   These entries established legends to
LC A/R RETURN   distinguish the elements of the stacked
LD S-T Inv RETURN   bars.
LE Cash RETURN

QV RETURN	This took us out of the Options menu, let us view the graph to check it, and then returned us to the Graph menu.
S	The S told 1-2-3 that we wanted to save the graph.
LB8X1A RETURN	This saved the graph as a newly created graph named LB8X1A.
NC LB8X1A RETURN	This saved the graph specifications under the name LB8X1A.
Q/FS LB8X1	This saved the worksheet with the graph specifications incorporated into it.

We then followed the same procedures to produce a stacked-bar graph for current liabilities, LB8X1L. If you have not done so, press Q to quit the Graph menu and return to READY. When you insert data on your own company into the balance sheet and income statements, the graphs will automatically be updated.

Building a Macro for Viewing the Graphs

If only one graph is embedded in a worksheet, it may be viewed by pressing the F10 function key. (Then press any key to return to the spreadsheet.) However, if the spreadsheet contains two graphs, the F10 key will bring up only the last one dealt with (the "current graph"). To view the other one, you must go through these steps:

/GNU	Tells 1-2-3 to change the current graph.
(Graph name) RETURN	Tells 1-2-3 the name of the graph you want to view. Press any key to return to the worksheet.

Q   Returns to READY mode.

F10   Puts the current graph on the screen.

     We can write a macro to short-circuit the process.
Recall that a macro is a collection of keystrokes saved
under a special name. Any time you enter that name, 1-2-3
automatically goes through the sequence of keystrokes specified in the macro. To create the macros for viewing our two
graphs, here are the steps we followed:

1. Put the pointer on Cell B48. This is the <u>location</u> of
    our first macro. The macro will take more space than
    the 9-space width of the column, but since the macro is
    a label, and since labels can extend into unused adja-
    cent columns, this presents no problem. However, it is
    best to leave enough blank cells to the right of the
    macro's cell so that you can read it on the screen and
    print out all the macro's keystrokes.

2. Our macro requires these keystrokes:

                   '/GNULB8X1A~Q~

    The apostrophe is necessary to indicate that you are
    entering a label, while the remainder is the set of
    operating keystrokes. Recall that in macro language,
    the tilde (~) represents the RETURN key.

3. After typing the macro into Cell B48, press the
     RETURN key. The macro is now entered in B48. (It
    extends over into C48 on the screen, but it is really
    in B48. Note that in order to be able to read a long
    macro on the screen or on a printout, it may be neces-
    sary to leave several cells blank.)

4. Now you must save the macro in a named range within the
    worksheet. Here are the keystrokes for that step:

                   /RNC\A RETURN RETURN

    Those keystrokes gave the Cell B48 (which is the range
    B48) the name \A.

At this point, your first macro is ready to use. Just type ALT A , and the current asset graph will appear on the screen. Press any key to go back to the worksheet and you will return to the worksheet in READY mode. The macro for the current liability graph was created in the same way, and it may be called up by pressing ALT B . Printouts of the two graphs are shown as Figures 8-2 and 8-3.

===

Figure 8-2

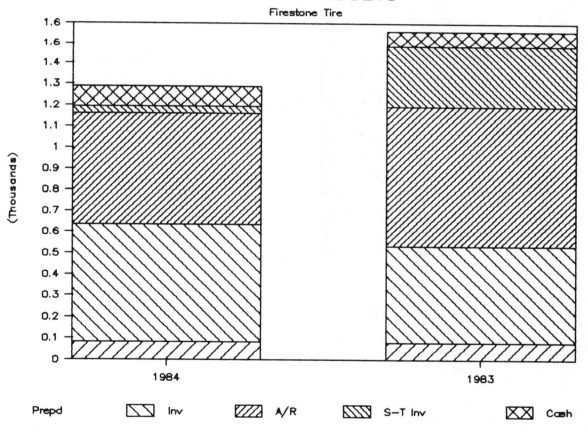

CURRENT ASSETS

Firestone Tire

===

Figure 8-3

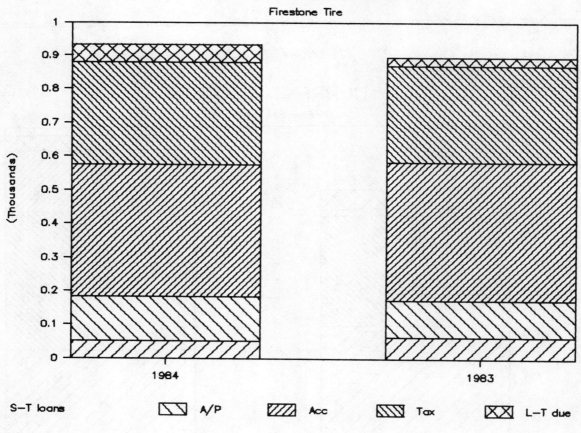

CURRENT LIABILITIES
Firestone Tire

Summary

This chapter developed a spreadsheet model to analyze a company's financial statements. We used two years of data for Firestone Tire, but we explained how you can erase Firestone's data and insert data for some other company, at which point the model will complete the analysis.

We used only two years of data, and we limited the detail shown in our statements. However, at this point you should be able to modify our model to fit your own needs. For example, you might want to examine five or even ten years of data, and you might want to construct some ratios different from the ones we used. Such changes should be as easy as 1-2-3!

Note: Before doing any of the following exercises, make sure you copy File LB8X1 onto your diskette and do these exercises on that file copy.

8-1 Firestone's dividend policy has not been reflected in either the income statement or the ratio analysis sections of File LB8X1. Dividends and dividends per share should be reflected in the income statement. (Before modifying the tables in File LB8X1 make sure you have turned off the Global Worksheet Protection feature. Before saving this file make sure you enable the Global Worksheet Protection feature. Save the file as LB8EX1.)

   a. Modify Table 8-5 for the year 1984 to include the following two-line items:

      1. Total dividends paid in 1984 (in millions) and
      2. Dividends per share in 1984. (Hint: Look at the addition to retained earnings in comparison to net income earned for the year. Div = $66 million; DPS = $1.42)

   b. Firestone's management would like to be able to compare its dividend payout ratio with the payout ratios of other companies in the tire industry. However, this ratio does not appear in Table 8-7. Modify Table 8-7 so this ratio is calculated for the year 1984. (Payout ratio = 64.71%)

8-2 Retrieve File LB8EX1. Convert the tables to template models by using the Range Erase command on the relevant input data sections in Tables 8-2 and 8-5. (Note that since you are only modifying unprotected data cells, you do not have to worry about turning on and off the Global Worksheet Protection feature.) Then input the following data, format the data cells to display one decimal place, press the F9 key to recalculate the remaining tables, and answer the questions that follow.

Balance Sheet for Lionel, Inc.

	1985	1984
Cash	15.5	14.0
Accounts receivable	67.2	58.4
Inventory	48.3	43.3
Net fixed assets	58.5	55.0
Short-term loans	16.8	15.1
Accounts payable	25.8	23.3
Accruals	17.0	15.4
Long-term debt due in 1 year	6.4	5.2
Long-term debt	51.3	47.8
Common stock	50.0	45.0
Retained earnings	22.2	18.9

Income Statement for Lionel, Inc.

	1985	1984
Sales	321.5	298.5
Cost of goods sold	278.5	254.0
Selling and general administrative expenses	29.0	30.0
Interest expense	4.9	4.0
Federal income taxes	3.6	4.2
Number of common shares outstanding	5000000	4500000

a. Give the values for the following ratios:

	1985	1984
Average collection period		
Total debt/Total assets		
Times interest earned		3.63X
Profit margin on sales		
Basic earning power ratio		
Return on total assets		
Return on total equity	7.62%	

b. Suppose the most recent industry average ratios for
    the ratios identified above are given below.
    Perform an analysis of Lionel's position compared
    to the industry position as well as a trend

263

analysis of these ratios. What corrective actions would you take if you were Lionel's management.

	Industry Average
Average collection period	60 days
Total debt/Total assets	53%
Times interest earned	3X
Profit margin on sales	3.2%
Basic earning power ratio	9.5%
Return on total assets	5.5%
Return on total equity	11%

Resave your file as LB8EX1. Since the graph specifications have already been saved on this file, you may press ALT A or ALT B to see the two stacked bar graphs for your new data. Remember that if you wish to print these 2 graphs you must save them as a separate picture file. Then you can go into the PrintGraph portion of the Lotus program to print them.

8-3 Go to the library and obtain a recent annual report for a company of your choosing. Then retrieve File LB8EX1. Convert the tables to template models by using the Range Erase command on the relevant input data sections in Tables 8-2 and 8-5. Input the data from the annual report in the appropriate cells of Tables 8-2 and 8-5. Remember, it is very likely that the input data you have will not exactly conform to the line items of Tables 8-2 and 8-5. If this is your first time doing this exercise it would be best to consolidate your data so that it "fits" to the line items on Tables 8-2 and 8-5. When you get comfortable using Lotus you can experiment with adding lines to the model and making the other modifications necessary. (Remember that when you are making changes only to the unprotected data cells you do not have to worry about turning off and on the Global Worksheet Protection feature. If you are modifying the model so that lines are being added, you will have to turn the Global Worksheet Protection feature off and then on when you are through.)

If you wish to save this file, you may save it as LB8EX1 or save it as a new file LB8EX2.

Chapter 9
Financial Forecasting

In Chapter 8 we developed a model to analyze past financial statements. Now we go on to develop forecasted, or pro forma, financial statements which can be used to help managers formulate plans for some future time period, say the next five to ten years. Computerized balance sheets and income statements can be revised easily and quickly to show the likely effects of different operating plans, and thus they provide management with an important planning tool.

Layout of the Spreadsheet

Figure 9-1 provides a schematic diagram of the spreadsheet used in this chapter, and Table 9-1 gives a listing of the file contents and instructions for its use. Table 9-2 is used for inputs, and Tables 9-3 through 9-5 give the model's output. We use data for the Artell Corporation, a company that develops artificial intelligence systems.

While the model's logic is rather complex, the model itself is easy to use. Inputs such as growth rates, interest rates, and regression coefficients are typed in, and when the F9 function key is pressed, the computer forecasts balance sheets and income statements and analyzes the funding requirements, thus generating Tables 9-3 and 9-4. Certain basic relationships can either be calculated as regression coefficients on the basis of historic data in the portion of the spreadsheet shown in Table 9-5, or these relationships can be entered directly into the input section. In our model, we calculated the regression coefficients in Table 9-5 for a set of variables assumed not to vary as a percentage of sales, but entered directly into the input section the percentages for those variables which in the case at hand do vary directly with sales and which, accordingly, can be expressed as a percentage of sales. Our model is set up to provide a 5-year forecast.

The Input Section

The input section is shown in Table 9-2, which begins in Cell A60. First, the forecasted annual growth rates in sales are entered for each of the 5 years of the forecast period. Thus, we entered 5 separate growth rates as estimated by Artell's marketing department. We then entered Artell's minimum current ratio and maximum debt ratio as set in the firm's bond indenture. Next, we entered the historic and current interest rates of the firm's debt, its tax rate, and its expected dividend and stock price growth rates. Finally, we input regression coefficients for those balance sheet and income statement items that vary directly as a percentage of sales; we read in the slope and intercept terms from Table 9-5 for those items which vary linearly with sales; and we input base year values for those items which do not vary with sales. As stated previously, we calculated the regression coefficients in this model using 1-2-3's regression analysis procedure; however, we could have entered them directly.
 A few points should be noted:

1. We assumed that dividends and stock prices would grow at a constant rate over the 5-year period. If we had forecasted different growth rates for these items in each year, we would have entered five growth rates as we did for sales growth.

2. A regression analysis is shown in Table 9-5 (Q1.X47). The Y-intercepts, slopes, and standard error terms of four regression models are shown. Each regression model has one independent variable and one dependent variable. Administrative expenses, receivables, inventory, and fixed assets are the dependent variables, and sales is the independent variable. Each regression model analyzes 10 years of historical data on sales plus one dependent variable, performing a series of simple linear regression analyses to determine the regression coefficient for each dependent variable as a function of sales. These regression models were used

266

to provide the regression coefficients in columns F and G for administrative expenses, receivables, inventory, and fixed assets.

==

Figure 9-1
Layout of Spreadsheet

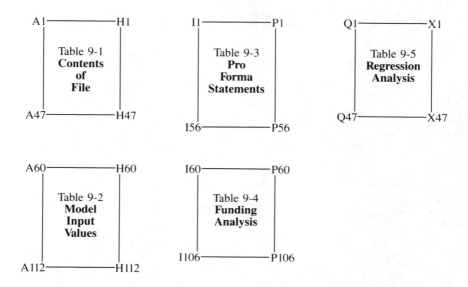

Table 9-1

Table 9-1. Contents of File LB9X1 and Instructions for Its Use (A1.H47)

    I. To position a table on the screen:
       1. Press function key F5, the "GoTo" key.
       2. Type the first cell shown in the range in the directory
          shown below, starting on line 39.
       3. Press the RETURN key.
       4. To return to the directory, press the F5 key and go to A39.

   II. The ranges for the tables will fit on a printed page. Thus, when
       you construct a table, you can print it by specifying the given
       range as the print range.

  III. The tables now have illustrative data. You can use the model with
       other data simply by entering new data in the highlighted cells
       in Tables 9-2 and 9-5. Then, when you complete the required
       input data sections with data for your own company, the other
       tables will be completed automatically. Note that all cells
       except input data cells in Tables 9-2 and 9-5 have been
       protected. If you need to modify the model, you may disconnect
       the protect feature with this command: /WGPD. If you attempt to
       write in a protected cell, you will hear a beep and receive an
       error message. Press ESC to return to READY mode. We recommend
       that you reprotect the worksheet after making your changes with
       the command /WGPE. Note also that the regression results
       calculated in Table 9-5 are used as inputs in Table 9-2. The
       other input data are entered directly into Table 9-2.

   IV. You should not use the Range Erase command to erase the input
       cells in Tables 9-2 and 9-5. If you do so, zeros and ERRS will
       appear throughout the worksheet. Due to the circularity of the
       model, some of the formulas cannot be recalculated after the new
       data have been entered. Therefore, you should simply replace the
       existing input values with your own data.

    V. Growth rates and ratios must be entered as fractions, not as
       percentages. No dollar signs or commas should be entered.

   VI. Here are the tables and their addresses:

        Cell Range   Number   Description of Exhibit
        -----------   ------   ----------------------------------
        A1.H47   9-1   Contents of file LB9X1
        A60.H112   9-2   Input section
        I1.P56   9-3   Projected financial statements
        I60.P106   9-4   Funding analysis
        Q1.X47   9-5   Regression analysis

```
     A         B         C        D       E      F        G        H
60  Table 9-2. Input Section (A60.H112)
61
62  Annual sales growth rates:                      Year 1 =   50.00%
63                                                  Year 2 =   50.00%
64                                                  Year 3 =   25.00%
65                                                  Year 4 =   15.00%
66                                                  Year 5 =   15.00%
67
68  Minimum current ratio                                       2.50
69  Maximum debt ratio (total debt to total assets)            50.00%
70  Interest rate on outstanding notes payable                  8.00%
71  Interest rate on new notes payable                         10.00%
72  Interest rate on outstanding bonds                         10.00%
73  Interest rate on new bonds                                 12.00%
74  Dividend growth rate                                       10.00%
75  Stock price growth rate                                    20.00%
76  Tax rate over the next five years                          50.00%
77
78
79  Regression parameters:
80
81       In this section, you should enter the regression coefficients for
82  the balance sheet and income statement items which vary directly with
83  sales.  For those items which are a fixed percentage of sales, you
84  should enter those percentages. But, for those items which vary
85  according to a simple linear relationship with sales, you should either
86  (1) enter the regression coefficients, if known, or (2) let 1-2-3 deter-
87  mine the regression coefficients for you by entering historic values of
88  those variables in Table 9-5 and cell references in the table below.
89
90                                                       a         b
91                                                  (intercept) (slope)
92                                                  ----------- --------
93           Cost of goods sold                         0.00      80%
94           Admin. & selling expenses                 25.45       6%
95           Cash                                        0.00       2%
96           Receivables                                 7.80      15%
97           Inventories                                17.44      18%
98           Net fixed assets                           35.89      23%
99           Accounts payable                            0.00       8%
100          Accrued wages and taxes                     0.00       5%
101
102  Starting (base year) input values:
103
104          Stock price                              $30.00
105          Dividend per share                        $0.80
106          Net sales                               $500.00
107          Interest expense                          $8.00
108          Notes payable                            $10.00
109          Bonds (long-term debt)                   $72.00
110          Common stock                            $150.00
111          Retained earnings                        $54.00
112          Total shares outstanding                     10
```

===

3. We assumed that the relationships between sales and
    financial statement accounts will be constant over the
    5 years. This assumption may not be valid; however,
    even if the relationships are not permanent, the fore-
    casting process will still be valuable in planning
    strategies and discovering potential problems, such as
    managing rapid growth and dealing with liquidity prob-
    lems.

4. Notice when you retrieve File LB9X1, the indicator CALC
    (manual calculation) appears at the bottom of your
    screen. After pressing the F9 key, the indicator CIRC
    (circular cell references) appears at the bottom of
    your screen. The spreadsheet contains several inter-
    dependent cells. For example, interest expense depends
    on both new notes payable and new bond issues, which at
    the same time are limited by the current ratio and
    maximum debt ratio limits set by management. As notes
    payable and bonds change, interest expense will change.
    The change in interest expense will increase or de-
    crease the addition to retained earnings, which will
    change the amount of funds required, which in turn will
    change the amounts of notes payable and bonds out-
    standing. This makes it necessary for 1-2-3 to calcu-
    late the spreadsheet several times (up to 15 iterations
    are sometimes necessary) to get the financial state-
    ments to balance. When making changes to the model,
    the CALC key may have to be pressed several times to
    insure that the financial statements balance.

    Sometimes, when you construct worksheets, the CIRC
    message will appear at the bottom of the screen when
    you do not expect it. It may be that the model you are
    building is circular, even though you did not realize
    it, or you may have entered a formula incorrectly,
    resulting in circularity in the model. If you need to
    know where circularity occurs in a model, type /WS for
    Worksheet Status. A screen will appear which provides
    information on the worksheet, such as the recalculation
    order and method, protection status, global formats,
    and the presence of circularity. Press /WS now. You
    will see that file LB9X1 is set for manual, natural
    order recalculation with 12 iterations, the global
    protection is on, the global format is commas with no

decimal places, and there is circularity in the model, with the first circular reference being K105. Press any key to return to the spreadsheet.

Note: The CIRC indicator will not normally appear at the bottom of your screen immediately after you retrieve a file, or be shown when you press /WS. However, once you enter data and press the CALC key, the circular reference will be indicated.

Normally the spreadsheet is recalculated every time a value is entered; however, the spreadsheet can be set on Manual recalculation so that each cell entry will not cause instant recalculation. After all new data are entered, press the CALC (function F9) key. We saved the file with the instruction to 1-2-3 to perform 12 iterations each time the CALC key is pressed. Even so, the CALC key may have to be pressed several times in order for the statements to balance. At times it is helpful to see the results of every iteration, and in that case you can follow this sequence: /WGRI1. This stands for main command menu, worksheet, global, recalculation, and iterate 1 time. Now the spreadsheet calculations will be performed only once each time the F9 key is pressed. To instruct 1-2-3 to calculate each time a new value is entered, type the command /WGRA.

5. As in Chapter 8, we protected the worksheet so that only the input cells can be changed. Also, as in Chapter 8, we entered a page-break code (/Worksheet Page) on Line 59 so that each exhibit can be printed out neatly on one page.

Balance Sheet and Income Statement Forecasts

After the input variable values are entered in Columns F and G, the CALC key is pressed, and many of the spreadsheet values are calculated immediately. Stock price and dividends per share both grow at constant rates, and the growth rate in sales is shown for each year.

On the income statements, shown in Table 9-3, net sales are calculated in the first iteration. Cost of goods sold and operating expenses (administrative and selling expenses) are tied directly to sales by their regression formulas and, therefore, they can also be calculated on the first iteration. Since the variables above EBIT are determined on the first ripple of spreadsheet calculations, EBIT will not change after the initial calculation.

Interest expense, however, will adjust to changes in financing, that is, as a result of additions to notes payable and bond issues. As these liabilities gradually approach their final values through several iterative spreadsheet calculations, interest expense will be adjusted automatically. This also means that the entire lower section of the income statement will be readjusted several times before reaching an equilibrium, where all constraints are satisfied.

On the balance sheets, also shown in Table 9-3, total assets are determined on the first iteration for each of the forecast years. All assets are based on sales and are calculated on the first pass of 1-2-3 through the spreadsheet, as the projected sales figures are determined.

In the liabilities and equity capital sections of the balance sheet, notes payable, bonds, and common stock all have been programmed to adjust to the firm's required external financing. An important part of this adjustment is the meeting of specified limits and goals, including the minimum current ratio and maximum ratio of debt to total assets.

When all adjustments are complete, the spreadsheet will be stable--if you press the CALC key, cell values will no longer change. After entering the initial data, position the worksheet with Cell I41 in the upper left corner of the screen. Total assets and total claims will both show on the balance sheet. Now press the CALC key (F9) while the last column (1990) shows these two totals to be exactly equal; the spreadsheet calculations will then be complete, and all values will be stable.

Table 9-3

Table 9-3. Projected Financial Statements, Artell Corporation (I1.P56)
(Millions of Dollars, Except for Per Share Amounts)

	1985	1986	1987	1988	1989	1990
Stock price	$30.00	$36.00	$43.20	$51.84	$62.21	$74.65
DPS	$0.80	$0.88	$0.97	$1.06	$1.17	$1.29
Sales growth rate	n.a.	50%	50%	25%	15%	15%

INCOME STATEMENTS

	1985	1986	1987	1988	1989	1990
Net sales	$500	$750	$1,125	$1,406	$1,617	$1,860
Cost of goods sold	400	600	900	1,125	1,294	1,488
Selling & admin.	55	70	92	109	121	136
EBIT	$45	$80	$133	$172	$202	$236
Interest expense	8	16	23	29	32	34
EBT	$37	$64	$110	$144	$171	$202
Taxes	18	32	55	72	85	101
Net income	$18	$32	$55	$72	$85	$101
Dividends	8	9	12	13	15	16
Add'n to RE	$10	$23	$43	$59	$71	$85
EPS	$1.85	$3.02	$4.52	$5.72	$6.79	$8.03

BALANCE SHEETS

	1985	1986	1987	1988	1989	1990
Cash	$10	$15	$23	$28	$32	$37
Receivables	82	120	175	217	249	285
Inventories	106	150	217	266	304	347
Total C.A.	$198	$285	$414	$512	$585	$669
Net fixed assets	153	212	300	366	415	472
Total assets	$351	$497	$714	$878	$1,000	$1,141
Accounts payable	$40	$60	$90	$113	$129	$149
Notes payable	10	16	20	22	24	26
Accruals	25	38	56	70	81	93
Total C.L.	$75	$114	$166	$205	$234	$267
Long-term debt	72	134	191	234	257	279
Common stock	150	172	237	261	261	261
Retained earnings	54	77	120	178	249	334
Total claims	$351	$497	$714	$878	$1,000	$1,141

273

Funding Analysis

When total assets equal total claims, go to the area shown
in Table 9-4 by pressing F5 I60 RETURN . (Note that if you
are currently in the same screen where I60 occurs, only the
cell pointer will move. You will then need to press the
down arrow key until I60 is in the left-hand corner of your
computer screen so that you can see a larger portion of the
analysis.) Here the pro forma ratio analysis is performed.
The current ratio and debt ratio should adhere to the limits
entered in the initial data. If the spreadsheet is working
properly, it should forecast the current ratio as being
close to the minimum (since excess liquidity reduces profitability). The debt ratio should be close to the maximum
unless growth is so slow that retained earnings hold down
the use of debt. Other key ratios are also calculated in
this section. The ratios included in the model show the
firm's liquidity, risk, assets turnover, and profitability.
        Also shown in Table 9-4 is an analysis of how the
funding requirements were met in each year. The maximum
amounts of each type of financing are computed, and then the
actual amounts used are shown. The maximum amounts were
based on the current ratio and debt ratio restrictions given
in the input section.

```
================================================================


                        Table 9-4




Table 9-4. Funding Analysis (I60.P106)


I. FUNDS RAISED (values shown here are calculated from Part III):

                        1985    1986    1987    1988    1989    1990
                        ----    ----    ----    ----    ----    ----
Extnl. funds req.        $0      $90    $126     $68     $24     $25
Surplus cash            n.a.      0       0       0       0       0
New notes payable       n.a.      6       3       2       2       2
New bonds               n.a.     62      57      43      23      23
New stock               n.a.     22      66      23       0       0
New shares sold         n.a.    0.60    1.52    0.45    0.00    0.00
Total shares out.      10.00   10.60   12.12   12.57   12.57   12.57

II. FINANCIAL RATIOS

Current ratio           2.64    2.50    2.50    2.50    2.50    2.50
T.A. turnover           1.42    1.51    1.57    1.60    1.62    1.63
Debt ratio            41.83%  50.00%  50.00%  50.00%  49.07%  47.93%
TIE                     5.62    4.97    5.71    6.02    6.41    6.86
ROA                    5.25%   6.44%   7.67%   8.19%   8.53%   8.85%
ROE                    9.05%  12.88%  15.34%  16.39%  16.75%  16.99%

III. CONSTRAINTS AND INPUTS

Interest rate on new bonds             12.00%
Int. rate on new notes payable         10.00%
Tax rate, next five years              50.00%
Maximum total debt/T.A.ratio           50.00%
Minimum current ratio                   2.50

Maximum debt           $176    $248    $357    $439    $500    $570
Financing needed          0      90     126      68      24      25
Maximum C.L.             79     114     166     205     234     267
Maximum new notes         4       6       3       2       2       2
Funding from
 bonds and stock          0      84     123      66      23      23
Funding from new
 notes payable            0       6       3       2       2       2
Add'l A/P & Accrls      n.a.     33      49      37      27      32
Maximum new bonds        28      62      57      43      32      46
Funding from
 new bonds                0      62      57      43      23      23
Funding from
 new stock                0      22      66      23       0       0
No. new shs. stock     0.00    0.60    1.52    0.45    0.00    0.00




================================================================
```

Regression Analysis

In the financial forecasting spreadsheet, several variables
are related to sales, but they do not change in direct
proportion to changes in sales. This means that an X percent in sales will lead to a change in the balance sheet
account, but not an X percent change. In such situations,
regression analysis is useful to help establish the relationship, and we used 1-2-3's built-in regression function
to determine the relationships. The four variables analyzed
in this manner were accounts receivable, administrative
expenses, inventory, and fixed assets. After computing the
regression equation coefficients for each variable against
sales, we used the model to predict inventory for each level
of sales, and we also created a graph that is useful both
for showing the relationship and for predicting inventory
based on expected sales. We could have created similar
graphs for administrative expenses, receivables, and fixed
assets.

Table 9-5 shows the section of the worksheet, Q1.X47,
used to calculate the regression coefficients. We entered
10 years of historic data on sales, administrative expenses,
accounts receivable, inventory, and fixed assets on Rows 11
through 20 in Columns R, S, T, U, and V. Then we ran four
separate linear regression analyses with sales, in Range
R11.R20, as the independent variable. For administrative
expenses, we specified the dependent variable range as
S11.S20; then we instructed 1-2-3 to calculate the intercept
term and to print the regression output in the range
Q26.T34. To run the regression, we typed the following
command:

    /DRXR11.R20 RETURN YS11.S20 RETURN ICOQ26 RETURN G

We ran the other three regressions by specifying new Y
values and output ranges. The output range was U26.X34 for
accounts receivable, Q39.T47 for inventory, and U39.X47 for
fixed assets.

Table 9-5

Table 9-5. Regression Analysis (Q1.X47)

Type in the years, if different, and the data for sales and the balance
sheet and income statement items. Then use the /Data Regression comman
to calculate regression coefficients in the area below the historic
data. Press the F10 key to view our graph of inventory versus sales.

Year	Sales	Admin. expenses	Accounts receivable	Inventory	Fixed assets	Predicted inventory
1975	175	35	33	44	78	48
1976	200	37	38	48	83	53
1977	215	38	44	53	86	55
1978	185	36	35	57	79	50
1979	235	39	43	60	91	59
1980	265	42	45	66	98	64
1981	300	45	52	73	106	71
1982	280	43	47	70	101	67
1983	350	46	61	78	118	79
1984	420	49	71	90	135	92

Administrative expenses: Accounts receivables:

        Regression Output: Regression Output:
Constant   25.45 Constant   7.80
Std Err of Y Est   0.98 Std Err of Y Est   1.99
R Squared   0.96 R Squared   0.97
No. of Observations   10.00 No. of Observations   10.00
Degrees of Freedom   8.00 Degrees of Freedom   8.00

X Coefficient   0.06   X Coefficient   0.15
Std Err of Coef   0.00   Std Err of Coef   0.01

Inventory: Fixed assets:

        Regression Output: Regression Output:
Constant   17.44 Constant   35.89
Std Err of Y Est   3.86 Std Err of Y Est   0.51
R Squared   0.93 R Squared   1.00
No. of Observations   10 No. of Observations   10
Degrees of Freedom   8 Degrees of Freedom   8

X Coefficient   0.18   X Coefficient   0.23
Std Err of Coef   0.02   Std Err of Coef   0.00

We then used the calculated regression equation to predict inventory levels at different sales levels:

Inventory = 17.44 + 0.18(Sales)

The predicted inventory levels are shown in Column X, and
they were plotted on the line graph shown, along with actual
inventory, in Figure 9-2. To obtain our graph on your
computer screen, just press the F10 key. In order to
return to your worksheet, press any key. The graph is a
line graph in which the option was taken to format actual
inventory in symbols, while the predicted inventory was
plotted with symbols but with lines connecting the symbols.
In this case, the line is the regression line itself, and
the graph shows just how well the sample data fit a
predicted line.
    Balance sheet and income statement variables could be
regressed against sales, the national economy, and other
economic variables, either in a series of simple regressions
or in a multiple regression analysis. With this information, forecasts of pro forma statements can be arranged in
spreadsheets similar to those behind the Artell forecasting
model.
    You may perform regression analyses on the variables
for your company by changing the labels and data in Columns
R through V and running 1-2-3's regression procedure. You
may include more than 10 years by adding more lines of data,
and you can analyze more than 4 variables by entering data
for those variables in the columns to the right of Column V.
If you do analyze additional variables, be sure to specify
your output range by entering the upper left corner cell
address of a blank range that is at least 9 rows by 4
columns.

===

Figure 9-2

Regression Fit
Predicted vs. Actual Inventory

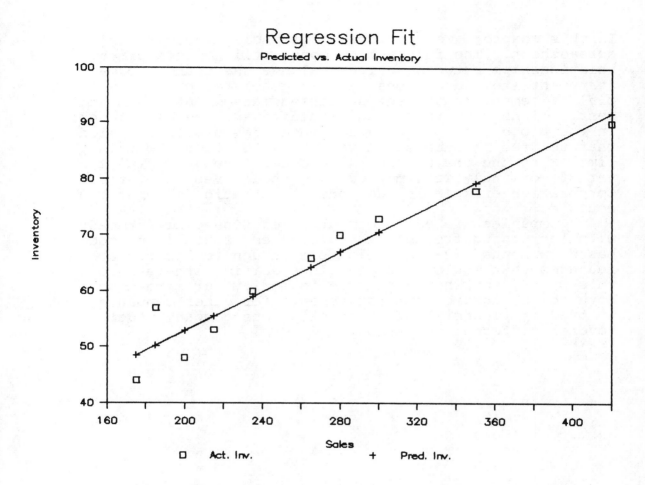

===

Summary

In this chapter, we developed a financial forecasting spreadsheet. The forecasting model utilizes historical relationships between various balance sheet and income statement items and sales, and it generates pro forma financial statements that meet specified management goals and restrictions concerned with liquidity and the use of debt. In the process, we calculated linear regression equations that related balance sheet variables to sales. Models similar to the one we used here could have an infinite variety of analytical methods and objectives; the Artell Corporation example is just one illustration of what you could do.

Companies are using computerized financial forecasts with increasing frequency. Spreadsheet forecasting models based on Lotus 1-2-3 are flexible enough to incorporate many features that would be useful in specific circumstances. At this point, you should be able to modify our spreadsheet both to obtain pro forma statements for other companies and to predict financial statements for one company under several different scenarios.

Chapter 9 Exercises

Note: Before doing any of the following exercises, make sure you copy File LB9X1 onto your diskette and do these exercises on that file copy.

9-1 Retrieve your copy of File LB9X1. Make the following data changes to Table 9-2 and answer the questions that follow. Remember to enter percentages as decimals.

Annual sales growth rates: Year 1 = 15.00%
Year 2 = 30.00%
Year 3 = 25.00%
Year 4 = 20.00%
Year 5 = 20.00%

Minimum current ratio   3.00
Maximum debt ratio   40.00%
Dividend growth rate   8.00%
Stock price growth rate 17.00%
Tax rate   46.00%

Regression parameters	(a)	(b)
Cost of goods sold	0.00	75%
Cash	0.00	4%
Accounts payable	0.00	5%
Accrued wages and taxes	0.00	4%

Starting (base year) input values:

Stock price	$ 27.00
Dividend per share	0.75
Net sales	450.00
Interest expense	6.00
Notes payable	8.00
Bonds (long-term debt)	78.00
Common stock	155.00
Retained earnings	49.00
Total shares outstanding	12

a. How have the modifications made to the input data changed the financing requirements for Artell Corporation?

b. What are the major factors affecting the financing requirement changes?

c. For the 1986-1990 period identify the following:

1. Maximum debt that could be used to meet Artell's financing requirements (1985 = $133, 1989 = $267)
2. Maximum new bonds that could be used to meet Artell's financing requirements
3. Funding from new notes payable (1986 = $11, 1990 = $6)
4. Funding from new bonds
5. Funding from new stock (1987 = $13, 1988 = $8)

Note: If you are making data changes on your own to experiment with the model, make certain that your data is consistent beginning with the first year. (We assume that the company is an ongoing concern which has had to follow the current ratio and total debt to total assets ratio restrictions that are given in the input data.)

Save your file as LB9EX1.

9-2 Retrieve File LB9EX1. Use the Range Erase command to erase the unprotected data cells in Table 9-2 but do not press the CALC key before entering the data. Then work the following problem. (If you do try to convert the model to a template model some of the formulas cannot be recalculated due to the model's circularity and ERRs will appear which cannot be removed. If this happens, you will have to start over.)
     Timber Tree Products is trying to forecast its financial statements for the period 1986-1990 in order to determine its projected financing requirements over the next four years. After entering the relevant data given below in the appropriate sections of Table 9-2, answer the questions that follow:

The following accounts vary directly as a percentage of sales:

% of Sales

Cost of goods sold	67
Cash	8
Accounts payable	8
Accrued wages and taxes	5

Annual sales growth rates:
Year 1 = 2%
Year 2 = 5%
Year 3 = 10%
Year 4 = 13%
Year 5 = 10%

Minimum current ratio	2.50
Maximum debt ratio	42%
Interest rate on O/S notes payable	11%
Interest rate on new notes payable	8%
Interest rate on O/S bonds	13%
Interest rate on new bonds	10.5%
Dividend growth rate	6%
Stock price growth rate	10%
Tax rate over the next 5 years	46%

Base Year (Input) Values:

Stock price	$ 22.00
Dividend per share	1.76
Net sales	325.00
Interest expense	7.70
Notes payable	5.00
Bonds (long-term debt)	55.00
Common stock	120.00
Retained earnings	47.00
Total shares outstanding	15

Answer the following questions regarding Timber Tree's financing requirements:

a. For the 1986-1990 period how much financing will Timber Tree need? (1988 = $12, 1989 = $15)

b. How much funding from new notes payable, new bonds, and new stock will Timber Tree need for the years 1986-1990?

c. What is the maximum debt, maximum current liabilities, maximum new notes, and maximum new bonds requirements for Timber Tree for the period 1986-1990? (Maximum CL: 1986 = $64, 1990 = $87; Maximum Bonds: 1987 = $8)

Chapter 10
A Cash Budgeting Spreadsheet

In this chapter, we develop a cash budgeting model to forecast the inflows and outflows of cash within a corporation
over a 12-month period. This cash budget can then be used
to predict the timing and dollar amounts of the firm's
short-term borrowings and investments. The cash budget
combines forecasts of monthly sales, predicted relationships
between sales and various expenses, and management's decisions regarding its liquidity position. The resulting forecast can then be used for comparison against actual month-
by-month cash flows.

Layout of the Spreadsheet

Figure 10-1 gives a schematic diagram of the layout of the
cash budgeting spreadsheet used in this chapter. Table 10-1
lists the file contents and provides instructions for its
use, while Tables 10-2 and 10-3 show printouts of the two
major sections of the spreadsheet model.
    This model is straightforward. Data on monthly sales,
receivables payment patterns, and monthly expenditures are
typed in the input section, Table 10-2, and when you press
the F9 function key, the computer does the arithmetic necessary to generate Table 10-3, the 12-month cash budget. You
will notice that the message CIRC will at some point appear
at the bottom of the screen. This indicates that simultaneous equations are present in the model. We will discuss
them later when we describe how the model works, but for
now, you should know that 1-2-3 is capable of solving simultaneous equations through an iterative process. We have

instructed 1-2-3 to go through 10 iterations of this model whenever we press the F9 key; however, we have found that we must often press the CALC key twice to obtain a solution to this model because of the degree of interaction and the number of months involved.

==

Figure 10-1
Layout of the Spreadsheet

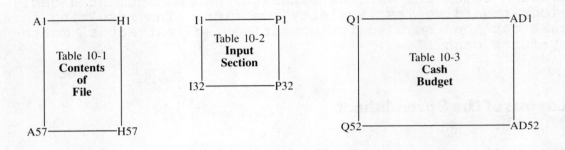

==

===

Table 10-1

Table 10-1. Contents of File LB10X1 and Directions for Its Use (A1.H57)

I. To position a table on the screen:

1. Press function key F5, the "GoTo" key.
2. Type the first cell shown in the range in the directory
   shown below, starting on line 46.
3. Press the RETURN key.
4. To return to the directory, press the F5 key and go to A46.

II. The ranges for Tables 10-1 and 10-2 will fit on one printed page.
Thus, you can print these two tables with one Print command by
specifying the print range as A1.P57. However, the cash budget
worksheet, Table 10-3, is too wide to fit on a single page with a
width of 72 characters. In order to be able to print this table
on one page, we reduced the column widths and printed it using
compressed print. We have saved a macro in this worksheet which
first prints Tables 10-1 and 10-2 using normal print and then
prints Table 10-3 using compressed print. This macro is named \P
and can be invoked by pressing ALT P.

III. The tables now have illustrative data. By using the Range Erase
command on the unprotected data in Tables 10-2 and 10-3, you
convert the cash budget to a template model. Then, when you enter
the data for your own company, the cash budget will be completed
automatically. Note that all cells except input data cells
have been protected. If you need to modify the model, you may
disconnect the protect feature with this command: /WGPD. If you
attempt to write in a protected cell, you will hear a beep and
receive an error message. Press ESC to return to READY mode.

IV. Note that unless you disconnect the protect feature, only the
data cells can be changed--all formulas are protected. Thus, you
cannot erase the entire cash budget at one pass; you can erase
only the unprotected input cells. Also, note that once you erase
the data in the worksheet, zeros and ERRs appear throughout.
When you enter new data, the ERRs will disappear.

V. We had to make several assumptions in creating this model.
One of our assumptions was that the firm would liquidate its
marketable securities before borrowing funds from the bank and
that any excess funds would first be used to repay bank loans.
Thus, at any given point in time, one of these two accounts will
have a zero balance.

VI. Here are the tables and their addresses:

Cell Range	Number	Description of Table
A1.H57	10-1	Contents of file LB10X1
I1.P32	10-2	Input section
Q1.AD52	10-3	Cash budget

VII. The macro, \P, which will print this worksheet is given below.

```
\P        /ppcfra1.p57~os\018~mr76~qagq
          /pppcfrq1.ad57~os\015~mr130~qagcfq
```

===

```
================================================================
                         Table 10-2




           I      J      K      L      M      N      O       P
 1   Table 10-2.  Input Data (I1.P32)
 2
 3   Input data in Column P
 4
 5    1. Sales one month before first month of budget period        640
 6    2. Sales two months before first month of budget period       555
 7    3. Beginning bank loan (either #3 or #4 must be zero)          267
 8    4. Beginning marketable securities                              0
 9    5. Cash sales as a proportion of total sales                  0.60
10    6. Proportion of sales collected one month after sale        0.30
11    7. Proportion of sales collected two months after sale       0.10
12    8. Annual interest rate on marketable securities             0.10
13    9. Inventory purchases as proportion of sales                0.62
14   10. Cash expense as proportion of inventory purchases         0.98
15   11. Annual interest rate on short-term bank loans             0.12
16   12. Beginning cash balance in first month of budget period      45
17   13. Cash as proportion of sales (target cash percentage)      0.05
18   14. Operating expenses, fixed component                         25
19   15. Operating expenses, variable component                   0.15
20
21   Enter the following values in the rows indicated for specific months:
22
23    1. Row 5    Sales forecast for each month
24    2. Row 6    Variance of actual sales from expected sales
25    3. Row 17   Cash inflow from sale of assets
26    4. Row 18   Cash inflow from securities issues
27    5. Row 28   Cash outflow, interest on long-term debt
28    6. Row 30   Cash outflow, principal paid on long-term debt
29    7. Row 31   Cash outflow, tax payments
30    8. Row 32   Cash outflow, fixed asset expenses
31    9. Row 33   Cash outflow, dividend payments
32   10. Row 34   Cash outflow, repurchase of stock




================================================================
```

The Input Section

The input section, entered in the range I1.P32, is divided
into two parts: variables which are constant in each month

and variables which take on different values in each month. The values of the variables which remain constant are entered in Column P of the input section; if you are using a color monitor, the base case input values will be green, while they will be highlighted on a monochrome monitor. Below the constant value input section is a listing of the variables which take on different values in each month. The values of these variables are entered directly into the cash budget on the appropriate lines.

In developing the cash budget, we made some assumptions relating to the model inputs. These assumptions were:

1. The firm makes both cash sales and credit sales, and the percentage of cash sales to total sales remains constant in each month. Also, the firm's receivables payment pattern is constant in each month; that is, cash is received in payment of credit sales with the same time lags in each month.

2. The cash budget summarizes all transactions during each month, and the bank loans or securities held reflect the position at the end of the month. Any excess funds in a particular month will first be used to repay bank loans and then, if no loans are outstanding, will be invested in marketable securities. Similarly, any cash shortage will be met first by liquidating marketable securities and then by borrowing from the bank. Thus, the values for bank loans and marketable securities cannot both be positive at the end of any given month.

3. The financial feedback system requires that beginning figures be entered for marketable securities and bank loans in Cells P7 and P8. Remember that one of these values must be zero and the other may be positive or zero. If you are using this spreadsheet for a company that has both short-term debt and marketable securities, enter zero for one value and the positive net amount for the other.

4. Current short-term interest rates will remain constant during the 12-month period. Hence, we entered only one value for the short-term investment rate and one for the short-term borrowing rate.

5. The firm's monthly inventory purchases are a constant percentage of that month's expected sales. We also assumed that the firm would take cash discounts, so we decreased cash outflows for inventory expenses by the amount of the discount.

6. The firm's monthly operating expenses are assumed to be related to sales according to a straight line regression formula. The fixed component, or the "a" value in the formula, is entered in Cell P18, and the variable component, or the slope of the equation, is placed in Cell P19. If you use this model for a company whose expenses are directly related to sales as a constant percentage of sales, then enter a zero in P18 and the variable percentage in P19.

7. Management's target cash balance is a constant percentage of expected monthly sales.

All of the cash flows from operations are based directly on sales, and these relationships are entered in the top section of the input screen. Expected monthly sales and the variance of actual sales from expected sales are entered manually in the cash budget, while operating cash flows have been specified in the cash budget as mathematical formulas. Non-operating cash flows, however, are not related to sales. The lower portion of the input section identifies the non-operating cash flows and the rows of the cash budget in which their values are to be entered. They include cash inflows from the sale of assets (fixed assets or bulk sales of working capital, but not "regular" sales inventory) and from securities issues and cash outflows for interest and principal payments on long-term debt, tax payments, fixed asset expenses (for example, planned repairs and overhauls), dividend payments, and stock repurchases.

Non-operating cash flows have two characteristics in common: (1) They are lump-sum flows, unlike the normal flow of operating expenses and sales revenues, which can be expressed as a proportion of sales, and (2) they are generally predictable because they are contractual (such as the payment of debt interest and principal) or else subject to management choice (such as dividend payments, stock repurchases, and the sale of fixed assets). Because they are not continuous throughout the year, non-operating cash flows are entered in the cash budget rows indicated, in the column for the month in which they will occur.

The Cash Budget

The completed cash budget is shown in Table 10-3. The expected, or most likely, level for sales in each month is entered in Row 5. Then a variance percentage is input in Row 6. The variance percentage is included to allow a scenario analysis to be performed by varying actual sales from expected sales and determining the effects of these changes on net monthly cash flows. These variance percentages would normally range from +1.0, indicating actual sales at twice the forecast level, to -1.0, indicating zero sales; +0.2 is a more reasonable range in most cases.

Finally, the remaining nonconstant inputs are entered. The cash budget is then calculated by pressing the F9 key twice.

In this example, net cash flows (the difference between cash inflows and cash outflows each month) are positive at the beginning of the year. These excess cash flows are used to reduce short-term borrowings from $267 at the beginning of January to zero by the end of February. Surplus cash, equal to $205 in January and $177 in February, is used first to pay off short-term bank loans and then to invest in marketable securities. In October, the company is forced to borrow again--after net negative cash flows have used up the stored liquidity represented by short-term marketable securities.

Notice that the cash budget spreadsheet automatically establishes the target cash balance for the month and then borrows, invests, or sells securities so as to leave the adjusted cash balance at the target level at the end of the month. The adjusted, or ending, cash balance carries over to become the beginning cash balance for the following month.

Table 10-3

Table 10-3. Cash Budget (Q1.AD52)

	JAN	FEB	MAR	APR	MAY	JUN	JUL	AUG	SEP	OCT	NOV	DEC
Most likely sales	$300	$110	$64	$85	$165	$198	$279	$301	$385	$574	$432	$225
Variance percentage	0.00	0.00	0.00	0.00	0.00	0.00	0.00	0.00	0.00	0.00	0.00	0.00
Actual sales	$300	$110	$64	$85	$165	$198	$279	$301	$385	$574	$432	$225
Inventory purchases	$186	$68	$40	$53	$102	$123	$173	$187	$239	$356	$268	$140
Cash receipts:												
Cash sales	$180	$66	$38	$51	$99	$119	$167	$181	$231	$344	$259	$135
Receivables												
1-Month 640	192	90	33	19	26	50	59	84	90	116	172	130
2-Months 555	56	64	30	11	6	9	17	20	28	30	39	57
Sale of assets		55				60		16				
Securities issues						40						
Interest on mkt sec	0	1	1	1	1	1	1	1	1	0	1	1
Total cash inflows	$428	$276	$102	$82	$132	$278	$244	$301	$350	$490	$471	$323
Cash expenditures:												
Inventory payment	$182	$67	$39	$52	$100	$120	$170	$183	$234	$349	$262	$137
Operating expenses	70	42	35	38	50	55	67	70	83	111	90	59
Interest expense:												
L-T debt						22						22
S-T debt	1	0	0	0	0	0	0	0	0	0	0	0
Debt repayment						40						
Tax payments			25			25			38			45
Fixed asset exp										156		
Dividends paid			6			6			6			6
Stock repurchases								32				
Total cash outflows	$253	$108	$104	$89	$150	$268	$236	$285	$361	$616	$352	$268
Net cash flow	$175	$168	($2)	($7)	($18)	$10	$8	$16	($11)	($126)	$118	$55
Plus beg cash balance	45	15	6	3	4	8	10	14	15	19	29	22
Ending cash balance	$220	$183	$3	($4)	($14)	$18	$18	$30	$4	($107)	$147	$76
Less target balance	15	6	3	4	8	10	14	15	19	29	22	11
Variance from target	$205	$177	$0	($8)	($22)	$8	$4	$15	($15)	($136)	$125	$65
Bank loan $267	$62	$0	$0	$0	$0	$0	$0	$0	$0	$40	$0	$0
Mkt sec $0	$0	$115	$115	$107	$84	$92	$96	$111	$96	$0	$85	$151
Adjusted cash balance	$15	$6	$3	$4	$8	$10	$14	$15	$19	$29	$22	$11

The cash budget model also contains a financial feedback system; for example, a cash surplus would result in additional securities purchased, which would increase interest income, which in turn would increase securities purchased. This iterative process continues until the changes are too small to cause further adjustments to the cash budget figures. The same iterative process occurs as a result of short-term borrowing. The final solutions for short-term borrowing and marketable securities are included when the model calculates Interest on marketable securities and Interest on short-term debt.

Summary

This cash budgeting model uses 1-2-3's iterative calculation process to solve a fairly complex system of simultaneous equations. The budget can be used in scenario analyses such as determining the effects of a changing payments pattern or various sales levels on net monthly cash flows; it can be modified for different companies; and it can be expanded to include additional budget accounts.

Chapter 10 Exercise

Note: Before doing this exercise, make sure you copy File LB10X1 onto your diskette and then do the following exercise with your copy of File LB10X1.

10-1 Retrieve File LB10X1. Make the following data changes to the model and answer the questions that follow. (Hint: When you change data in Tables 10-2 and 10-3, position the cell pointer in S5 and use the command /WTB (Worksheet Title Both) to freeze the month and account labels on the screen.)

The Clayton Company is planning to request a line of credit from its bank. The following sales forecasts have been made for 1987.

November 1986	175
December 1986	200
January 1987	150
February 1987	150
March 1987	300
April 1987	450
May 1987	600
June 1987	300
July 1987	300
August 1987	75
September 1987	150
October 1987	100
November 1987	175
December 1987	125

Collection estimates were obtained from the credit and collection department as follows: collected within the month of sale, 5%; collected the month following the month of sale, 80%; and collected the second month following the month of sale, 15%. Monthly inventory purchases represent 66% of the sales for the month and Clayton Company always pays for its inventory purchases in the month it is purchased because its supplier offers a 2% discount with cash payments made within 30 days of the purchase.

In December 1986 Clayton had a loan balance of $80 with an annual interest rate of 11%. On January 1, Clayton's cash balance on hand was $25; the company has a target cash balance amounting to 3% of sales and any excess cash above this is first used to pay off bank loans and then is invested in marketable securities with an annual interest rate of 9%. Clayton's fixed operating costs amount to $22 per month and its variable operating costs vary directly with sales and total approximately 17% of sales.

Clayton's recent forecasts have overstated actual sales by 5% (input variance as -0.5); thus, Clayton has built in a line item called variance percentage to take this into account.

The following data outlines nonoperating receipts and outlays Clayton forecasts for the next year.

Receipts
Sale of assets:	2/87	$25
	6/87	$30
	11/87	$20
Sale of securities:	4/87	$10
	9/87	$5

Expenditures
Interest expense:
(Long-term debt)	6/87	$10
	12/87	$10
Principal payment:	8/87	$35
Tax payment:	3/87	$15
	6/87	$15
	9/87	$27
	12/87	$36
Fixed asset expenses:	1/87	$75
	11/87	$135
Dividend payment:	3/87	$4
	6/87	$4
	9/87	$4
	12/87	$4
Stock repurchases:	10/87	$80

Save your file as LB10EX1.

a. In what months does Clayton need to borrow money?

b. In what months does Clayton have excess money in
    which it invests in marketable securities? (July,
    August, September, and October; the marketable
    securities balance in August totals $177.)

c. How do the answers for Parts a and b vary if all
    of the following occur:
    1. Clayton has a $0 bank loan balance in December
        and $0 invested in marketable securities.
    2. The collection percentages change.

        Cash sales   3%
        % of sales collected in
          following month   70%
        % of sales collected
          2 months after sale   27%

    3. Clayton receives a 5% discount for paying cash
        for inventory within 30 days of the purchase.
    4. Variable operating expenses vary directly with
        sales, totaling approximately 20% of sales.

    (Clayton invests in marketable securities in
    February, July, August, September, and October.
    The marketable securities balance in October
    totals $136.)

Chapter 11
Lease versus Borrow Analysis

In this chapter we build a 1-2-3 spreadsheet for analyzing leasing versus borrowing to finance fixed asset investments. The lease versus borrow decision is made after the project has been accepted as part of the capital budgeting process. The decision involves determining the net cash outflows under each financing method and then choosing the method which has the lower present value of cash outflows.

Layout of the Spreadsheet

The layout of the spreadsheet is shown in Figure 11-1. Table 11-1 describes the contents of File LB11X1 and provides instructions for its use, while Tables 11-2 through 11-8 show printouts of the major sections of the spreadsheet model.

The model is straightforward. The data values are entered in Table 11-2, and Tables 11-3 through 11-7 are automatically calculated when the F9 (CALC) key is pressed. The loan amortization schedule is generated in Table 11-3, and depreciation schedules based on 3-year, 5-year, and 10-year ACRS class lives are generated in Table 11-4. Table 11-5 analyzes the cash flows which result from borrowing money and purchasing the asset. Table 11-6 then calculates the present value costs of leasing and borrowing. Table 11-7 analyzes the cash outflows associated with the lease so that the rate of return implicit in the lease can be determined. Finally, Table 11-8 illustrates a data table and its usefulness in sensitivity analysis.

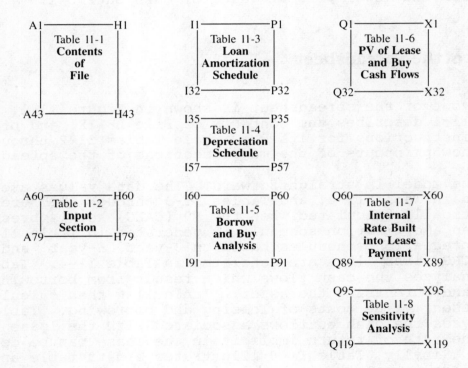

Figure 11-1
Layout of the Spreadsheet

A1 ——————— H1
Table 11-1
**Contents
of
File**
A43 —————— H43

I1 ——————— P1
Table 11-3
**Loan
Amortization
Schedule**
I32 —————— P32

Q1 ——————— X1
Table 11-6
**PV of Lease
and Buy
Cash Flows**
Q32 —————— X32

I35 —————— P35
Table 11-4
**Depreciation
Schedule**
I57 —————— P57

A60 —— Table 11-2 —— H60
**Input
Section**
A79 —————— H79

I60 —————— P60
Table 11-5
**Borrow
and Buy
Analysis**
I91 —————— P91

Q60 —— Table 11-7 —— X60
**Internal
Rate Built
into Lease
Payment**
Q89 —————— X89

Q95 —————— X95
Table 11-8
**Sensitivity
Analysis**
Q119 —————— X119

===

Table 11-1

Table 11-1. Contents of File LB11X1 and Directions for Its Use (A1.H43)

I. To position a table on the screen:

    1. Press function key F5, the "GoTo" key.
    2. Type the first cell shown in the range in the directory shown below, starting on line 32.
    3. Press the RETURN key.
    4. To return to the directory, press the F5 key and go to A32.

II. The ranges for the tables will fit on a printed page. Thus, when you construct a table, you can print it by specifying the given range as the print range.

III. The tables now have illustrative data. By using the Range Erase command on the data in Table 11-2, you convert all the tables to template models. Then, when you complete Table 11-2 for your company, the other tables will be completed automatically. Note that all cells except input data cells in Table 11-2 have been protected. If you need to modify the model, you may disconnect the protect feature with this command: /WGPD. If you attempt to write in a protected cell, you will hear a beep and receive an error message. Press ESC to return to READY mode.

IV. Note that unless you disconnect the protect feature, only the data cells can be changed--all formulas are protected. Thus, you cannot erase the entire loan analysis. You can erase only the unprotected cells in the input section. Also, note that once you erase data in the input section, zeros and ERRs appear throughout the worksheet. They will disappear when you enter new data.

V. Here are the tables and their addresses:

Cell Range	Number	Description of Exhibit
A1.H43	11-1	Contents of file LB11X1
A60.H79	11-2	Input section
I1.P32	11-3	Loan amortization schedule
I35.P57	11-4	Depreciation schedule
I60.P91	11-5	Borrow and buy analysis
Q1.X32	11-6	PV of lease and buy cash flows
Q60.X89	11-7	Internal rate built into lease pymt
Q95.X119	11-8	Sensitivity analysis

===

The Input Section

Values for 11 variables are entered in Column H of the input section. These values include the price of the asset, the loan term and interest rate, the down payment made on the asset, the annual lease payment, the lease term, the expected residual value of the asset, the ITC percentage, annual maintenance expense, and the firm's tax rate. Also entered is a code which specifies whether the asset falls into the 3-year, 5-year, or the 10-year ACRS class life category. Then the initial loan balance is calculated as the net price minus the down payment, and the discount rate to be used in the analysis is calculated as the after-tax cost of debt. The 11 input values provide 1-2-3 with all the information necessary to perform the lease analysis and to complete the other tables. All of the cells in the spreadsheet are protected except those for the 11 inputs in Table 11-2, which are highlighted.

After entering the new values, press the CALC key to obtain the key results--the present values of the cash outflows from leasing and borrowing. These values are displayed below the list of input values, in Cells D78, D79, and H79. The lowest present value cost indicates the preferred type of financing.

There are several assumptions embodied in the lease analysis model, including the following:

1. If the asset is purchased, the owner will normally put some money down on the asset in Year 0 and also receive an investment tax credit (ITC). The down payment and ITC percentage are entered in the model, and the loan amount is calculated as the invoice price of the asset less the investment tax credit and the down payment. If no down payment is made and no ITC applies, then the borrowed amount calculated will be equal to the purchase price of the asset.

2. Since the ITC, if applicable, is used to reduce the loan amount, it is both a cash inflow and a cash outflow in Year 0. Hence, the ITC is important in deter-

mining the initial loan balance, but it has no impact on the Year 0 cash flow analysis. Thus, if the asset is purchased the Year 0 cash outflow is the down payment.

3. The asset will be fully depreciated, so the residual value will be taxed as ordinary income. Therefore, it must be entered as an after-tax amount.

4. The owner of the asset (the lessee if it is leased) receives all of the benefit from the depreciation tax shelter. This annual benefit is equal to the annual depreciation amount times the tax rate.

===

Table 11-2

	A	B	C	D	E	F	G	H
60	Table 11-2.	Input Section (A60.H79)						
61								
62	Table of input values:							
63		1.	Price of asset					$200,000
64		2.	Term of loan in years					20
65		3.	Loan interest rate					12.00%
66		4.	Down payment					$10,000
67		5.	Initial loan balance (calculated value)					$170,000
68		6.	Annual lease payment					$21,356
69		7.	Term of lease in years					20
70		8.	Residual value at loan maturity (after-tax)					$25,000
71		9.	Investment tax credit (ITC) percentage					10.00%
72		10.	Investment class: 1=3-year; 2=5-year; 3=10-year					3
73		11.	Maintenance expense (each year if owned)					$1,500
74		12.	Tax rate					40.00%
75		13.	Discount rate (calculated value)					7.20%
76								
77	Discounted net cash outflows from leasing & borrowing:							
78		Leasing $133,663			Net advantage to leasing:			
79		Borrowing $129,503						($4,160)

===

5. The asset will be depreciated using ACRS. The asset will fall into either the 3-year, 5-year, or 10-year class life.

6. Lease payments are constant in each year and occur at the _end_ of the year. Thus, the initial cash outflow from leasing occurs in Year 1. The model can be modified easily to handle other situations, such as beginning-of-year lease payments. For a 20-year lease, if payments are made at the beginning of the year in Table 11-6, enter the formula +H68 in Cell R9 and put a zero in R29, then in Table 11-7, enter the formula -H63+H68 in R69 and zero in R89. To go back to end-of-year payments, enter a zero in R9 and the formula -H63 in R69, copy R28 into R29, and copy R88 into R89.

7. Loan payments are made at the _end_ of each year.

8. All tables in the spreadsheet are set up for a 20-year analysis. If the borrowing or leasing periods are shorter than 20 years, the analysis will be performed over the required number of years and zeros will appear in the remaining cells. The model would require modification to analyze longer lease periods; to extend the model, you should insert enough blank rows for the additional periods at the end of Tables 11-3, 11-5, 11-6, and 11-7, then copy the Year 20 row of each table into the new rows.

9. The net after-tax cash flows from leasing and borrowing are discounted at the same rate, the after-tax cost of debt. This rate, which is calculated, will be less than the rate used to discount risky investments, because many of the cash flows in the lease versus borrow analysis are contractual, hence certain.

10. If the dollar amounts in the analysis exceed the cell range and cause overflows (asterisks in the cells), divide all dollar amounts by 1,000, that is, convert $10,000,000 to $10,000. Be sure to convert all dollar amounts. Then multiply the final output by 1,000. The lease versus borrow decision will be the same even if you do not remember to multiply the output by 1,000, but the magnitude of advantage will be off by a factor of 1,000.

In our example, we analyze lease versus borrow cash flows for a new backhoe that will be acquired by the Owens Construction Company.

The Loan Amortization Schedule

The loan amortization schedule, shown in Table 11-3, is found in the spreadsheet range I1.P32. This schedule separates the annual loan payments into their interest and principal components. The initial loan balance, term, and interest rate are given at the top of the table, after which the annual loan payment is calculated using the @PMT function. Note that like the lease payment in our model, the loan payment is assumed to have occurred at the end of the year.

Each cell in Column I, the year number, is compared with the term of the loan. If the year number is equal to or less than the term of the loan, the annual payment is entered in Column J. On the other hand, if the year number is larger than the loan term, a zero is entered in Column J. Owens' backhoe is expected to be used and paid for, if purchased, over a period of 20 years, so the loan payment is displayed for every year.

Interest is calculated on the outstanding loan balance in Column K as the previous loan balance times the interest rate. The cells in Column L compute the principal portion of each loan payment as the loan payment minus the interest portion. The principal payment is subtracted from the previous loan balance to determine the new loan balance shown in Column M.

==

Table 11-3

Table 11-3. Loan Amortization Schedule (I1.P32)

Loan balance	$170,000
Term of loan (years)	20
Interest rate on loan	12.00%
Annual loan payment	$22,759

Year	Payment	Interest	Principal	Loan Balance
0				$170,000
1	$22,759	$20,400	$2,359	167,641
2	22,759	20,117	2,643	164,998
3	22,759	19,800	2,960	162,038
4	22,759	19,445	3,315	158,724
5	22,759	19,047	3,713	155,011
6	22,759	18,601	4,158	150,853
7	22,759	18,102	4,657	146,196
8	22,759	17,544	5,216	140,980
9	22,759	16,918	5,842	135,138
10	22,759	16,217	6,543	128,596
11	22,759	15,431	7,328	121,268
12	22,759	14,552	8,207	113,060
13	22,759	13,567	9,192	103,868
14	22,759	12,464	10,295	93,573
15	22,759	11,229	11,531	82,043
16	22,759	9,845	12,914	69,128
17	22,759	8,295	14,464	54,664
18	22,759	6,560	16,200	38,465
19	22,759	4,616	18,144	20,321
20	22,759	2,439	20,321	0

==

Depreciation Schedule

The depreciation schedule is found in the range I35.P57 and
is shown in Table 11-4. The asset purchase price and the
applicable ITC percentage are displayed at the top of the

depreciation schedule; these values are copied from the input section. Next, the ITC amount is calculated as the purchase price times the ITC percentage, and the depreciable basis is determined as the purchase price minus one-half the ITC.

Three depreciation schedules are computed--one for a 3-year class asset, one for a 5-year class asset, and one for a 10-year class asset. The appropriate depreciation figures are then used in the borrow and buy analysis.

===

Table 11-4

Table 11-4.   Depreciation Schedule (I35.P57)

Purchase price	$200,000
ITC percent	10.00%
ITC dollar amount	$20,000
Amount to depreciate	$190,000

Year	3-Year Class: Percent	Deprec	5-Year Class: Percent	Deprec	10-Year Class: Percent	Deprec
1	25.00%	$47,500	15%	$28,500	8%	$15,200
2	38.00%	72,200	22%	41,800	14%	26,600
3	37.00%	70,300	21%	39,900	12%	22,800
4			21%	39,900	10%	19,000
5			21%	39,900	10%	19,000
6					10%	19,000
7					9%	17,100
8					9%	17,100
9					9%	17,100
10					9%	17,100

===

Borrow and Buy Analysis

Table 11-5 analyzes the annual after-tax cash outflows associated with borrowing and purchasing the asset. The annual
loan payments and interest expenses are copied from Table
11-3. For the depreciation expense figures, an IF statement
is used to determine the asset's ACRS class, after which the
appropriate depreciation expense from Table 11-4 is chosen;
a zero is entered if the year value exceeds the asset's
class life. Maintenance costs are entered by referencing the
input cell in Table 11-2; an IF statement is used to tell
1-2-3 to enter a zero for maintenance expense if the year
value exceeds the term of the loan.

The tax-deductible expenses for each year (maintenance,
depreciation, and interest) are summed in Column N. The
total tax savings from the deductible expenses, deductible
expenses times the tax rate, is given in Column O.

In Year 0, the net cash outflow is the loan down payment since there are no other cash flows in that year. (The
firm does receive an investment tax credit but that amount
is applied directly to the purchase price of the asset, so
the firm does not consider it as a cash inflow.) In all
other years, the net cash outflow is equal to the loan
payment, plus the maintenance cost, minus the tax savings.
In the final year of the analysis, the net cash outflow is
reduced by the asset's residual value (a negative cash
outflow).

==

Table 11-5

Table 11-5. Borrow and Buy Analysis (I60.P91)

Tax Rate   40.00%
Down payment included in Year 0 net cash flow
Residual value included in final period

Year	Loan Payment	Maint Cost	Deprec	Interest	Total Tax-Ded Expenses	Total Tax Saving	Net Cash Outflow
0							$10,000
1	$22,759	$1,500	$15,200	$20,400	$37,100	$14,840	9,419
2	22,759	1,500	26,600	20,117	48,217	19,287	4,973
3	22,759	1,500	22,800	19,800	44,100	17,640	6,619
4	22,759	1,500	19,000	19,445	39,945	15,978	8,282
5	22,759	1,500	19,000	19,047	39,547	15,819	8,441
6	22,759	1,500	19,000	18,601	39,101	15,641	8,619
7	22,759	1,500	17,100	18,102	36,702	14,681	9,578
8	22,759	1,500	17,100	17,544	36,144	14,457	9,802
9	22,759	1,500	17,100	16,918	35,518	14,207	10,052
10	22,759	1,500	17,100	16,217	34,817	13,927	10,333
11	22,759	1,500	0	15,431	16,931	6,773	17,487
12	22,759	1,500	0	14,552	16,052	6,421	17,839
13	22,759	1,500	0	13,567	15,067	6,027	18,232
14	22,759	1,500	0	12,464	13,964	5,586	18,674
15	22,759	1,500	0	11,229	12,729	5,092	19,168
16	22,759	1,500	0	9,845	11,345	4,538	19,721
17	22,759	1,500	0	8,295	9,795	3,918	20,341
18	22,759	1,500	0	6,560	8,060	3,224	21,036
19	22,759	1,500	0	4,616	6,116	2,446	21,813
20	22,759	1,500	0	2,439	3,939	1,575	(2,316)

==

Present Value Analysis

The net cash outflows from leasing and the present value
costs of leasing and buying are analyzed in Table 11-6.
Annual lease payments are entered in Column R, the tax
savings associated with the lease payments are computed in
Column S, and the net cash outflows associated with leasing
are calculated in Column T. The present values of the

annual lease outflows are computed in Column U, and the
borrow and buy outflows in Column V. Note that the Year 0
cash flow for borrowing is equal to the down payment, if
any, made on the purchase of the asset. The annual present
value figures are summed to determine the present value cost
of each alternative.

==

Table 11-6

Table 11-6. Present Value of Lease and Buy Cash Flows (Q1.X32)

Discount rate =   7.20%   (from table of input values)

Year	Lease Payment	Tax Saving	Net Cash Outflow	Present Value Lease	Present Value Buy
0	$0	$0	$0	$0	$10,000
1	21,356	8,542	12,814	11,953	8,787
2	21,356	8,542	12,814	11,150	4,327
3	21,356	8,542	12,814	10,401	5,373
4	21,356	8,542	12,814	9,703	6,271
5	21,356	8,542	12,814	9,051	5,962
6	21,356	8,542	12,814	8,443	5,679
7	21,356	8,542	12,814	7,876	5,888
8	21,356	8,542	12,814	7,347	5,620
9	21,356	8,542	12,814	6,854	5,377
10	21,356	8,542	12,814	6,393	5,155
11	21,356	8,542	12,814	5,964	8,139
12	21,356	8,542	12,814	5,563	7,745
13	21,356	8,542	12,814	5,190	7,384
14	21,356	8,542	12,814	4,841	7,055
15	21,356	8,542	12,814	4,516	6,755
16	21,356	8,542	12,814	4,213	6,484
17	21,356	8,542	12,814	3,930	6,238
18	21,356	8,542	12,814	3,666	6,018
19	21,356	8,542	12,814	3,420	5,821
20	21,356	8,542	12,814	3,190	(577)
				$133,663	$129,503

==

308

IRR on Lease

The normal situation is for the lessor to offer the lessee a payment schedule. However, that payment schedule is developed so as to provide the lessor with some target rate of return on the funds invested in the lease. The lease analysis model could be set up to take as an input either the dollar amount of the lease payment per period or as the rate of return on the lease. Our model is set up to take the lease payment in dollars. (If the rate, but not the dollars, was known, you could calculate the payment separately and then input it.)

Table 11-7, Q60.X89, calculates the interest rate built into the lease payment schedule. The IRR function contains an interesting 1-2-3 feature. Notice that the range of cash flows after the initial investment is indicated by an absolute cell reference followed by a relative reference. By using this form of @IRR statement, the first formula in S70 can be copied into cells S71.S89, and the range will be self-adjusting. The calculated IRR, which is the implied interest rate in the lease agreement, appears in Column S of the final year of the lease term and also in Cell V89.

```
==============================================================
```

                              Table 11-7

        Table 11-7. Internal Rate Built into Lease Payment (Q60.X89)

        Year O Balance = Price - Year O lease payment

                    Direct
                    Cash Flow
              Year to Lessor   IRR
              ---- ----------   ----
                0   (200,000)
                1   21,356   0.00%
                2   21,356   0.00%
                3   21,356   0.00%
                4   21,356   0.00%
                5   21,356   0.00%
                6   21,356   0.00%
                7   21,356   0.00%
                8   21,356   0.00%
                9   21,356   0.00%
               10   21,356   0.00%
               11   21,356   0.00%
               12   21,356   0.00%
               13   21,356   0.00%
               14   21,356   0.00%
               15   21,356   0.00%
               16   21,356   0.00%
               17   21,356   0.00%
               18   21,356   0.00%
               19   21,356   0.00%
               20   21,356   8.64%   IRR =   8.64%


```
==============================================================
```


Sensitivity Analysis

The lease versus borrow spreadsheet can be used to answer
what-if questions about different variables that affect the
outcome. For example, you may want to determine the effects

of changes in loan interest rates on the decision to lease or borrow, or determine the breakeven loan interest rate that would make the present value costs of leasing and borrowing equal.

For the sensitivity analysis, we can set up a data table showing present values of borrowing cash flows for different loan rates. A data table of this type is shown in Table 11-8. The formula +D79 is entered in Cell T99. D79 is the cell that will be recalculated based on varying loan interest rates. In Cell S99, we have entered the formula +H65 (the initial input value of the loan rate). We then formatted that cell with the command /RFT RETURN so the formula is displayed rather than a numerical value. Then, in the range S100 + S119 we entered the interest rates which we wanted to use to evaluate the loan. We entered the rates 1 percent to 20 percent using the Data Fill command /DF S100.S119 RETURN .01 RETURN .01 RETURN RETURN.

To create the data table we typed the following sequence: /DT1 for command menu, data, table, and 1 input cell. In response to the prompt for the table range, we entered S99.T119, pressed the RETURN key, and responded to the prompt for an input cell by typing H65. When this is entered, the spreadsheet will calculate present values for borrowing over the interest rate range 1 to 20 percent. Note that (1) the interest rate range formulas have previously been entered; if this were not the case, you would have to enter these formulas. (2) In order to run the Data Table feature, you must disengage the protection feature on the worksheet by typing /WGPD . (3) Any changes made to the worksheet will not ripple through the data table when the CALC key is pressed; the only way to see the results of your changes in the data table is by going through the Data Table command sequence again. The results show that a loan rate greater than 15 percent would be required in order for leasing to be the best financing under current assumptions; therefore, at all interest rates less than 15 percent, borrowing is the correct financing decision.

In addition to data table analysis, the model can be used for simple what-if analysis: Simply by changing input values, you can modify the model to analyze the decision under different conditions, such as determining the effects of a different lease payment, different residual values, or different loan interest rates.

```
=================================================================

                            Table 11-8


            Table 11-8. Sensitivity Analysis (Q95.X119)

                             Loan        PV
                             Rate     Borrowing
                             +H65     $129,503
                             1.00%     101,086
                             2.00%     104,823
                             3.00%     108,251
                             4.00%     111,401
                             5.00%     114,303
                             6.00%     116,984
                             7.00%     119,465
                             8.00%     121,766
                             9.00%     123,906
                            10.00%     125,900
                            11.00%     127,761
                            12.00%     129,503
                            13.00%     131,135
                            14.00%     132,668
                            15.00%     134,111
                            16.00%     135,471
                            17.00%     136,755
                            18.00%     137,969
                            19.00%     139,119
                            20.00%     140,210



=================================================================
```

Summary

In this chapter, we described a Lotus 1-2-3 model that
analyzes the decision as to whether to lease or borrow to
acquire the use of an asset. We discussed the nature of the
lease versus borrow decision in terms of being a financing
decision, which is somewhat different from an investment
decision. In a financing decision, most of the cash flows
are predictable. Thus, although both financing and investment decisions use present value methods, the discount rates
applied to future cash flows can be lower for financing

decisions.   The discount rate used in a lease versus borrow analysis is frequently stated as the after-tax cost of debt.

Lease versus borrow decisions require the simultaneous use of several types of financial analyses, including loan amortization tables, depreciation schedules, after-tax cash flows, and the calculation of present values. The spread-sheet model in this chapter links the various analytical tables in a logical sequence so that most of the work is completed automatically. The user enters the input data, presses the CALC key, and immediately views the key results of the analysis. The specific analyses in the lease versus borrow model are (1) the loan amortization schedule, (2) the depreciation schedule, (3) the table of cash flows attribut-able to borrowing, (4) the table of leasing cash flows and annual present values of lease and borrow cash flows, and (5) an analysis of the implied rate of interest in the lease.

A variety of what-if questions can be analyzed with this spreadsheet. New data can be entered for one or sev-eral input variables, making it easy for management to see the changed results. Data tables also increase the model's usefulness, since results can be generated for any formula value based on different input values. Using a data table, we can look at the effects of loan rate changes on the lease versus borrow decision.

Chapter 11 Exercises

Note: Before doing these exercises, make sure you copy File LB11X1 onto your diskette and then work the exercises on that copy.

11-1 a. Indicate whether leasing or borrowing is advantageous under each of the situations given below and the amount of the net advantage.

       1. The term of the loan and lease is 10 years and the annual lease payment is equal to $30,000. (Borrow, net advantage = $5,136)

       2. Use the same facts as in #1, but change the asset's after-tax residual value at the loan's maturity to $10,000.

       3. The term of the loan and lease is 15 years, the annual lease payment is equal to $22,000, the loan interest rate is 10%, the tax rate is 46%, the asset's after-tax residual value is $20,000, and the price of the asset is $225,000. (Lease, net advantage = $6,250)

    b. For the situation described in #3 of Part a, identify the approximate loan rate where the costs of leasing versus borrowing is equivalent. (Hint: This requires you to update the data table in Table 11-8 for this situation. Remember to disable the Global Protection feature on your worksheet before attempting to run the data table. The loan rate would be somewhere between 7 and 8 percent.)

11-2 The Overland Company has decided to acquire a new truck. One alternative is to lease the truck on a 4-year contract for a lease payment of $10,000 per year, with payments to be made at the beginning of each year. The lease would include maintenance. Alternatively, Overland could purchase the truck outright for

314

$40,000, financing with a bank loan for the net purchase price and amortizing the loan over a 4-year period at an interest rate of 10 percent per year. Under the borrow-to-purchase arrangement, Overland would have to maintain the truck at a cost of $1,000 per year, payable at year-end. The truck qualifies for a 6% investment tax credit; it falls into the ACRS 3-year class; and it will have a salvage value of $10,000, which is the expected market value, after 4 years, at which time Overland plans to replace the truck irrespective of whether it leases or buys. Overland has a tax rate of 40 percent. (Remember, the salvage value is before taxes.)

Retrieve File LB11X1. Disable the Global Protection feature and convert the model to a template model by using the Range Erase command on the unprotected data cells. Then with the information given above, input the data in Table 11-2 from the facts given and answer the questions below. (Hint: Remember the model is set up for end-of-year lease payments, so you will have to convert the model to accommodate beginning-of-year lease payments as discussed on Page 302. Also remember the lease term is 4 years versus the 20-year term discussed in the chapter. Re-run your data table after you have made the data changes and the worksheet has been recalculated.)

a. What is Overland's PV cost of leasing? ($22,038)

b. What is Overland's PV cost of owning? ($21,196)

c. Should the truck be leased or purchased?

d. At approximately what loan rate would the costs of borrowing and leasing be equivalent?

Chapter 12
Capital Structure

This chapter presents a model designed to analyze the effects of a change in capital structure on the firm's stock price and financial position. Inputs, including capital structure and component cost rates, are entered, after which the model forecasts the firm's balance sheets and income statements over a 5-year period (the forecast period could be expanded with some simple modifications). The model also forecasts earnings and dividends per share, coverage ratios, cash flows, degrees of operating and financial leverage, breakeven sales volume, and an estimated stock price.

The model in this chapter is in several respects more complex than the other models in the book. This is because capital structure is itself an especially complicated subject. In his 1984 Presidential Address to the American Finance Association, Stewart Myers entitled his talk "The Capital Structure Puzzle." Capital structure is indeed a puzzle, and a complex one to boot.

As you work with the model, you will see that the required inputs include estimates of the cost of debt and equity under different capital structures, and one of the generated outputs is an estimate of the stock price. You should recognize that no one--not you, we, your instructor, your boss, or the best guru on Wall Street--can measure accurately the cost of equity at a given capital structure, much less tell precisely how it will change if the capital structure is changed. Still, judgments have to be made on these issues, and the beauty of our capital structure model is that it can be used to analyze the effects of different assumptions about the capital structure/cost rate relationship, with the output showing the sensitivity of EPS, coverage ratios, and ultimately stock prices to different conditions. The plain and simple truth is that finance is to a large extent a matter of informed judgment. Still, models such as this one can give financial decision makers better insights into the possible effects of alternative courses of action.

Layout of the Spreadsheet

The layout of the spreadsheet is shown in Figure 12-1.
Table 12-1 shows the file's contents and provides instruc-
tions for its use; Table 12-2 shows the input section; and
Tables 12-3 through 12-5 display the model's output.

==

Figure 12-1
Layout of Capital Structure Model

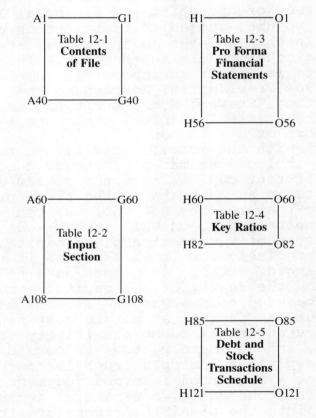

==

==

Table 12-1

Table 12-1. Contents of File LB12X1 and Directions for Its Use (A1.G40)

I. The following five sections, or tables, are on this file:

Cell Range	Number	Description of Table
A1.G40	12-1	Contents of file LB12X1
A60.G108	12-2	Input section
H1.O57	12-3	Pro forma financial statements
H60.O82	12-4	Key ratios and performance measures
H85.O121	12-5	Debt/stock transactions

II. To position a table on the screen:

1. Press function key F5, the "GoTo" key, then type the first cell shown in the range for the table, and then press the RETURN key.

2. To return to the contents directory, press the HOME key.

III. The ranges for the tables will fit on a printed page. Thus, when you construct a table, you can print it by specifying the given range as the print range.

IV. The tables now have illustrative data. You can use the model with other data simply by entering new data in the highlighted cells in Table 12-2. When you enter data for your own company, Tables 12-3 through 12-5 will be completed automatically. Note that all cells except the input data cells in Table 12-2 have been protected. The input cells which you may change are highlighted. If you need to modify the model, you may disconnect the protect feature with this command: /WGPD. If you attempt to write in a protected cell, you will hear a beep and receive an error message. We recommend that you reprotect the worksheet after making your changes with the command /WGPE. You should not use the Range Erase command to erase the input cells in Table 12-2. If you do so, zeros and ERRS will appear throughout the worksheet. Due to the circularity of the model, some of the formulas cannot be recalculated after the new data have been entered. Therefore, you should simply replace the existing input values with your own data.

==

Basic Assumptions and Input

Certain basic assumptions are programmed into the model.
You should be aware of them so that you will understand the
model's limitations and also so that you can change assumptions (by changing certain formulas) if they do not apply in
the situation with which you are working. We combine our
discussion of assumptions with a discussion of the input
data section, Table 12-2. As in previous models, the cells
in which data can be entered are highlighted, while all
other cells have been protected to prevent formulas from
being accidentally changed or erased. The entries in this
section form the basis for the projected 5-year balance
sheets and income statements.

1. <u>Years</u>. We developed the model for a base year (1985)
   plus a 5-year forecast period (1986-1990). It would be
   easy to change the years to begin with a different base
   year and relatively easy to extend the length of the
   forecast period.

2. <u>Inflation, growth in units sold, tax rate</u>. Base year
   values for these variables are entered, and the model
   then copies them into the forecast year. However, we
   left these cells unprotected so that you may override
   the model and specify different rates for each year
   simply by entering values where appropriate.

==

Table 12-2

<pre>
          A   B   C   D   E   F   G
60   Table 12-2. Input Section (A60.G108)
61
62
63   Forecast Period
64   Base Year   ---
65   Input data: 1985   1986   1987   1988   1989   1990
66   ----   ----   ----   ----   ----   ----
67   Inflation rate   4.50%   4.50%   4.50%   4.50%   4.50%   4.50%
68   Growth: units sold 5.00%   5.00%   5.00%   5.00%   5.00%   5.00%
69   Sales in units   5946   6243   6555   6883   7227   7589
70   Sales price/unit $0.90 $0.94 $0.98 $1.03 $1.07 $1.12
71   Tax rate   40.00%   40.00%   40.00%   40.00%   40.00%   40.00%
72   Fixed costs
73   except deprec $500 $549 $602 $661 $725 $795
74   Variable costs as
75   % of sales: 40.00%   40.00%   40.00%   40.00%   40.00%   40.00%
76   Common equity cost 14.00%   14.00%   13.90%   13.80%   13.70%   13.60%
77   Equ flot or repur cost, %   10.00%   10.00%   10.00%   10.00%   10.00%
78   Embedded L-T debt cost 9.00% 9.31%   9.47%   9.61%   9.74%
79   Marginal L-T debt cost 11.00% 10.90%   10.80%   10.70%   10.60%
80   Embedded preferred cost 0   0   0   0   0
81   Marginal preferred cost 10.00% 10.00%   10.00%   10.00%   10.00%
82   Short-term debt cost   9.00% 9.00%   9.00%   9.00%   9.00%
83
84   Ratios of capital accounts to nonspontaneous NWC plus FA:
85   Debt ratio   50.00%   50.00%   47.50%   45.00%   42.50%   40.00%
86   Preferred ratio   0.00%   0.00%   0.00%   0.00%   0.00%   0.00%
87   Com equity ratio   50.00%   50.00%   52.50%   55.00%   57.50%   60.00%
88   Total (check)   100.00%   100.00%   100.00%   100.00%   100.00%   100.00%
89   Year-end price $9.00
90   5-yr. div gro rate 6.50%   6.50%   6.50%   6.50%   6.50%   6.50%
91   Div/share (Do) $0.50
92   L-R payout rate   50.00%
93   Beg shares out   967.50
94   Beg current assets $6,500
95   Beg fixed assets $6,500
96   Beg A/P & accruals $1,500
97   Beg ret earnings $1,000
98   Current ratio   2.00
99   Avg debt maturity 10
100 Avg life of fixed
101   assets   7
102
103 Calculated values:
104
105 Current asset growth rate   9.73%   9.73%   9.73%   9.73%   9.73%
106 Fixed asset growth rate   5.87%   5.87%   5.87%   5.87%   5.87%
107 Year currently outstdg
108   debt all redeemed   1996   1997   1998   1999   2000
</pre>

==

3. <u>Growth in assets</u>. We do not input separately an asset growth rate. Rather, we assume that all assets are fully utilized, and hence that any growth in unit sales requires an equal percentage increase in assets. However, current assets increase both as a result of growth in units sold and with inflation. Thus, the growth in current assets is a function of both inflation and sales growth:

$$\text{Current asset growth rate} = \text{Sales growth} + \text{Inflation} + \left(\frac{\text{Sales}}{\text{growth}}\right) * (\text{Inflation})$$

For example, if unit sales were growing at a 10 percent rate and inflation were 5 percent, the current asset growth rate would be:

C.A. growth rate = 0.10 + 0.05 + (0.10)(0.05) = 15.5%.

Since all fixed assets are not replaced each year, they do not increase with inflation. However, a portion of the fixed assets will wear out and require replacement each year, and the replacement cost of these worn out assets will increase due to inflation. Thus, the growth rate in fixed assets is a function of sales growth and, to a lesser degree, inflation. We assume that fixed assets wear out and are replaced at a steady rate. The average life of the fixed assets is entered in Cell B101. The fixed asset growth rate is then calculated as:

$$\text{Fixed asset growth} = \text{Sales growth} + \frac{\text{Inflation}}{\text{Avg. life of fixed assets}} + (\text{Sales growth}) * (\text{Inflation})$$

For example, if unit sales are growing at a 10 percent rate, if inflation is 5 percent, and if the average life of fixed assets is 7 years, then

$$\text{Fixed asset growth} = 0.10 + \frac{0.05}{7} + (0.10)(0.05) = 11.2\%.$$

4. **Fixed operating costs.** Fixed operating costs, excluding depreciation, are shown in B73.G73, and they include such items as salaries and overhead. These items will increase with the rate of inflation; however, they will also increase with the rate of sales growth, because assets are assumed to be fully utilized in the base year. As assets grow as a result of sales increases, more resources will be required to manage them; hence, salaries and overhead expenditures will increase. Thus, fixed costs are calculated as: Previous year's fixed costs*(1 + Sales growth rate)*(1 + Inflation rate).

5. **Variable costs.** Variable costs are assumed to be a fixed percentage of sales. Thus, variable costs will increase automatically with both unit sales growth and inflation. We input the variable cost rate (B75.G75), then 1-2-3 calculates dollar amounts later in the model.

6. **Sales price and unit sales.** Sales prices are assumed to grow at the rate of inflation and unit sales at the unit sales growth rate entered on Line 68. Sales prices could easily be changed to grow (or decline) at some other rate, or specific sales prices could be entered for each year. You would use /WGPD to unprotect the worksheet and then type in the specific sales prices or formulas in B70.G70.

7. **Debt, preferred, and common equity costs.** The debt and preferred stock outstanding at the start of the analysis, has an "embedded" cost. For instance, the embedded cost of debt is the average interest cost of the currently outstanding debt; we calculate the embedded cost of debt as interest paid divided by total debt outstanding. New debt and preferred issues (marginal debt and preferred) have some other cost rates, and these values must be entered for individual years. Note that both a long-term and a short-term debt rate must be entered. The short-term rate is the rate of

interest on notes payable. All short-term debt is assumed to mature at the end of each year, and it must be reissued at the then current short-term interest rate.

The cost of common equity capital must also be entered (B76.G76). All cost rates--debt, preferred, and common equity--should, in general, be higher if more debt is used in the capital structure. We generally assume a rising yield curve and hence use a lower marginal interest rate for short-term than for long-term debt. As all textbooks indicate, and as all financial experts know, it is very difficult to specify the level of these values, and the model offers no help in this regard. Keep in mind that the quality of a model's output is dependent on the quality of its input--in short, remember the word GIGO, or "Garbage In, Garbage Out". We have used this model in several consulting assignments, and, once people are comfortable with the arithmetic, the discussion (and controversy) centers on the proper debt, preferred, and common cost rates.

8. <u>Embedded cost of debt and preferred</u>. If the firm has debt and/or preferred stock outstanding at the start of the model run, their costs must be entered. These embedded cost rates will normally be different from the costs of new (marginal) debt or preferred issues. Also, all long-term debt is assumed to have a constant maturity; in our model, we assume a 10 year maturity, but this can be changed by entering a different maturity in Cell B99. A sinking fund provision built into the model requires that one-tenth of each layer of debt be retired in each year. Note that the percentage of debt retired in each year depends on the maturity of the debt; the amount of debt refunded each year is calculated as the sum of each debt layer divided by its maturity. The refunded debt is then reissued at the current cost of debt for that year. The debt refunding and total debt outstanding schedules are shown in Table 12-5 (H85.O121). All financing is assumed to be done at the end of the year, and the financing done is based on both the net new capital required to support asset growth and on debt refunding. The model forces the capital raised to be consistent with the prescribed target capital structure.

9. Capital structure ratios. You can specify different capital structures for each year in the range B85.G87. Since our principal concern is to analyze the effects of changes in capital structure, we normally change these ratios in various ways while holding the operating factors (inflation, sales growth, and so forth) constant. Always keep in mind the fact that cost rates for new debt and preferred, and for all common equity, will change as the capital structure changes. Various theories suggest specific relationships, and the empirical data are fuzzy. Therefore, judgment is required here.

10. Capital account balances. As a firm's sales grow, certain current liability items (accounts payable and accruals) increase spontaneously. These items represent sources of free financing, and firms normally use all the free spontaneous financing they can get. Therefore, the firm's capital structure decision focuses primarily on its costly sources of financing-- notes payable, long-term debt, preferred equity, and common equity. In our model, we assume that the firm can and does use a specified amount of payables-plus- accruals. We then subtract funds raised from these sources from total assets to obtain the amount of remaining assets that must be financed with nonspontaneous (costly) capital, and we apply our capital structure ratios to this nonspontaneous capital. (Note: Another way of looking at this is to think of spontaneous funds as supporting current assets, to then define net working capital as current assets minus spontaneous funds, and then to think of the capital structure decision as relating to the financing of fixed assets plus net working capital. The point is, we want to focus on how the firm raises capital other than by spontaneously generated funds.)

    In the model, accounts payable and accruals are assumed to grow at the current asset growth rate, and total debt, preferred stock, and total common equity are calculated as percentages of total assets minus spontaneous funds. The breakdown of total debt between long-term and short-term debt is based on the current ratio entered in Cell B98: The debt ratio determines total nonspontaneous debt, and the specified current ratio allocates total nonspontaneous debt between long-term debt and notes payable. Thus, the current ratio specified as an input is a policy variable which determines the debt maturity breakdown.

11. <u>5-year dividend growth rate</u>. Companies normally treat the dividend growth rate as a policy variable over the short or intermediate term, and they often have a long-run target payout policy. (The long-run target payout could be unspecified, because it has relatively little effect on short-run operations.) We specify the base year 5-year dividend growth rate in Cell B90, assume that it will be maintained for 5 years, and then let this growth rate control payout over the 5-year forecast period. Then we specify (in Cell B92) a target payout ratio for the years beyond the forecast period. If the model runs indicated discontinuities--such as an average 20 percent payout over the 5-year forecast period versus a 50 percent long-run payout--we would change either the 5-year growth rate or the long-run payout rate, or both, to close the gap, because abrupt dividend policy changes are undesirable. Note that we could enter different growth rates for each year in the 5-year time horizon without other changes in the model. Thus, we could close any gap between the short and long-run payout gradually, on a year-by-year basis. In practice, we discuss this with senior management. In school cases, we make assumptions.

12. <u>Long-run dividend growth rate</u>. The model calculates the return on equity in each year as the net income for the year divided by beginning-of-year equity. We then assume that the ROE for the last year of the forecast period (1990 in our example) will be maintained in the future. This assumption, along with the dividend policy (payout) assumption, allows us to use the constant growth model to value the stock at the end of the fifth year. The constant growth rate is calculated by the model in Cell O74 as follows: $g = (1 - \text{Long-run target payout rate})(\text{Year 5 ROE}) = (1 - B92)*O71$. Thus, we assume that the firm will reach a steady state after the fifth year and that earnings and dividends will grow at the long-run rate g thereafter.

326

13. <u>Dividends</u>. Dividends are paid on the number of shares of stock outstanding at the beginning of the year. Dividends are paid out of net income, and the remaining earnings for the year are either retained to support asset growth or used to repurchase common stock.

14. <u>Other inputs</u>. Base year current assets, fixed assets, accounts payable, accruals, shares outstanding, and retained earnings are also needed to get the model started (B93.B97). The average debt maturity (B99) is used to determine when the initial outstanding debt will mature and the proportion of each layer of outstanding debt which will be refunded in each year.

15. <u>Stock and bond issues/retirements</u>. Depending on its earnings, payout policy, asset growth, and capital structure, the firm will have to issue or repurchase stock and sell or refund debt. Debt flotation costs are assumed to be amortized and thus are built into the cost rates assigned to debt, so they are included in the interest expense calculation. The equity flotation cost rate (which can be varied) is entered in C77.G77 and is assumed to apply to both new issues and repurchases. We assume that equity flotation costs are expensed in the year they occur, but since they are not tax deductible, they appear on the income statement as a deduction after taxes (K51.O51).

Common stock is assumed to be bought or sold at the end-of-year stock price. New common equity needed to maintain the target capital structure is met first by retaining earnings, then by selling stock. If the required amount of common equity declines, or if it increases by less than the retained earnings for the year, then common stock is repurchased.

Once you have entered all input values, you must press the CALC key to solve the model. We used /WGRM and set it for five iterations, which is sufficient to produce stable results. Tables 12-3 through 12-5 will automatically be generated in a few seconds.

We also need to sound a word of caution here. Due to interdependencies built into the model, you should not use the Range Erase command to erase input data. Instead, you should replace the existing data in Table 12-2, Range

A60.G108, with your own data. Erasing the input data will cause ERRs to appear throughout the model. Normally, that would cause no problems. However, when a model uses circular equations, an initial value for at least one of the variables involved is needed to get the iteration process started.

Pro Forma Financial Statements

Pro forma balance sheets and income statements for the 5-year forecast period are shown in Table 12-3 (H1.O57). The income statement and balance sheet calculations are based on the input entered in Table 12-2.

The balance sheet (H3.O31) is computed by (1) increasing current and fixed assets by their growth rates (A105.G105 and A106.G106, respectively), (2) setting total capital equal to total assets, (3) increasing accounts payable and accruals by the current asset growth rate, (4) determining notes payable as current assets divided by the current ratio, minus accounts payable and accruals, (5) multiplying total capital less spontaneous funding by the capital structure percentages to determine the amounts of nonspontaneous debt, preferred stock, and common equity, (6) determining the amount of long-term debt as nonspontaneous debt minus notes payable, and (7) determining the breakdown of common equity between common stock and retained earnings. Step 7 depends on retained earnings as calculated in the income statement (H34.O57), but retained earnings depend on the total amount of dividends paid out, which is dividends per share times the number of beginning shares outstanding. However, the number of beginning shares outstanding depends on stock repurchases and issues from the previous year, which in turn depend on retained earnings. Because of these interactions, the model has circular references; hence, it must be solved iteratively. We used the /WGR command, set at Manual with five iterations, so after data have been entered, the model will solve when you press the CALC key.

Table 12-3

Table 12-3. Pro Forma Financial Statements (H1.057)

Balance Sheets for Years Ending December 31, 1985-1990
(Dollars in Millions)

	Actual 1985	1986	1987	1988	1989	1990
Assets:						
Current assets	$6,500	$7,132	$7,826	$8,587	$9,422	$10,338
Fixed assets	6,500	6,881	7,285	7,713	8,165	8,644
Total assets	$13,000	$14,014	$15,111	$16,299	$17,587	$18,982
Claims:						
A/P and accruals	$1,500	$1,646	$1,806	$1,982	$2,174	$2,386
Notes payable	1,750	1,920	2,107	2,312	2,537	2,783
Total CL	$3,250	$3,566	$3,913	$4,293	$4,711	$5,169
Long-term debt	4,000	4,264	4,213	4,131	4,014	3,855
Preferred stock	0	0	0	0	0	0
L-T debt plus pref	$4,000	$4,264	$4,213	$4,131	$4,014	$3,855
Common stock	4,750	4,832	5,247	5,669	6,093	6,516
Retained earnings	1,000	1,352	1,739	2,206	2,769	3,442
Tot common equity	$5,750	$6,184	$6,985	$7,875	$8,862	$9,958
Total claims	$13,000	$14,014	$15,111	$16,299	$17,587	$18,982

Income Statements for Years Ending December 31, 1986-1990
(Dollars in Millions)

	1986 1	1987 2	1988 3	1989 4	1990 5
Sales revenues	$5,872	$6,443	$7,069	$7,757	$8,511
Fixed costs (except dep)	549	602	661	725	795
Variable costs	2,349	2,577	2,828	3,103	3,405
Depreciation	983	1,041	1,102	1,166	1,235
EBIT	$1,991	$2,223	$2,479	$2,763	$3,077
S-T interest	173	190	208	228	251
L-T interest	360	397	399	397	391
EBT	$1,459	$1,636	$1,872	$2,137	$2,435
Taxes	583	655	749	855	974
Pref dividends	0	0	0	0	0
Flotation expense	8	41	42	42	42
NI for common	$867	$940	$1,081	$1,240	$1,419
Total dividends	$515	$554	$613	$677	$745
Net cash flow	$1,850	$1,981	$2,183	$2,406	$2,654

Retained earnings for the year are calculated by reducing net income by the amount of common dividends paid out. This figure is then compared to the increase in common equity needed to achieve the target capital structure, in an IF statement in the range K119.O120. If earnings minus dividends is less than the necessary increase in common equity to achieve the target capital structure, common stock must be sold. If earnings minus dividends is greater than the necessary increase in common equity to achieve the target capital structure, earnings equal to the needed increase in common equity are retained and the rest are used to repurchase stock.

The income statement (H34.O57) is relatively straightforward except for the depreciation and interest calculations. We calculate depreciation expense on a straight line basis over the average life of the fixed assets. Thus, the depreciation formula is simply fixed assets divided by the average life. We could have used ACRS to depreciate the assets for tax purposes and straight line to depreciate them for reporting purposes. If we had done this, there would have been a difference between the amount of depreciation expense deducted for tax purposes and reported depreciation, and this difference would have depended on the fixed asset growth rate. At relatively high growth rates, tax depreciation would be higher, causing taxes to be lower, and an item called "deferred taxes" would have appeared on our balance sheet. Because we did not want to go into that amount of detail, we used an effective tax rate of 40 percent, rather than the 46 percent statutory tax rate, to adjust taxes downward to more accurately reflect the firm's true tax bill.

Since we assume all financing occurs at the end of the year, interest for the year is calculated on debt outstanding at the beginning of the year. We also assume that one-tenth of the long-term debt outstanding at each cost level is refunded and then reissued at the new marginal debt cost for that year. The debt schedule in Table 12-5 (H85.O121) shows the layering of long-term debt; it is from this schedule that long-term interest is calculated. (Short-term interest is simply the notes payable balance times the current short-term interest rate.) The first part of the debt schedule shows exactly how much long-term debt is outstanding at each cost level. Long-term interest is calculated by multiplying each layer by its appropriate cost and then summing the long-term components. Short-term and long-term interest are shown as separate line items on the income statement. The formulas could be changed to accommodate a different debt maturity structure; for example, if 5-year debt were used, one-fifth of each layer of debt would have to be rolled over each year.

Key Ratios and Performance Measures

The model calculates several key ratios and other measures of financial performance; they are shown in Table 12-4 in the range H60.082. These values include the stock price at the end of each year, the market/book ratio, EPS, DPS, payout ratios, price/earnings ratios, return on beginning common equity (ROE), growth rates, TIE, degree of operating and financial leverage (DOL and DFL), breakeven quantity, and the after-tax weighted average cost of capital. Most of these calculations are straightforward, but a few warrant explanation.

First, the dividend per share (DPS, in K68.068) for each year during the forecast period is calculated as the dividend per share in the prior year times 1 plus the dividend growth rate, and total dividends are equal to DPS times the beginning number of shares outstanding. The Year 5 stock price (Cell O64) is then calculated using the constant dividend growth model. The stock price at the end of each of the first four forecast years (Years 1 through 4) is then calculated as the present value of the dividends to be received in the remaining years of the forecast period plus the present value of the Year 5 stock price, discounted at the equity capital cost rate for the year as specified in C76.F76. The number of shares of stock issued or repurchased (K119.O120) is then computed as follows:

1. The new common equity required to keep the capital structure on target is calculated. For 1986, it is equal to K28-J28, or common equity at the end of 1986 minus common equity at the end of 1985.

331

==

Table 12-4

Table 12-4. Key Ratios and Performance Measures (H60.082)

	1985	1986	1987	1988	1989	1990
Year-end stk price	$9.00	$9.63	$10.44	$11.30	$12.23	$13.22
Year-end book val	$5.94	$6.34	$6.88	$7.48	$8.15	$8.89
M/B ratio	1.51	1.52	1.52	1.51	1.50	1.49
EPS	n.a.	$0.90	$0.96	$1.06	$1.18	$1.30
DPS	$0.50	$0.53	$0.57	$0.60	$0.64	$0.69
Payout ratio		59.43%	58.86%	56.74%	54.63%	52.52%
P/E ratio		10.75	10.83	10.62	10.39	10.14
Return on beg equity (ROE)		15.08%	15.21%	15.48%	15.75%	16.01%
1-yr. EPS growth rate		n.a.	7.52%	10.48%	10.62%	10.77%
1-yr. stk price growth rate		7.01%	8.38%	8.30%	8.21%	8.10%
Div growth rate beyond 1990						8.00%
TIE ratio		5.53	5.60	6.21	6.96	7.87
DOL		1.18	1.18	1.18	1.18	1.18
DFL		1.22	1.22	1.19	1.17	1.15
Breakeven quantity		972	1,021	1,072	1,125	1,182
At. wt. avg. cost of cap.		7.85%	7.83%	7.96%	8.08%	8.19%

==

2. Next total dividends paid during the year are subtracted from net income for the year. For 1986, this is K53-K56.

3. Then, the required increase in common equity (K28-J28) is compared with retained earnings for the year (K53-K56). If retained earnings exceeds required equity, then a surplus of equity will exist, and stock will be repurchased. If required equity exceeds retained earnings for the year, new shares must be issued.

4. The number of shares issued or repurchased is calculated by dividing the equity shortfall or surplus by the calculated price per share (K64 for 1986).

5. The calculations called for in Steps 1-4 are performed in the IF statements given in the range K119.O120.

Debt and Stock Transactions Schedule

We assume that all long-term debt has a 10-year maturity, and that one-tenth of each layer of outstanding long-term debt matures and is refunded each year at the marginal interest rate specified for the current year (C79.G79). (Short-term debt is rolled over at the current year's short-term rate.) The first schedule in Table 12-5 (H92.O102) shows the total amount of debt outstanding at the beginning of each year, and the second schedule (H106.O114) shows the net amount of debt refunded during each year. These values are then used in the interest calculation formula in the income statement, Table 12-3 (H34.O57). Table 12-5 also shows the details on stock issues and/or repurchases and shares outstanding as discussed in the last section.

Scenario Analysis

It would be relatively easy to construct data tables which changed an input variable and showed the effects of this change on one or more output variables, or data tables that showed the effects of two input variables on one output variable. However, when we use this particular model in practice, we always want to change more things than data tables permit. Therefore, we find it preferable to employ scenario analysis. We run the model under several different scenarios, assuming pessimistic, optimistic, and most likely operating conditions. Then we use three capital structures--with low, medium, and high levels of debt--in each scenario. We also use the Range Value Copy command to display the results of each scenario analysis in an empty section of the worksheet, adding another set of output to this section each time we complete one of the scenarios. Then we print out the results of all the scenarios. We could then graph the different scenarios to get a better idea of what was happening.

==

Table 12-5

Table 12-5. Debt Refunding/Stock Transactions Schedule (H85.0121)

In this table we use beginning-of-year numbers, whereas the balance
sheet uses end-of-year values. Thus, the value of total debt outstanding
for 1986 is the long-term debt value from the 1985 balance sheet.

		1986	1987	1988	1989	1990
Total L-T debt outstanding						
at cost of:	9.00%	$4,000	$3,600	$3,200	$2,800	$2,400
	11.00%	0	664	597	531	465
	10.90%	0	0	416	374	333
	10.80%	0	0	0	426	384
	10.70%	0	0	0	0	433
Total L-T debt outstanding		$4,000	$4,264	$4,213	$4,131	$4,014
Net amount refunded						
at cost of:	9.00%	$0	$400	$400	$400	$400
	11.00%		0	66	66	66
	10.90%			0	42	42
	10.80%			0	0	43
	10.70%			0	0	0
Total amount refunded		$0	$400	$466	$508	$551
Beg shares out		967.50	976.02	1015.72	1053.06	1087.80
Shares issued		8.52	39.70	37.33	34.74	31.92
Shares repurchased		0.00	0.00	0.00	0.00	0.00
Ending shares out.	967.50	976.02	1015.72	1053.06	1087.80	1119.72

==

Summary

In this chapter we presented a relatively comprehensive, but
complex, capital structure model. This model can be used to
analyze the effects of different capital structures on a

firm's stock price and ratios. It can also be used to analyze the effects of different sales and dividend growth rates holding capital structure constant. One conclusion we have drawn from our use of the model is that changes in operating decisions generally have vastly larger impacts on stock price and other output variables than do capital structure changes.

    We should close by repeating our earlier warning--GIGO, or "Garbage In, Garbage Out". The model performs the necessary arithmetic correctly, but its forecasts will give you a reasonable picture of the results of various capital structure changes if--and <u>only</u> if--your assumptions are reasonable. Also, when our consulting clients have questioned the usefulness of the model because of the difficulty of obtaining inputs such as future debt and equity cost rates, we have simply asked whether they would prefer to make capital structure decisions by flipping a coin or by trying to analyze effects with a model such as this one. We generally win the argument. The state of the art in capital structure theory and analysis is not very advanced, but at least the model lets people see the effects of various assumptions and theories. It is not the model's fault that finance theory has so many limitations!

Chapter 12 Exercises

Note: Before doing the following exercises, make sure you copy File LB12X1 on your diskette then do these exercises on that copy.

12-1 Make the following data changes and answer the questions that follow.

	1985	1986	1987	1988	1989	1990
Inflation rate	6%					
Variable costs	55%					
Flotation costs		5%				
Equity cost	15%	15%	15.1%	15.2%	15.3%	15.4%
Embedded long-term debt		9.75%				
Marginal long-term debt		10.5%	10.6%	10.7%	10.8%	10.9%
Short-term debt		8.75%	8.75%	8.75%	8.75%	8.75%
Debt ratio	40%	40%	42.5%	45%	47.5%	50%
Preferred equity ratio	0%	0%	0%	0%	0%	0%
Common equity ratio	60%	60%	57.5%	55%	52.5%	50%
Current ratio	2.5					
Average life of fixed assets	10					
Sales in units	7000					
Year-end stock price	$8.00					

In comparison to the base case data that was previously entered what happens to the following ratios during the 1986-1990 period?

a. TIE ratio (New data: 1987 = 5.84X, 1990 = 5.16X)

b. DOL ratio

c. DFL ratio (New data: 1989 = 1.23)

d. Breakeven quantity (New data: 1986 = 1,296, 1988 = 1,429)

e. After-tax weighted average cost of capital

f. Number of shares issued or repurchased

g. M/B ratio (New data: 1986 = 1.04, 1990 = 1.06)

h. Year-end stock price

i. Payout ratio

j. P/E ratio (New data: 1987 = 8.34, 1989 = 7.43)

k. ROE

12-2 Assume the same data changes occur as in Exercise 12-1 except for the following:

a. The capital structure is 50% debt ratio and 50% common equity ratio in 1985 and 1986, and in 1990 the target capital structure is to be 46% debt and 54% equity. Assume equal changes in the capital structure over the forecast period.

b. Assume the same starting equity and marginal long-term debt costs (1986) as in Exercise 12-1; however, due to a decrease in the debt ratio the capital costs decline over the forecast period so that in 1990 marginal long-term debt costs 10.3% and common equity has a cost of 14.8%. (Note that in reality the equity and debt costs in the base year for the firm in Exercise 12-2 would be somewhat higher than the firm in Exercise 12-1 due to its higher beginning debt ratio.

   What happens to these same 11 ratios mentioned in Exercise 12-1 during the 1986-1990 forecast period, when these data changes are made?

Chapter 13
Capital Budgeting

In this chapter we present a capital budgeting model which analyzes investment projects on the basis of five criteria: net present value (NPV), internal rate of return (IRR), profitability index (PI), regular payback period, and discounted payback period. The model can be used to analyze both new investment decisions and replacement decisions by entering the initial cost of the new or replacement asset and the incremental cash flows which are expected to be generated by it.

Layout of the Spreadsheet

Figure 13-1 is a schematic diagram of the capital budgeting spreadsheet. Table 13-1 describes the spreadsheet and provides instructions on its use. Data are entered in the range shown in Table 13-2, and the output generated by the model is shown in Tables 13-3 through 13-7. A data table used to test the sensitivity of the analysis to changes in various input variables is given in Table 13-8. Note that the model is designed to analyze a capital budgeting project over a time period of 10 years or less.

Figure 13-1
Layout of the Spreadsheet

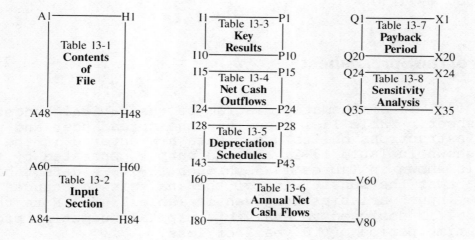

Table 13-1. Contents of File LB13X1 and Directions for Its Use (A1.H48)

   I. To position a table on the screen:

      1. Press function key F5, the "GoTo" key.
      2. Type the first cell shown in the range in the directory
         shown below, starting on Line 36.
      3. Press the RETURN key.
      4. To return to the directory, press the F5 key and go to A36.

  II. Table 13-6 should be printed using compressed print and a right
      margin of 134. All other tables will fit on a single page and
      can be printed by specifying the given range as the print range.

 III. The tables now have illustrative data. By using the Range Erase
      command on the data in Table 13-2, you convert all the tables
      to template models. Then, when you enter data for your company's
      own project, the other tables will be completed automatically.
      This model can be used both with expansion projects and with
      replacement projects by entering data in the appropriate cells
      and zeros for the items which do not apply to your particular
      analysis. Note that all cells except the input data cells in
      Table 13-2 have been protected. If you need to modify the model,
      you may disconnect the protect feature with this command: /WGPD.
      If you attempt to write in a protected cell, you will hear a beep
      and receive an error message. Press ESC to return to READY mode.

  IV. Note that unless you disconnect the protect feature, only the
      data cells can be changed--all formulas are protected. Thus, you
      cannot erase entire tables at one pass; you can erase only the
      unprotected cells in Table 13-2. The other cells contain formulas
      and, hence, are protected. Also, note that once you erase the data
      in the worksheet, zeros and ERRs appear throughout. When you
      enter new data, the ERRs will disappear.

   V. Here are the exhibits and their addresses:

Cell Range	Number	Description of Table
A1.H48	13-1	Contents of File LB13X1
A60.H84	13-2	Input section
I1.P10	13-3	Key results
I15.P24	13-4	Net cash outflows
I28.P43	13-5	Depreciation schedules
I60.V80	13-6	Annual net cash flows
Q1.X20	13-7	Payback period
Q24.X35	13-8	Sensitivity analysis

===

The Input Section

All of the data needed in the model to estimate the net cash flows associated with the investment are entered in the range A60.H84 as shown in Table 13-2. The first five items refer to the purchase price, value, and expected life of the old asset and are used in determining the annual depreciation expense and current book value of the old asset. The assumption is made that the old asset is being depreciated by the straight line method but the new asset will be depreciated using the ACRS method. If the investment is an expansion project, hence no old asset is involved, zeros should be entered for these items.

Next, the firm's cost of capital and tax rate are entered. The remaining eight items relate to the new asset. The purchase price and ITC percentage are used, along with the required increase in net working capital and the salvage value of the old asset, to determine the initial cash expenditure and the depreciable basis of the new asset. This information and the asset's ACRS class life are needed to calculate the annual depreciation expense for the new asset. The ACRS class life may be specified to be either 3, 5, or 10 years.

Next, the expected annual increases in sales and costs are entered. Inflation should be considered when inputting this data--the model does not adjust for inflation, so the data should reflect inflationary expectations and their effects on sales revenues and costs. If either of these values is negative--for instance, if costs are expected to decline because the new asset will be more efficient than the old asset--then a negative value should be input. Finally, the expected salvage value and estimated economic life of the new asset are entered. The salvage value is entered on a before-tax basis and is assumed to be received at the end of the final year of the project's life.

===

Table 13-2

```
         A        B         C        D        E       F      G          H
60   Table 13-2. Input Section (A60.H84)
61
62   Input Values:
63
64        1.   Purchase price of old asset                        $7,500
65        2.   Market value of old equipment                      $1,000
66        3.   Expected salvage value of old asset                   $0
67        4.   Expected life of old asset at time of purchase        15
68        5.   Number of years since purchase of old asset          10
69        6.   Cost of capital                                   10.00%
70        7.   Tax rate                                          46.00%
71        8.   Purchase price of new asset, incl install & freight  $12,000
72        9.   ITC percentage, new asset                         10.00%
73       10.   Required increase in net working capital           $1,000
74       11.   Depreciation, new asset: 3, 5, or 10 (ACRS class)      5
75       12.   Increase in sales due to new asset                    $0
76       13.   Cost increase (reduction) due to new asset       ($3,000)
77       14.   Salvage value of new asset, before-tax            $2,000
78       15.   Estimated life of new asset                            5
79
80
81   Calculated Values:
82
83        Current book value of old asset                         $2,500
84        Depreciable basis of new asset                         $11,400
```

===

After all of the input data have been entered, the
current book value of the old asset and the depreciable
basis of the new asset are determined by the spreadsheet.
These values are calculated in Table 13-2 and are used as
inputs in the other tables. The current book value of the
old asset is equal to the original purchase price times the
fraction of the asset's remaining life. The depreciable
basis of the new asset is the purchase price less one-half
of the investment tax credit applied to the purchase price.

We should elaborate on several assumptions which are
embodied in the logic of the model.

1. Annual depreciation expenses for the old asset are
    calculated using the straight line method, while the
    ACRS method is used to determine annual depreciation
    expenses for the new asset. The new asset may be
    depreciated over a 3-, 5-, or 10-year class life.
    Depreciation schedules are actually calculated for the
    asset over all three class lives, but only the appro-
    priate depreciation expense values are used to deter-
    mine the annual net cash flows of the project.

2. The required increase in net working capital is neces-
    sary only over the new project's economic life. The
    increase in net working capital is included as an
    initial cash outflow and is recovered in the final year
    of the project's life. If the investment leads to a
    net reduction in working capital, then this amount is
    entered as a negative number, reducing the initial cash
    outlay; however, this amount is then included as an
    outflow in the last year.

3. Any changes in sales or costs are assumed to be con-
    stant over the life of the asset. Therefore, these
    values are entered only once in the input section and
    are copied for each year of the analysis. The model
    can be changed to allow incremental sales and costs to
    vary from one year to the next by entering the annual
    amounts in the appropriate cells in Table 13-6. Note,
    however, that these cells are protected; thus, it is
    necessary to use the Range Unprotect command to unpro-
    tect these cells before entering the new data.

4. In the calculations of the NPV, IRR, and PI, the
    assumption is made that all cash flows occur at the end
    of the year. The assumption that cash flows occur at
    discrete intervals is necessary for these calculations.
    In calculating the regular payback period and dis-
    counted payback period, however, cash flows are assumed
    to occur evenly throughout the period. Thus, the regu-
    lar payback period and discounted payback period can
    include a fraction of a year.

5. The life of the new asset in a replacement decision
    must equal the remaining life of the old asset. This
    assumption is necessary in order that the projects may

be compared without using replacement chains or certainty equivalent analysis.

Key Results

The five capital budgeting measures--regular payback period, discounted payback period, IRR, NPV, and PI--are displayed in the table of key results shown in Table 13-3 (I1.P10). The regular payback period and discounted payback period are calculated in Table 13-7, and the calculated value is copied into Table 13-3. The IRR and NPV of the asset are computed by the 1-2-3 @IRR and @NPV functions using the net cash flows determined in Table 13-6; the cost of capital input in Table 13-2 is shown with the IRR for comparison purposes. The cost of capital input in Table 13-2 is also used as the discount rate in the NPV calculation. The profitability index, PI, is equal to the present value of the cash flows in Years 1 through 10 divided by the initial cash outflow in Year 0.

===

Table 13-3

Table 13-3. Key Results (I1.P10)

Payback period	4.09 years	Disc. payback per.	4.87 years
IRR:	11.3%	versus	10.00% cost of capital
NPV:	$383	versus $10,110	initial cash outflow (project cost)
PI:	1.04		

===

The table of key results (I1.P10) makes it easy to observe the effects of changes in the original input values for a replacement decision. If you enter new input data and

345

press the F9 function key, the new values of the capital budgeting measures will be computed and displayed automatically. When using the model for your own data, be aware that you may have to modify the discount rate guess in Cell J6, the cell that displays the project's IRR.

Initial Net Cash Outflows

Table 13-4 (I15.P24) consists of a short analysis which determines the initial net cash outflow attributable to the purchase of the expansion or replacement asset, or the net cost of the project. The net cash outflow is equal to the purchase price of the new asset less the investment tax credit, plus the after-tax proceeds from the sale of the old asset in a replacement decision, plus any increase in net working capital. Note that the firm can receive a positive tax credit from the sale of the old asset if the asset's market price is less than its book value. (Potential re- quired modifications: recapture of ITC on old asset, project cost spread over several years.)

==

Table 13-4

Table 13-4. Net Cash Outflows (I15.P24)

Cost of new equipment	$12,000
Investment tax credit	(1,200)
Market value of old equipment	(1,000)
Tax effect of sale of old equipment	(690)
Increase in net working capital	1,000
Total initial outflow	$10,110

==

Depreciation Schedules

Straight line and ACRS depreciation schedules are shown in Table 13-5, using 1986 depreciation schedules. The model assumes that the old project is being depreciated over its remaining useful life by the straight line method and that the new asset's depreciation expense is being determined by ACRS over either a 3-, 5-, or 10-year class life. When you enter the code for the ACRS depreciation schedule on the input table (by entering a 3, 5, or 10 in cell H74), the model selects the correct depreciation amounts in columns L, N, or P. All three ACRS depreciation schedules are calculated with each iteration of the model, but only the selected depreciation stream is used in determining the depreciation expense and tax savings used in the net cash flow calculations in Table 13-6. (Potential required modifications: depreciation schedules if tax laws are revised, use of ACRS for old asset.)

===

Table 13-5

Table 13-5. Depreciation Schedules (I28.P43)

Old: Straight line   New: ACRS Depreciation

Year	Dep.	3-Year		5-Year		10-Year	
1	$500	25.00%	$2,850	15.00%	$1,710	8.00%	$912
2	500	38.00%	4,332	22.00%	2,508	14.00%	1,596
3	500	37.00%	4,218	21.00%	2,394	12.00%	1,368
4	500			21.00%	2,394	10.00%	1,140
5	500			21.00%	2,394	10.00%	1,140
6	0					10.00%	1,140
7	0					9.00%	1,026
8	0					9.00%	1,026
9	0					9.00%	1,026
10	0					9.00%	1,026

===

Annual Net Cash Flows

The annual net cash flows attributable to the project are
calculated in the range I60.V80 as shown in Table 13-6. The
net cash flow for Year 0 is simply the initial cash outflow
calculated in Table 13-4. For every other year in the
analysis, the annual incremental cash flow is calculated as
the change in after-tax income plus the change in depreciation expense. The change in before-tax income is computed
as the change in sales minus the change in costs and depreciation expense. Incremental after-tax income is the change
in before-tax income minus the change in taxes. In the
final year, the after-tax salvage value of the new machine
and the return of the net working capital investment are
also included in the calculation of net cash flow.

==

Table 13-6

Table 13-6. Annual Net Cash Flows (I60.V80)

Year	0	1	2	3	4	5	6	7	8	9	10
Change in sales		$0	$0	$0	$0	$0	$0	$0	$0	$0	$0
Change in costs		(3,000)	(3,000)	(3,000)	(3,000)	(3,000)	0	0	0	0	0
Deprec on new machine		1,710	2,508	2,394	2,394	2,394	0	0	0	0	0
Deprec on old machine		500	500	500	500	500	0	0	0	0	0
Change in depreciation		1,210	2,008	1,894	1,894	1,894	0	0	0	0	0
Change in before-tax income		$1,790	$992	$1,106	$1,106	$1,106	$0	$0	$0	$0	$0
Change in taxes		823	456	509	509	509	0	0	0	0	0
Change in after-tax income		$967	$536	$597	$597	$597	$0	$0	$0	$0	$0
Add: Change in depreciation		1,210	2,008	1,894	1,894	1,894	0	0	0	0	0
AT salvage value, new machine		0	0	0	0	1,080	0	0	0	0	0
Return of working capital		0	0	0	0	1,000	0	0	0	0	0
Net cash flow	($10,110)	$2,177	$2,544	$2,491	$2,491	$4,571	$0	$0	$0	$0	$0

==

The expected after-tax salvage value for the new machine is calculated in this section using the before-tax salvage value entered in Table 13-2 and the firm's tax rate. If the machine is sold for a price of less than its book value, the model will recognize the tax effects of this loss, resulting in a higher after-tax than before-tax salvage value. The before-tax and after-tax salvage values will be equal only when the asset is sold at its book value. The return of the net working capital investment has no tax effects.

As was mentioned earlier, the model assumes that any changes in sales and costs will be constant in each year over the life of the asset. If this is not true of the investment project you are analyzing, then you must modify the model by unprotecting the cells relating to the changes in sales and costs and entering the expected changes for each year individually. The model is designed to function properly if the values of these items are entered as constants in the input section or individually in Table 13-6.

Calculation of the Payback and Discounted Payback Period

The cumulative cash flows from the asset are generated in Column S of Table 13-7 (Q1.X20) and are used to calculate its payback period. When the cumulative cash flow changes from a negative to a positive value, the calculation of the payback period is triggered in Column T. The model assumes that the annual cash flows occur evenly over the year.

The payback period is calculated by

1. Listing each year's cash flow in Column R, starting with the initial negative flow in Year 0.

2. Accumulating the cash flows in Column S.

3. Checking each year to see whether the current year's cumulative flow is greater than 0 and the previous year's accumulation was negative.

4. If the cumulative cash flow does change from negative to positive in the current year, calculating the proportional part of the year for which the cumulative

349

cash flow was positive and subtracting this value from the number for the current year.

In our example, the cumulative cash flow changes from negative to positive during the fifth year of the project. The model determines that the cash flow was positive for 91 percent of the year; therefore, the payback period is 5 - .91 = 4.09 years. For any project life from 1 to 10 years, the correct payback period is shown in Cell T20. If the cost of the investment is not repaid within 10 years, the payback period displayed is equal to 0.

The discounted payback period is similar to the regular payback, but it shows how long it takes for payback to occur if capital costs are included. Each cash flow is discounted by the cost of capital, and then the discounted payback is calculated similarly to the regular payback. In our example, the regular payback is just over 4 years, but the discounted payback is almost 5 years. Thus, the projected cash flows would have to come in for almost 5 years in order for the project to break even after financing costs.

===

Table 13-7

Table 13-7. Calculation of Payback Period (Q1.X20)

Year	Cash Flow	Cumul. Cash Flow	Payback Calcul.	Disc. Cash Flow	Cumul. Disc. C.F.	Disc. Payback
0	($10,110)	($10,110)		(10,110)	(10,110)	
1	2,177	(7,933)	0.00	1,979	(8,131)	0.00
2	2,544	(5,390)	0.00	2,102	(6,029)	0.00
3	2,491	(2,898)	0.00	1,872	(4,157)	0.00
4	2,491	(407)	0.00	1,702	(2,456)	0.00
5	4,571	4,164	4.09	2,838	383	4.87
6	0	4,164	0.00	0	383	0.00
7	0	4,164	0.00	0	383	0.00
8	0	4,164	0.00	0	383	0.00
9	0	4,164	0.00	0	383	0.00
10	0	4,164	0.00	0	383	0.00

Payback Period in Years =   4.09   4.87

===

Sensitivity Analysis

Scenario and sensitivity analyses can be performed simply by
changing various inputs, such as the annual changes in sales
and costs. Then, by pressing the F9 function key, the
results of this new scenario can be viewed in the table of
key results. However, if you want to calculate the results
of a change in one or two input variables at several different levels of another input variable, it is often more
efficient to create a data table, such as the one shown in
Table 13-8. Here we have created a table which calculates
the NPV of the project at several different costs of capital
and for several different values for the change in operating
costs associated with the project. A data table can be very
useful in helping the user to quickly determine which input
variables would have the greatest impact on the decision and
the range of values for which the investment would be
profitable.

===

Table 13-8

Table 13-8.   Sensitivity Analysis (Q24.X35)

Data Table:	Cost of Capital +J8	Change in Operating Costs				
		(6,000)	(4,500)	(3,000)	(1,500)	0
	0%	$12,264	$8,214	$4,164	$114	($3,936)
	5%	9,067	5,560	2,053	(1,453)	(4,960)
	10%	6,524	3,453	383	(2,688)	(5,758)
	15%	4,472	1,756	(959)	(3,674)	(6,389)
	20%	2,795	373	(2,050)	(4,472)	(6,894)
	25%	1,410	(769)	(2,947)	(5,125)	(7,304)

===

Summary

In this chapter, we have presented a capital budgeting model which analyzes a proposed investment project using five criteria: the net present value, the internal rate of return, the profitability index, the regular payback period, and the discounted payback period. This model can be used to analyze both expansion and replacement projects. We have also developed a data table which can be used to perform sensitivity analyses on the model's input variables. This type of analysis allows the user to see which input variables are the most critical and therefore require the most careful analysis and estimation.

Chapter 13 Exercises

Note: Before doing the following exercises, make sure to copy File LB13X1 onto your diskette, then use your copy to do the following exercises.

13-1 Convert File LB13X1 to a template model by using the Range Erase command on the input data in Cells H64.H78 in Table 13-2, then press the F9 (CALC) key. Now work the following exercise by entering the data from the problem into the corresponding cells in Table 13-2.

You have been asked by the president of your company to evaluate the proposed acquisition of a new tractor. The tractor's basic price is $50,000, and it will cost another $10,000 to modify it for special use by your company. The tractor falls into the ACRS 3-year class and qualifies for a 6% investment tax credit. It will be sold after 3 years for $20,000. Use of the tractor will require an increase in net working capital of $2,000. The tractor will have no effect on revenues, but it is expected to save the firm $20,000 per year in before-tax operating costs, mainly labor. The firm's marginal tax rate is 40%. The project's cost of capital is 10%. (Hint: This is not a replacement decision; thus, all data referring to the old asset should be input as 0.)

a. What is the amount of the total initial outflows? ($58,400)

b. What are the cash flows for Years 1, 2, and 3? ($17,820; $20,846; $34,614)

c. Identify the following:

1. The project's payback period (2.57 yrs.)
2. The project's discounted payback period (2.96 yrs.)
3. The project's IRR (10.9%)
4. The project's NPV ($1,034)
5. The project's profitability index (1.02)

d.   Should the tractor be purchased?

e.   Redo the data table in Table 13-8 so the changes
     you have made for the problem are taken into
     account. Change the operating costs in Cells
     T29.X29 to read: (40,000) (30,000) (20,000)
     (10,000) and 0. (Remember to disengage the
     Worksheet Global Protection feature before doing
     the data table.)

f.   If the project's cost of capital is 12% should the
     tractor be purchased? What is the NPV of the
     project at this new cost of capital? [NPV =
     ($1,233)]

13-2   Convert File LB13X1 to a template model by using the
       Range Erase command on the input data in Cells H64.H78
       in Table 13-2 then press the F9 (CALC) key. Now work
       the following exercise by entering the data from the
       problem into the corresponding cells in Table 13-2.

       Malibu Shipyards is considering the replacement of an
       8-year old riveting machine with a new one that will
       increase the earnings before depreciation from $30,000
       to $58,000 per year. The new machine will cost
       $60,000 and have an estimated life of 8 years with a
       salvage value of $8,000 at the end of 8 years. The
       machine will be depreciated over its 3-year ACRS
       recovery period and the applicable investment tax
       credit on the purchase of the new machine is 10%. The
       applicable corporate tax rate is 40 percent, and the
       firm's cost of capital is 12 percent. The old machine
       was bought 8 years ago at a price of $48,000, it has a
       remaining book value of $24,000, and a remaining life
       of 8 years. The old machine is being depreciated
       using the straight-line method toward a zero salvage
       value, or by $3,000 a year. If replaced, the old
       machine can be sold now for $15,000. (Hint: You will
       have to modify the discount rate guess in Cell J6 from
       its current value to .6. Remember to disengage the
       Global Protection feature before making this
       modification.)

a. Identify the following:

1. The project's payback period (1.58 yrs.)
2. The project's discounted payback period (1.85 yrs.)
3. The project's IRR (58.3%)
4. The project's NPV ($62,035)
5. The project's profitability index (2.75)

b. What is the amount of the total initial outflow? ($35,400)

c. What are the cash flows for Years 1-8? (Y1 = $21,300; Y2 = $24,264; Y3 = $24,036; Y4 - Y7 = $15,600; and Y8 = $20,400.)

d. Should the riveting machine be purchased?

e. Redo the data table in Table 13-8 so the changes you have made for the problem are taken into account. (Hint: Disengage the Global Protection feature and do the following: Change the title of the Data Table from Operating Costs to Revenues; change the revenue numbers of the heading as follows--40,000, 30,000, 20,000, 10,000, and 0; and change the input cell 2 from H76 to H75.)

Chapter 14
Bond Refunding

This chapter presents a model for determining the profitability of refunding an outstanding bond after a decline in
interest rates. The model computes the present value of the
costs associated with refunding the old issue and compares
this cost to the present value of the interest that will be
saved as a result of the refunding.

Layout of the Model

A schematic diagram of the bond refunding model is shown in
Figure 14-1. Table 14-1 describes the contents of the file
LB14X1. Model inputs are entered in Table 14-2, key results
of the model are displayed in Table 14-3, the complete bond
refunding analysis is shown in Table 14-4, and the internal
rate of return of the decision is computed in Table 14-5.
Finally, a sensitivity analysis is performed in Table 14-6.

357

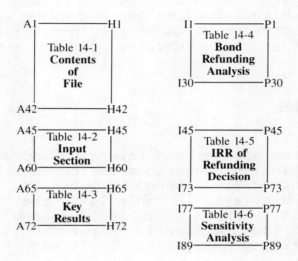

```
========================================================================


                              Figure 14-1
                          Layout of the Model




          A1———————————H1          I1————————P1
                                        Table 14-4
              Table 14-1                  Bond
              Contents                  Refunding
                 of                     Analysis
                File               I30————————P30


          A42——————————H42

          A45    Table 14-2   H45    I45————————P45
                  Input                  Table 14-5
          A60    Section      H60        IRR of
                                        Refunding
          A65    Table 14-3   H65        Decision
                  Key               I73————————P73
          A72    Results      H72
                                   I77————————P77
                                        Table 14-6
                                       Sensitivity
                                        Analysis
                                   I89————————P89




========================================================================
```

```
================================================================
```

Table 14-1

Table 14-1. Contents of File LB14X1 and Directions for Its Use (A1.H42)

I. To position a table on the screen:

    1. Press function key F5, the "GoTo" key.
    2. Type the first cell shown in the range in the directory
       shown below, starting on Line 33.
    3. Press the RETURN key.
    4. To return to the directory, press the F5 key and go to A33.

II. The ranges for the tables will fit on a printed page. Thus, when
you construct a table, you can print it by specifying the given
range as the print range.

III. The tables now have illustrative data. By using the Range Erase
command on the data in Table 14-2, you convert all the tables to
template models. Then, when you enter data for your own company,
the other tables will be completed automatically. Note that
all cells except the input data cells in Table 14-2 have been
protected. If you need to modify the model, you may disconnect
the protect feature with this command: /WGPD. If you attempt to
write in a protected cell, you will hear a beep and receive an
error message. Press ESC to return to READY mode.

IV. Note that unless you disconnect the protect feature, only the
data cells can be changed--all formulas are protected. Thus, you
cannot erase the entire worksheet at one pass; you can erase only
the unprotected input data cells in Table 14-2. The other cells
are formulas, hence protected. Also, note that once you erase
the data in the worksheet, zeros and ERRs appear throughout.
When you enter new data, the ERRs will disappear.

V. Here are the tables and their addresses:

Cell Range	Number	Description of Table
A1.H42	14-1	Contents of file LB14X1
A45.H60	14-2	Input section
A65.H72	14-3	Key results
I1.P30	14-4	Bond refunding analysis
I45.P73	14-5	IRR of refunding decision
I77.P89	14-6	Sensitivity analysis

```
================================================================
```

The Input Section

All of the data needed in the refunding analysis are entered in the range A45.H60 as shown in Table 14-2. The model requires that you enter information on the principal value of the outstanding bond issue, the flotation costs of the old and new issues, the original maturity of the old issue, the years remaining to maturity of the old issue, the coupon interest rates on each issue, the call premium percentage, the firm's tax rate, and the current short-term interest rate. You also enter the number of months during which both issues will be outstanding; the model computes the fraction of a year during which the issues overlap. Another key piece of information the model requires is the maturity of the new bond issue; however, you do not input this.

===

Table 14-2

	A	B	C	D	E	F	G	H
45	Table 14-2. Input Section (A45.H60)							
46								
47								
48	Principal value of old bond issue outstanding							$60,000,000
49	Coupon interest rate, old issue							15.00%
50	Years remaining to maturity, old issue							20
51	Flotation costs, old issue							$3,000,000
52	Original years to maturity, old issue							25
53	Call premium as percent of par value							10.00%
54	Maturity of new bond issue (from Cell H50)							20
55	Coupon interest rate, new issue							12.00%
56	Overlap period in months							1
57	Overlap period in years (calculated value)							0.0833
58	Flotation costs, new issue							$2,650,000
59	Tax rate							40.00%
60	Current short-term interest rate							11.00%

===

An important assumption embodied in this model is that the new bond will be issued with the same maturity as the remaining maturity of the old bond. To insure that this assumption will not be violated, we have set up the model so that when the remaining maturity of the old bond is entered, this value is automatically entered as the maturity of the new bond issue. If the new bond had a substantially longer maturity than the remaining life of the old bond, then a cash flow mismatch would occur, and it would be necessary to modify the model to incorporate some type of "replacement chain" analysis.

Key Results

Five quantities are displayed in the table of key results shown in Table 14-3. The five values are:

1. The net present value of the refunding decision is reported in Cell H68. It was calculated in Cell P29.

2. The IRR on the investment required to undertake the refunding is reported in Cell H69. It was calculated in Cell L72.

3. The present value of the cash outlay required to refund the outstanding debt issue is reported in Cell H70.

4. The present value of the after-tax interest savings over the life of the new issue due to refunding is reported in Cell H71.

5. The discount rate used in the analysis, which is equal to the after-tax yield on new long-term debt, is reported in Cell H72.

```
================================================================
                          Table 14-3


  Table 14-3.   Key Results   (A65.H72)


     NPV of refunding decision                         $5,907,974
     IRR of refunding decision                             19.59%
     Cash outlay required to refund the debt issue     $5,357,843
     PV of after-tax savings due to refunding         $11,265,817
     Discount rate (after-tax cost of new debt)             7.20%



================================================================
```

Bond Refunding Analysis

There are three parts to the bond refunding analysis shown
in Table 14-4 (I1.P30). The first section (I4.P19) shows
the factors that determine the net investment required to
undertake the refunding. The second part (I21.P27) calculates the net present value of the interest savings. The
final section (I29.P30) computes the net present value of
the refunding decision.

        Turning to the first section of Table 14-4, note that
most outstanding corporate bond issues contain a provision
for a call premium, which is a penalty imposed on the firm
for early retirement of the debt issue. The call premium is
expressed as a percentage of the principal value of the
debt; this percentage was an input in Table 14-2, and it is
used here to calculate the actual call premium. Since the
premium is a tax-deductible expense, the premium outlay is
reduced by the amount of the tax savings due to its tax
deductibility.

```
================================================================
```

Table 14-4

Table 14-4. Bond Refunding Analysis (I1.P30)

	Amount before Tax	Amount after Tax	Cash Flow, from Year	to Year	PV Factor, 7.20%	Present Value
Cost of Refunding:						
Call prem, old	6000000	3600000	0	0	1.000	$3,600,000
Flot cost, new	2650000	2650000	0	0	1.000	2,650,000
Tax sav, new flot	-132500	-53000	1	20	10.431	(552,860)
Tax sav, old flot	-2400000	-960000	0	0	1.000	(960,000)
Tax benefits lost	120000	48000	1	20	10.431	500,703
Extra interest	750000	450000	0	0	1.000	450,000
Int on S-T invest	-550000	-330000	0	0	1.000	(330,000)
PV of net investment						$5,357,843

Interest Savings:

	Amount before Tax	Amount after Tax	Cash Flow, from Year	to Year	PV Factor, 7.20%	Present Value
Interest, old bond	9000000	5400000				
Interest, new bond	7200000	4320000				
Net interest saved	1800000	1080000	1	20	10.431	$11,265,817

NPV of Refunding Decision = PV of Savings - PV of Costs = $5,907,974

```
================================================================
```

The flotation cost of the new issue is a cash expense at the time the new bond is sold. However, this cost is not an immediate tax-deductible expense—it must be amortized over the life of the issue. Further, since the old bond is being retired before it matures, the firm will be able to write off the unamortized flotation cost of the old issue as a tax-deductible expense at the time of refunding. However, this immediate write-off of the old flotation cost means that the firm will lose an annual tax-deductible expense which it would have had if the refunding had not occurred; this item is shown as "lost tax benefits" in Table 14-4.
Extra interest refers to the interest paid on the old bonds after the new issue is outstanding but before the refunding actually occurs. During the same period, the

company has surplus cash on hand from the new issue, and this cash is invested in short-term marketable securities at the rate entered in Cell H60. The after-tax short-term interest reduces the cash outlays for refunding. Note that the overlap period could be set at 0; if the firm planned to issue the new bond on the day money is needed to pay off the old bond, zero should be used. The present value of the net investment as shown in P18 is the sum of the present values of each of the factors involved in the refunding process.

The second part of Table 14-4 (I21.P27) calculates the net interest saved each year as the before-tax and after-tax difference between the old and new bonds' interest. These cash flows occur in each year until the bonds mature, and they are discounted at the firm's after-tax cost of new debt to determine the present value interest savings.

Finally, in Cell P29 we show the NPV of the refunding operation; it is determined as the difference between the present value interest savings and the present value cost of refunding.

IRR of the Refunding Decision

The internal rate of return from the refunding operation is calculated in Table 14-5 (I45.P73). The cash flows corresponding to each year are entered in Column J. The model can analyze a bond refunding with a maximum remaining maturity of up to 20 years; the maturity period could be extended with some simple modifications. The Year 0 value represents the present value of the investment required to refund the old issue, and the remaining cash flows are the annual after-tax reductions in interest. The model calculates the holding-period IRR for each year up to and including the year in which the bond matures, and it displays these values in Column K. The IRR would be zero for the remaining years if there were less than 20 years left to maturity on the old bond. In Column L, the year is compared to the number of years remaining to maturity. If these two values are equal, the IRR from Column K is listed; otherwise, a zero is displayed. The IRR of the refunding operation is equal to the only non-zero value in Column L.

If you make changes to the model, you may find that the model cannot compute the IRR and that an ERR message will appear in Column K of this exhibit. This problem can be overcome by changing the guess in the IRR function.

==

Table 14-5

Table 14-5.   IRR of Refunding Decision (I45.P73)

Year	Cash Flow	@IRR	IRR
0	-5357843		
1	1080000	-79.84%	0.00%
2	1080000	-43.91%	0.00%
3	1080000	-21.48%	0.00%
4	1080000	-8.09%	0.00%
5	1080000	0.26%	0.00%
6	1080000	5.72%	0.00%
7	1080000	9.43%	0.00%
8	1080000	12.04%	0.00%
9	1080000	13.92%	0.00%
10	1080000	15.31%	0.00%
11	1080000	16.34%	0.00%
12	1080000	17.14%	0.00%
13	1080000	17.75%	0.00%
14	1080000	18.22%	0.00%
15	1080000	18.60%	0.00%
16	1080000	18.89%	0.00%
17	1080000	19.13%	0.00%
18	1080000	19.32%	0.00%
19	1080000	19.47%	0.00%
20	1080000	19.59%	19.59%

IRR = 19.59%

==

Sensitivity Analysis

When analyzing a potential refunding operation, the decision should be made on the basis of the NPV; if the NPV is negative, the refunding should not proceed. However, this question will arise: How low must interest rates decline before the refunding would become profitable, that is, show a positive NPV? The analysis to answer this question involves yet another question: How long will it take rates to fall to such levels, hence will we have to change inputs such as the remaining maturity of the old bond and its call price to analyze the refunding?

Even if the NPV of the analysis done thus far is positive, this does not mean that the company should proceed with the refunding--it might be more profitable to wait until interest rates fall even further, in which case the NPV will be even larger.

Based on our experience, we concluded that it would not pay to attempt to incorporate all of these potential analyses into the present model--rather, we concluded that it would be best to discuss briefly how modifications could be done and then to demonstrate just one. Here are the potential modifications that occurred to us:

1. <u>Under present conditions NPV is negative.</u> In this case, construct a Data Table 1 with the interest rate on the new bond as the input variables in the left column, Cell H55 the Input 1 cell, and NPV from Cell P29 being the output variable. Interest rates used in the analysis would go down from the current rate. The data table analysis will show NPV at different interest rates, so you can use it to see how low rates must fall to make refunding profitable.

2. <u>NPV is currently positive, but interest rates may fall further.</u> Construct the data table discussed above, but use both higher and lower rates than the current rate on new bonds. Further, if you can assign probabilities to different interest rates, you can calculate the expected value of waiting awhile before refunding. We set this example up in Table 14-6 (I77.P89), using interest rates of 10, 12, and 14 percent, with probabilities of 25, 50, and 25 percent, respectively. We also assumed that the delay period is only a few weeks, so conditions other than interest rates remain constant. Note that if interest rates rise and the NPV becomes negative, the company will not refund and hence the NPV will be zero, not a negative number. As we set the example up, the expected value of waiting for a few weeks exceeds the NPV of refunding immediately:

$6,777,289 > $5,907,974. However, the NPV of refunding immediately is riskless, but the expected NPV if the company waits is risky--this is indicated by the standard deviation shown in P88.

3. <u>Examine a longer time horizon.</u> The type analysis set forth above can be extended, but the analysis becomes more complex because the years to maturity of the old bond change, the call price normally changes (declines), and the fact that if the refunding is delayed, the calculated NPV must itself be discounted back to the present to make it comparable to the NPV of refunding today. Our approach, when doing such analysis, is to use the /Range Value command rather than to create data tables. We simply make a series of modifications to the model to develop NPVs for various years to maturity, use /RV to copy values (as opposed to formulas) to some designated section of the worksheet, and then compare the results.

===

Table 14-6

Table 14-6. Sensitivity Analysis (I77.P89)

Data Table:	Coupon Interest Rate +P29	Probability	x	Expected NPV
	10%15293208	25%		$3,823,302
	12% 5907974	50%		$2,953,987
	14%-1930583	25%		$0

Expected NPV of Refunding Decision if wait 1 month = $6,777,289

Standard deviation = $1,636,371

===

367

Summary

In this chapter, we presented a model which determines the profitability of refunding an outstanding bond issue after a substantial decline in interest rates. An important matter in bond refunding is choosing the best time to refund an issue. Although the analysis may indicate that it is profitable to refund an issue today, it may be even more profitable to delay the refunding. A sensitivity analysis may be helpful in deciding whether or not to delay refunding.

Chapter 14 Exercises

Note: Before doing the following exercises, make sure you copy File LB14X1 onto your diskette, then do the following exercises on that copy.

14-1 Retrieve File LB14X1 from your diskette. Convert the model to a template model by using the Range Erase command to eliminate data input from the corresponding cells in Table 14-2. Then press the F9 (CALC) key-- this converts your model to a template model.

Data Retrieval Computer Company has outstanding a $75 million bond issue which has a 13% coupon interest rate and 15 years remaining to maturity. This issue which sold 5 years ago, had flotation costs of $3.75 million, which the firm has been amortizing on a straight-line basis over the 20-year original life of the issue. The bond has a call provision which makes it possible for the company to retire the issue at this time by calling the bonds in at a 9.75% call premium. Investment bankers have assured the company that it could sell an additional $60 million to $75 million worth of new 15-year bonds at an interest rate of 11%. To insure that the funds required to pay off the debt will be available, the new bonds would be sold 1 month before the old issue is called, so for 1 month, interest would have to be paid on 2 issues. Current short-term interest rates are 9.5 percent. Predictions are that long-term interest rates are unlikely to fall below 11%. Flotation costs on a new refunding issue would amount to $3.2 million. Data Retrieval's marginal tax rate is 46%. Should the company refund its $75 million of 13% bonds?

a. What is the cash outlay required to refund the debt issue? ($5,857,257)

b. What is the discount rate used in the bond refunding analysis? (5.94%)

c. What is the present value of the after-tax savings due to refunding? ($7,897,855)

d. What is the net present value of the refunding decision? ($2,040,598)

e. What is the internal rate of return of the refunding decision? (10.9%)

14-2 Continuing the problem above, identify for each situation given below, whether the proposed bond refunding is profitable and the NPV of the refunding decision if circumstances changed as follows. (Remember to only change the data item in each situation, that is, hold everything else constant.)

a. If the coupon rate of the old issue were 12.5% versus 13%? (Refund, NPV = $83,009)

b. If the years remaining to maturity of the old issue was 10 years versus 15 years? (Refund, NPV = $24,154)

c. If both a and b occurred? [Do not refund, NPV of refunding decision = ($1,453,634)].

Chapter 15
Option Pricing and Bond Duration Models

In this chapter we present two models: the Black-Scholes Option Pricing Model and a bond duration model. These models each solve a single but complex equation, and they were originally developed to help our students work end-of-chapter text problems. Because these models were developed for use with textbook problems, they differ somewhat in format from the other models.

Black-Scholes Option Pricing Model

An option is a contract which gives the holder the right to buy (or sell) the underlying asset to the option writer for a given length of time at a fixed price. Options have become important financial securities since 1973, when they were first traded on the Chicago Board Options Exchange and when Fischer Black and Myron Scholes derived an option valuation formula known as the Black-Scholes Option Pricing Model. Subsequently, options trading has been broadened to include hundreds of individual securities and indices of securities, as well as dozens of commodities. This growth has been made possible to a large extent by the Black-Scholes model, which consists of the following three equations:

$$V = P[N(d_1)] - Xe^{-R_F t}[N(d_2)]. \qquad (15\text{-}1)$$

$$d_1 = \frac{\ln(P/X) + [R_F t(\sigma^2/2)]t}{\sigma\sqrt{t}}. \qquad (15\text{-}2)$$

$$d_2 = d_1 - \sigma\sqrt{t}. \qquad (15\text{-}3)$$

Here

V = calculated value of the call option. This is the price an investor should be willing to pay for the asset.

P = current price of the underlying asset.

X = exercise, or striking, price of the asset.

R_F = risk-free interest rate.

t = time in years until the option expires.

σ^2 = variance of the rate of return on the asset.

$N(d_1)$ = probability that a deviation less than d_1 will occur in a standard normal distribution.[1] Thus, $N(d_1)$ and $N(d_2)$ represent areas under a standard normal distribution function.

e = exponential function = 2.7183... .

ln(P/X) = natural logarithm of P/X.

Layout of the Model

Figure 15-1 shows the layout of the option pricing model. Table 15-1 (A1.H38) shows the contents and instructions for this model, which is stored as File LB15X1. Data values are entered in Table 15-2 (A60.H83), and, since the output is a single number, the key result of the calculation is displayed here also, in Cell G75. Table 15-3 (I1.O86) shows the table of normal probabilities along with some values required for the Black-Scholes model.

==

Figure 15-1
Layout of Black-Scholes Option Pricing Model

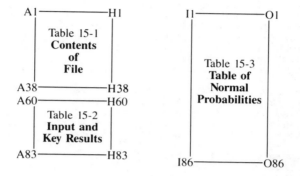

==

==

Table 15-1

Table 15-1. Contents of File LB15X1 and Directions for Its Use (A1.H38)

   I. To position a table on the screen:

      1. Press function key F5, the "GoTo" key.
      2. Type the first cell shown in the range in the directory
         shown below, starting on line 32.
      3. Press the RETURN key.
      4. To return to the directory, press the F5 key and go to A32.

  II. We have inserted a page break on Line 58. This allows you to
      specify the entire worksheet as a print range. Table 15-1 will
      be printed on the first page, Table 15-2 on the second page,
      the first 57 lines of Table 15-3 on the third page, and the
      remainder of Table 15-3 on the fourth page.

 III. The calculation of the option price in this model requires normal
      probability values. Rather than have the user look up the values
      in a statistics book, we incorporated a normal probability table
      into this model. This table is given in Table 15-3. The final
      two columns of Table 15-3 are calculated values which depend on
      the input data; these values are then used as inputs in the
      Black-Scholes model.

  IV. The worksheet has been protected using the Global Protect
      command. Only those cells in Table 15-2 in which data should
      be entered have been unprotected. These cells are highlighted.
      If you want to make any other changes to the worksheet, you must
      first disable the protect feature with the command: /WGPD.

   V. Here are the tables and their addresses:

         Cell Range   Number   Description of Table
         ----------   ------   --------------------------
         A1.H38   15-1   Contents of file LB15X1
         A60.H83   15-2   Input section and key results
         I1.O86   15-3   Table of normal probabilities

==

Using the Model

To use the model, you first enter in Cells G67.G71 of Table
15-2 the values for the five input variables--asset price
(P), exercise price (X), risk-free interest rate (R_F), time

to expiration (t), and expected variance of returns on the asset (σ^2), and then you press the F9 key to have the model calculate the option's value. The theoretical option value will be displayed in Cell G75. Below the option price are eight calculated values; these values are elements of the Black-Scholes model as expressed in Equations 15-1, 15-2, and 15-3 above, and they are calculated by the model. The values of $N(d_1)$ and $N(d_2)$ are taken from the normal probability table found in Table 15-3.

==

Table 15-2

```
            A         B          C         D         E         F           G           H
60   Table 15-2. Input Section and Key Results (A60.H83)
61
62   Black-Scholes Option Pricing Model
63
64
65   Input Values:
66
67      Current price of underlying common stock        P =     $20.00
68      Exercise price                                  X =     $20.00
69      Risk-free rate of interest                      r =      0.12
70      Time to expiration                              t =      0.25
71      Variance of stock returns                     s^2 =      0.16
72
73
74   Key Result:
75                     Theoretical Option Value =              $1.88
76                                                             =====
77
78   Calculated Values:
79
80      ln(P/X) =        0.00000              d1 =            0.25000
81      (s^2)/2 =        0.08000              d2 =            0.05000
82    s*(t^0.5) =        0.20000            N(d1) =           0.59869
83     e^(-rt) =         0.97045            N(d2) =           0.51993
```

==

375

Table 15-3

Table 15-3. Table of Normal Probabilities (I1.086)

z	Cumul Prob	d1 = 0.250	d2 = 0.050
0.00	0.000000	0.000000	0.000000
0.05	0.019935	0.000000	0.000000
0.10	0.039820	0.000000	0.019935
0.15	0.059605	0.000000	0.000000
0.20	0.079243	0.000000	0.000000
0.25	0.098686	0.098686	0.000000
0.30	0.117888	0.000000	0.000000
0.35	0.136803	0.000000	0.000000
0.40	0.155391	0.000000	0.000000
2.90	0.498131	0.000000	0.000000
2.95	0.498408	0.000000	0.000000
3.00	0.498647	0.000000	0.000000
3.05	0.498853	0.000000	0.000000
3.10	0.499030	0.000000	0.000000
3.15	0.499182	0.000000	0.000000
3.20	0.499311	0.000000	0.000000
3.25	0.499422	0.000000	0.000000
3.30	0.499515	0.000000	0.000000
3.35	0.499595	0.000000	0.000000
3.40	0.499662	0.000000	0.000000
3.45	0.499719	0.000000	0.000000
3.50	0.499767	0.000000	0.000000
		0.098686	0.019935
		0.098686	0.019935

Note: We have printed only a portion of the table. The actual Table 15-3 contains 50 additional lines. If you printed the entire table, Lines 1 through 57 would be printed on one page and Lines 58 through 86 on a second page.

We illustrate the option model with a stock price of $20, an exercise price of $20, a time to expiration of 0.25 years, a risk-free interest rate of 12 percent, and a variance of stock returns of 0.16. When these values are entered in the input section of the Black-Scholes model, the theoretical value computed is $1.88. The steps required to calculate the value of an option are: (1) Retrieve File LB15X1; (2) press F5, and go to A60; (3) enter the five input data in the range G67.G71; and (4) press the F9 (CALC) key. You can perform scenario analyses simply by changing input values and hitting the F9 key to obtain the new option price.

Duration

In introductory finance courses, people are generally taught that the prices of outstanding bonds decline if interest rates rise, and that the longer a bond's maturity, the greater the effect on price of a given interest rate change. This is called "interest rate risk," and it has a number of important implications. However, while maturity and interest rate risk are indeed related, a bond's <u>duration</u> is a much better indicator of its interest rate risk than is its maturity. Duration is a sort of weighted average of the time when cash flows from the bond (interest payments and maturity value) will be received. Here is the formula:

$$\text{Duration} = \sum_{t=1}^{n} \frac{t(\text{PVCF}_t)}{\sum_{t=1}^{n} \text{PVCF}_t} = \sum_{t=1}^{n} \frac{t(\text{PVCF}_t)}{\text{Bond's value}}.$$

Here n is the periods (years or semiannual periods) to maturity, t is the year each cash flow occurs, and PVCF_t is the present value of each CF_t.

We needed to develop a duration model to help some investors (bankers and pension fund administrators) appraise the riskiness of their portfolios, and we also wanted to develop a model that our students could use in connection with course work. First, we wrote a model that calculated a bond's duration and price given its yield to maturity, years to maturity, and coupon interest rate. This first model was not especially complicated, and we could use it to analyze different bonds.

However, the model had to be modified for every bond that was analyzed, and that meant (1) that no one could use it unless they knew how to use 1-2-3 and (2) that it would take quite a long time to analyze all the bonds in a large portfolio. At that point, we decided to write two macros to overcome these problems.

The top part of Table 15-4 gives instructions for using the model, the input and output sections, and the spreadsheet itself. This model is stored as LB15X2. Users are required to enter (in the range C21.C27) the YTM, the maturity in years (fractions such as 2+7/12 for 2 years plus 7 months can be used), and the coupon interest rate. The output is displayed just to the right of the inputs (G21.G23). We used the Worksheet Global Protect command to protect the model, with only the required input cells (plus a few others for highlighting purposes) unprotected with the Range Unprotect command.

We used two macros in this model, permitting us to use the model to analyze bonds which pay interest on either an annual or semiannual basis. If interest is paid annually, the macro \A is used, while the macro \S is used if interest is paid semiannually. When the three required data items have been entered, the user presses, simultaneously, the ALT key and A if interest is paid annually and ALT S if interest is paid semiannually. The model then executes a macro which provides as output the bond's duration, its value, and the APR return (which is relevant for semiannual bonds). You should retrieve our model and run a few test cases, using various inputs, to get a feel for what it does.

378

==

Table 15-4

```
      A            B            C            D          E          F        G        H
 1  Duration, Price, and APR                          (LB15X2)
 2
 3
 4      1. This model calculates bond prices, APRs, and durations where
 5  YTM is known. The maturity must be 31 years or less, and either
 6  annual or semiannual compounding can be used.
 7
 8      2. First, input into the indicated cells (1) the YTM, (2) the years
 9  to maturity, and (3) the coupon rate. Use the stated, or nominal, YTM,
10  not APR, for semiannual bonds.
11
12      3. Then put Cell A19 in the upper left corner of your worksheet
13  and press, simultaneously, the ALT key and the A key if the
14  analysis is on an annual basis, and ALT plus S if the analysis
15  calls for semiannual compounding. A beep will occur when results
16  are ready; this takes about 25 seconds for long maturities on an XT.
17
18
19  INPUTS (enter %s as decimals):            OUTPUT (Press ALT plus A or S):
20
21  YTM (semiannual):        9.50%        Duration:             2.25051727
22  periodic yield:          4.75%        Calculated price:     1,052.73
23  par value:           $1,000.00        APR YTM:                  9.73%
24  maturity, yrs:      2.58333333
25     t =             5.16666666         !!!SEMIANNUAL!!!
26  coupon rate:            10.00%
27  Interest pmt.:          $50.00                          Sum =      Price
28                                                 PVCF*t/  Duration   t =
29      t          CF          PVCF       PVCF*t   Value    (t = Mat)  Mat.
30  ----------------------------------------------------------------------------
31   0.000                                                             1,000.00
32   0.167       50.00        49.61        4.13    0.004    0.004         49.61
33   1.167       50.00        47.36       27.63    0.026    0.030         96.98
34   2.167       50.00        45.22       48.99    0.047    0.077        142.20
35   3.167       50.00        43.17       68.35    0.065    0.142        185.36
36   4.167       50.00        41.21       85.85    0.082    0.223        226.57
37   5.167    1,050.00       826.15    2,134.23    2.027    2.251      1,052.73
38   6.167        0.00         0.00        0.00    0.000    0.000          0.00
39   7.167        0.00         0.00        0.00    0.000    0.000          0.00
40   8.167        0.00         0.00        0.00    0.000    0.000          0.00
41   9.167        0.00         0.00        0.00    0.000    0.000          0.00
42  10.167        0.00         0.00        0.00    0.000    0.000          0.00
43  11.167        0.00         0.00        0.00    0.000    0.000          0.00
44  12.167        0.00         0.00        0.00    0.000    0.000          0.00
45  13.167        0.00         0.00        0.00    0.000    0.000          0.00
```

==

The two macros are printed out in Table 15-5. Look at macro \S, which is in Cells B105.B113. You could look at the screen, but it is just as easy to follow it in Table 15-5. Here's a step-by-step rundown:

1. We use the Global Protect feature to keep people from messing up the model. However, as inputs change, so must the spreadsheet cells. Therefore, we begin the macro with '/wgpd, which disables the Global Protect feature. (Incidentally, the label prefix does not show in the table, but if you put the pointer on Cell B105 and looked at the control panel, you would see that we did type an apostrophe before the /.)

2. Still in B105, we told 1-2-3 to have the pointer go to A21 and enter the label YTM (semiannual): . This is to indicate that a semiannual payment bond is being analyzed.

3. Lines 2 through 4 of the macro (B106.B108) simply put things on a semiannual basis by dividing by 2.

4. Line 5 (B109) puts the pointer on D32 and then performs some arithmetic.

5. Line 6 (B110) copies a formula and then, in effect, causes the CALC key (F9) to be pressed twice.

6. Next, the step in B111 sends the pointer to E25 and puts in a label indicating semiannual payments.

7. Then we have the pointer go to C21, which is where we want it to be when we analyze the next bond.

8. Finally, we turn the Global Protect feature back on and have the computer beep to let us know that the analysis is complete.

```
================================================================

                        Table 15-5


   \A      /wgpd{goto}a21~YTM (annual):~          Named range table:
           {goto}c22~+c21~
           {goto}c25~+c24~                        \A      B95
           {goto}c27~+c23*c26~                    \S      B105
           {goto}d32~+c32*a32~
           /c~d33.d93~{calc}{calc}
           {goto}e25~!!!ANNUAL!!!~
           {goto}a18~{right 2}{down 3}
           /wgpE{beep}

   \S      /wgpd{goto}a21~YTM (semiannual):~
           {goto}c22~+c21/2~
           {goto}c25~+c24*2~
           {goto}c27~+c23*c26/2~
           {goto}d32~+c32*a32/2~
           /c~d33.d93~{calc}{calc}
           {goto}e25~!!!SEMIANNUAL!!!~
           {goto}a18~{right 2}{down 3}
           /wgpE{beep}




================================================================
```

    If you simultaneously press ALT and the F2 function
key, 1-2-3 will execute a macro in steps. The word STEP
will appear at the bottom of the screen. Then, when you
press ALT A or ALT S, 1-2-3 will pause at each keystroke.
Try it. Press ALT F2 and then ALT S. Now you must press
the RETURN or any other key repeatedly, and the macro will
execute step by step. This is a good way to see what is
happening if you need to debug a macro that does not do what
it should. You can use Control Break (Ctrl plus Break
simultaneously) to stop the macro and ALT F2 to get out of
the STEP macro execution mode at any time, even while the
macro is running.

Summary

This chapter presented two separate models to solve complicated equations used often in finance, the Black-Scholes
option pricing model and the calculation of a bond's duration. Although the models are rather complex, they are
quite easy to use. We should point out that we would not
bother to write 1-2-3 models to solve equations such as
these if we were only going to use them once or twice, since
it would be faster to solve them with a financial calculator. However, if you (or someone) will be solving an
equation many times, then it often pays to develop a computerized solution process.

Chapter 15 Exercises

Note: Before doing the following exercises, make sure you copy Files LB15X1 and LB15X2 onto your diskette, then do the exercises on these copies.

15-1 Retrieve File LB15X1. Convert the model to a template model by using the Range Erase command on the input data in Cells G67.G71. Then press the F9 key (CALC) key--this converts the model to a template model--make the following changes and identify the option's value in each situation, converting the model to a template model after each situation.

   a. Current price of stock $25
       Exercise price $19.50
       Risk-free rate of interest   10%
       Time to expiration   0.20
       Variance of stock returns   0.22

       (Theoretical Option Value = $6.10)

   b. Current price of stock $22
       Exercise price $22
       Risk-free rate of interest   9%
       Time to expiration   0.15
       Variance of stock returns   0.12

       (Theoretical Option Value = $1.32)

   c. Current price of stock $15
       Exercise price $13
       Risk-free rate of interest   9%
       Time to expiration   0.12
       Variance of stock returns   0.09

       (Theoretical Option Value = $2.18)

15-2 Retrieve File LB15X2. Convert the model to a template model by using the Range Erase command on the input data in Cells C21, C24, and C26. Then press the F9 (CALC) key--this converts the model to a template

383

model--make the following changes, identify the
duration, calculated price, and APR yield to maturity
(which will be different only for semi-annual bonds)
in each situation, converting the model back to a
template model after each situation. Remember in
order to use the model you must invoke the macro \A if
the bond is an annual one and you must invoke the
macro \S if the bond is semi-annual.

a. YTM   11.5%
    Maturity, years   23 years, 3 months
    Coupon rate   12.625%
    1. Annual basis? (D = 8.1356; P = $1,183.43, APR
        = 11.5%)
    2. Semi-annual basis? (D = 8.1843; P = $1,121.68,
        APR = 11.83%)

b. YTM   16.9%
    Maturity, years   3 years, 7 months
    Coupon rate   18.25%
    1. Annual basis? (D = 2.7641, P = $1,106.83, APR
        = 16.9%)
    2. Semi-annual basis? (D = 2.6093, P =
        $1,110.74, APR = 17.61%)

c. YTM   10.7%
    Maturity, years   4 years, 10 months
    Coupon rate   11.75%
    1. Annual basis? (D = 3.9059, P = $1,056.86, APR
        = 10.7%)
    2. Semi-annual basis? (D = 3.7764, P =
        $1,058.08, APR = 10.99%)

384

Appendix A
DOS Commands for Lotus 1-2-3

Table of Contents

Assigning File Names   386
DOS Prompts   388
Directories   388
Formatting Diskettes   395
Erasing Files   397
Changing the Name of a File   399
Copying Files   399

- -

The original version of 1-2-3 had certain built-in features
that permitted you to format diskettes, copy diskettes, and
do other "housekeeping" tasks within the 1-2-3 program itself. However, those features were deleted from Release 2,
so the disk operating system (DOS) must be used to accomplish those important tasks. In this appendix we distill
the two-inch-thick DOS manual into what we consider to be
the most useful material for someone using 1-2-3. We use
DOS 3.1, but the commands we discuss are generally identical
to those in DOS 2.1.
     We suggest that you use this appendix as follows:

1. Take 5-10 minutes to skim through it.

2. If you will be using your computer frequently, then go
    ahead and read the appendix. Go though it in two
    passes, though. On the first pass, read it and
    experiment (using a diskette that has files you do not
    want or can replace), but do not get hung up--if you
    do not understand something, just go on to the next
    topic. Then, on the second pass, try to understand and
    be able to do everything. We recommend the two-pass
    approach because there is a "simultaneity problem" with

the material--it is often necessary to know something
about two topics to understand either, yet it is
difficult to cover both simultaneously.

3. If you will not be using the computer frequently, then,
   after skimming the appendix, just go back to 1-2-3 and
   then, if and when the need arises, come back to the
   appendix, look up the command you need--say formatting
   a diskette, or copying a diskette--and just read the
   relevant section.

4. We do not recommend trying to memorize the various DOS
   commands. If you use them frequently, you will learn
   them anyway, and if you do not use DOS frequently, you
   will forget them. So, just use the appendix as a
   reference source whenever you need a DOS command.

If you are using the book as part of a course, your instructor will give you more specific instructions on how you
should approach the appendix given the class requirements.

Assigning File Names

DOS is, in essence, a filing system that permits you to
store, retrieve, copy, and make changes to files on floppy
or hard disks. A "file" can be a letter, term paper, class
record, forecasted balance sheet, or what have you. Each
file has a name--a "file name"--of from one to eight characters, which may include the following letters, numbers,
and/or special symbols:

```
A to Z
0 to 9
$ # & @ ! % ( ) - _ { }  `  '  ~  ^
```

However, if you are using DOS 2.1 rather than 3.1, your file
names will be restricted to letters, numbers, and the underline symbol. Never use * or ? in a file name, as these
symbols can cause the file to be erased by mistake. Also,

you should not use the following names as file names, because DOS reserves these terms for other purposes: CON, AUX, COM1, COM2, LPT1, LPT2, LPT3, and NUL. In either case, LB4X12 is an acceptable file name, as are TEXACO, TAX#1, and 1. RUBBERMAID, however, is not acceptable, because it is too long. Blank spaces are not permitted, and while you can type either upper- or lowercase letters, they will all be converted to capitals by the DOS system.

File names can also have <u>extensions</u>--these consist of one, two, or three characters that are added to the basic file name following a period. Thus, TAX#1.WK1 is a "legal" file name using WK1 as the extension. <u>However, when you use 1-2-3, you should not use your own extensions</u>. 1-2-3 adds the extension .WK1 automatically whenever you save a 1-2-3 file, and then it uses this extension to call up files and list them in the menu when you use the 1-2-3 /File Retrieve command. If you do use your own extension, 1-2-3 cannot add the .WK1 and you must retrieve the file by typing in its full name--the file will not show up on the menu when you type /FR as a Lotus command. Thus, if you saved a 1-2-3 worksheet as TAX.EFB, it would be saved. However, when you typed /FR, the file would not appear in the menu, and you would have to type in the full name in order to retrieve it. Therefore, do not use extensions with 1-2-3 file names.

Note: Release 1A of 1-2-3 used the extension .WKS rather than .WK1. If you have a file created under Release 1A and retrieve it under Release 2, it will automatically be translated into Release 2 and, when saved, be saved under .WK1. This makes it extremely easy to use old files on the new system.

You must assign a file name to each file you create in order to save it. You can then store it on a floppy or hard disk under that file name and retrieve it whenever you want to use it. Lotus 1-2-3 actually uses the DOS filing system--commands such as /FR or /FS are really Lotus commands to the computer to go into the DOS system.

It is important to note that when you use file names within the 1-2-3 system, you do not have to type the extensions because 1-2-3 automatically assumes .WK1. However, if you are using file commands (such as copy) under DOS, you must specify the extension or you will get a "file not found" message.

DOS Prompts

When you turn on the computer, the DOS prompts appear on your
screen as A> or B> if you are using a PC and as A>, B>, or
C> if you are using an XT or AT. These prompts tell you (1)
that you are in DOS (or "the system"), (2) that DOS is
waiting for a command, and (3) which drive you are currently
in--A, B, or C. The drive you are in is called the "current
drive." You can change the current drive--say, from A to
B--by typing, at the A prompt, b: RETURN. Immediately, the
prompt will change from A> to B>.


```
A>              (original prompt)
A>b: RETURN     (type b: RETURN to change drives)
B>              (new prompt)
```


Directories

Anyone who does much work with 1-2-3 will create a number of
files; often these files will be stored on several disks,
including the hard disk if you are using your own XT or AT.
Also, computers that are hooked up to a network will draw
from the network's hard disk file storage system.
Frequently, you will need to find out what files are on a
disk. This information can be obtained by using the Directory command. Here are some tips on using this command:

1. With the DOS prompt on the screen, type dir and
      RETURN . You will be given a listing of all files on
      the current disk in the current directory:


```
A>dir RETURN
```

The above command will give you a list of the files on
the diskette in Drive A. Make sure you have a diskette
in this drive when typing this command, or else you
will get an error message on your screen.

388

2. If there are many files on the disk--say, the 35 for this book--the names will fill more than one screen and will go by too fast for you to read. You can obtain one screenful of the list at a time by using the command dir/p rather than dir:

A>dir/p RETURN

The p stands for "pause". After reading the first screen of the list, strike any key to view the next screenful of directory information.

3. The directory listing gives the file name, extension, number of bytes used, and, if you log on the date and time when you start each computer session, the date/time when each file was last saved.

4. At the bottom of the list, the number of files on the disk is reported, along with the unused disk capacity.

5. If you want to find out what is on a disk in a drive that is not the current drive--say Drive C is the current drive and you want the directory of a floppy diskette in Drive A--just type dir followed by the directory name and a colon, as C>dir a:RETURN . Alternatively, you can change drives by typing, at the C prompt, C>a:RETURN and then, at the A prompt, A>dir RETURN or A>dir/p RETURN .

Subdirectories for Hard Disks
(Read this section only if you are using an XT, an AT, or a computer that is on a network.)

DOS makes it possible for you to divide up the space on a disk into compartments called subdirectories. A disk is like a file cabinet, subdirectories are like the drawers in the cabinet, and files are like individual file folders. Generally, we do not use subdirectories with floppy diskettes, because a floppy, having a normal capacity of only 360K, just will not hold an unwieldy number of medium-sized files. However, with XTs and ATs, which have 10 to 20

389

or more megabytes of disk storage capacity, one can store
thousands of files, making it essential to employ subdirectories. In general, we create a subdirectory for each
different type of program that we use, such as Lotus 1-2-3
and our word processing package. We further divide each
subdirectory into files pertaining to a particular book or
project. To illustrate, we have the hard disk, Drive C, on
one of our XTs set up as shown in Figure A-1.

===

Figure A-1

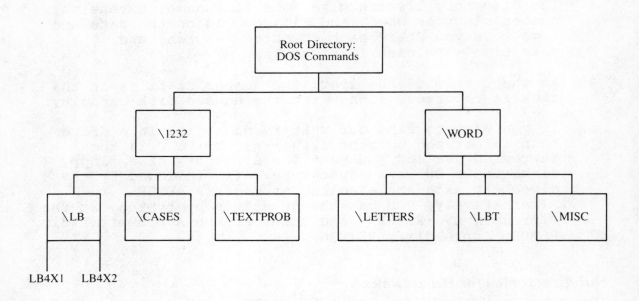

===

DOS defines this as a "tree structure," with a "root" and
several branches and subbranches. Our "root directory",
which is signified by \, contains just the DOS command
files--files which provide the computer with instructions
for printing, formatting, and so forth--plus the locations
of our two subdirectories, which contain the basic Lotus

1-2-3 Release 2 program and the software for WordStar, the word processing program we use. Our second-order subdirectories contain various 1-2-3 and word processing files which we have created ourselves. Our 1-2-3 files are divided into those for this book (stored in subdirectory \LB), solutions for a number of cases (\CASES), and solutions to a group of end-of-chapter problems for our finance textbook (\TEXTPROB). (Although the root directory does not have a name, we find it convenient to think of it as being named \ , since the backslash signifies the root directory. The backslash is also used to separate the subdirectory name from the second-order subdirectory. For example, the complete name of the subdirectory in which our Lotus 1-2-3 book files are stored is \1232\LB.)

When we turn on our XT, we leave the door on Drive A open. This causes the computer to load the disk operating system from Drive C, giving us a C> on the screen. At this point, we are in the root directory, the one with DOS commands. We change directories--say, to \1232--by typing, at the C prompt:

cd\1232 RETURN

A new C prompt appears. It looks exactly like the first one, but it is for the \1232 subdirectory. Now we type Lotus RETURN, which calls up the Lotus program file and loads the Lotus Access menu on the screen. At this point, we insert the Lotus System diskette in Drive A, and we access 1-2-3 by pressing the RETURN key, and we get a blank worksheet. We then take the Lotus System diskette out and put it away.

We could work with the worksheet at this point, but if we did, the file we created would be stored in the 1-2-3 subdirectory which we have named \1232. When we first purchased our computer, we saved everything in this file, and it soon became hard to find individual files. So we went to the subdirectory-within-a-subdirectory system. Now, whenever we want to work with the files for this book, we go into the \1232\LB subdirectory. To get there, we access 1-2-3 as described above and then type /FD. The / invokes the 1-2-3 main command menu, F invokes the File menu, and by entering D you display the current directory. The prompt

Enter current directory: C:\1232

appears on our screen. We then type

C:\1232\LB RETURN

Note that if you have not created this subdirectory and you
type in this command, Lotus will respond with the following
error message: "Directory does not exist." In that case,
just press the ESC key to return to READY mode. In other
words, you must have previously created a subdirectory in
the disk operating system; we will tell you how to do this
in the next section. Also, note that you can specify the
root directory to be the current directory by entering c:\
as the current directory.
     Since we have created the second-order subdirectory
\1232\LB, we are switched immediately to it--the current
directory becomes \1232\LB. Now we type /FR (which invokes
the 1-2-3 main command menu, the File menu, and the File
command "Retrieve"). The files in subdirectory \1232\LB
appear on Line 3 of the control panel.
     Now suppose we want to retrieve the file LB3X2. We can
(1) use the arrow keys to find and put the pointer on LB3X2,
and then enter it, or (2) type LB3X2 RETURN. If there are
only a few files in the directory, we find it easier to use
the arrow key. If there are lots of files, it is easier to
type in the file name. Incidentally, 1-2-3 shows five file
names in the control panel at a time. If there were 33
files, they would actually be laid out in a matrix as
follows:

```
file #1     file #2     file #3     file #4     file #5
file #6     file #7     file #8     file #9     file #10
file #11    file #12    file #13    file #14    file #15
file #16    file #17    file #18    file #19    file #20
file #21    file #22    file #23    file #24    file #25
file #26    file #27    file #28    file #29    file #30
file #31    file #32    file #33
```

In this case, it would be easier to use the down arrow to scroll down the rows and search for a file than to use only the left- and right-arrow keys. You can write files to a disk in a specific sequence by copying them on one by one in the desired sequence. However, if you alter a file, DOS may move it. For example, if you add something to a file, causing it to use more bytes, it may no longer fit into its old space on the diskette. In that case it will be moved, which will of course change its position in the list of files. Erasing files can similarly alter the order in which they are stored. Also, if a new file is added, it may go into a blank space somewhere in the middle rather than at the end of the list of files.

Note: When you turn on the computer and go through the procedure to access 1-2-3, you will automatically go into a directory. You can use the 1-2-3 command /WGDD to specify the default directory, or the directory you want to be in upon startup. If during a given week we plan to be working primarily on this book, we set \1232\LB as the default directory. If during some other week we plan to work on our casebook, we set as the default directory \1232\CASES.

Making and Removing Subdirectories on an XT or AT

Making a subdirectory is very easy. For example, to make our subdirectory LB, we simply typed, at the C>, the Make Directory command:

C>md\1232\LB RETURN

Now a listing of the \1232 subdirectory would show that we have a second-order subdirectory called \LB. To make \LB the current directory, we would type this change directory command:

C>cd\1232\LB RETURN

393

Note that \1232\LB is the full name of this directory. To
return to the root directory, we type cd\ RETURN.
   To remove a subdirectory, follow these steps:

1. Erase all files from the subdirectory. A directory
    cannot be removed unless it is empty of files. Using
    our example, you can erase the file LB3X2 by typing:

          C>erase c:\1232\LB\LB3X2 RETURN

    or you can erase all the files in the subdirectory by
    typing:

          C>erase c:\1232\LB*.* RETURN

    The *.* ("star-dot-star") command tells 1-2-3 you want
    to erase all the files in the directory regardless of
    the file name or extension. (Note that in both Erase
    commands shown we do not actually need the "c:" because
    the C prompt appears. However, we have found that it
    is better to put the drive notation in the command to
    prevent mistakes.)

2. You cannot remove the current directory (or the root
    directory), so you must be in some directory other than
    LB when you remove the LB directory. We would normally
    go into the root directory, by typing cd\ RETURN ,
    before removing a directory like LB.

3. With all files erased and some directory other than the
    one to be removed designated as the current directory,
    you would type the following at the C prompt to remove
    subdirectory LB:

          C>rd\1232\LB RETURN

Finding Out What Subdirectories Are Stored on a Hard Disk

The DOS Tree command will provide a listing of all subdirectory levels on the hard disk. With our setup as described in Figure A-1, we would type cd\ RETURN to go into the root directory and then, at the C prompt, type:

C>tree RETURN

DOS would then provide us with a <u>directory path listing</u>. It would first list the "path" \1232 and then the subdirectories under \1232. Next would be subdirectories under our second-order subdirectories; since we have none, at each level we would see the word "None." After the \1232 listings, we would get similar information on our subdirectory, \WORD.

Formatting Diskettes

A diskette is like a phonograph record in the sense that it has "tracks" on which information is stored. However, blank diskettes must be set up, or "formatted", to install a set of tracks that will be compatible with your computer. If you are using a PC with two disk drives, and if, when you turn on the machine, you have the DOS diskette in Drive A, you will receive an A prompt, A>. To format a diskette in Drive B, you then type, at the A>,

A>format b: RETURN

You are then prompted to put a diskette into Drive B and press RETURN, and the diskette will be formatted.
    If you are using an XT, you should get a C prompt on your screen when you turn on the computer. Again, put the diskette to be formatted in Drive B and type:

395

```
                    C>format b: RETURN
```

(Note that you could have typed format a:RETURN with the
same result since Drives A and B are interchangeable on a
single floppy drive system such as the XT.)

When you press the RETURN key, the computer will start
formatting. A red light will appear on Drive B, and you
will hear a clicking noise. Formatting takes about 30
seconds. Then the computer will ask whether you want to
format another disk. If not, type N , and you will return
to C>. If the answer is yes, type Y and repeat the
process.
        If you already have the machine on and are working with
1-2-3, then you can use these keystrokes to get to the
system:

/S   This takes you out of 1-2-3 and puts you back
                into "the system," or DOS. You will receive a
                DOS prompt. The current directory will be A
                on a PC or the subdirectory in which the 1-2-3
                programs are stored on an XT. If you are
                working on a PC, type format b: RETURN , then
                skip to the next paragraph. If you are on an
                XT, follow the steps below to format your
                diskette.

CD\ RETURN   This returns you to the root directory, where
                the DOS commands are stored. You will still
                see a C prompt on the screen, but you will now
                have access to the DOS commands.

format b: Typed at the C>, this tells DOS that you want
                to format a diskette in Drive B. You should
                see this on your screen:

                        C>cd\
                        C>format b:

                The b: is absolutely critical--if you do not
                have it, you will format your hard disk, which

                              396

will destroy everything on it--DOS, 1-2-3, and any files you may have created. <u>So be sure the b: is there!</u> Also, be sure <u>your 1-2-3 System disk is not in Drive B, or it too will be destroyed if it is not write protected</u>.

RETURN   This statement will appear on the screen:

       Insert new diskette for Drive B:
       and strike any key when ready.

Now put the diskette to be formatted into Drive B. <u>Make sure it is a blank diskette with no useful information, because formatting destroys all information on a diskette</u>.

RETURN   When you press the RETURN key, the diskette will be formatted, and you will then be asked if you want to format another diskette. Type N , and you will return to C>.

Once you have formatted your storage diskette, you can return to 1-2-3 by typing exit RETURN . (If you had not been using 1-2-3, you would need to access 1-2-3. With our setup, this means typing, at the C prompt, cd\1232 RETURN and lotus RETURN RETURN , at which point we get a worksheet on the screen.)

Erasing Files

You can erase 1-2-3 files using the regular 1-2-3 command sequence. With a 1-2-3 worksheet (blank or otherwise) on the screen, type /FEW , enter the appropriate file name, and type Y to tell 1-2-3 that you really do want to erase the file.
You can also erase files using the DOS Erase command. From the DOS prompt, type:

erase file directory:file name RETURN

(Be careful when using the DOS Erase command. It is important that you specify the correct file directory.) If the
file is on a hard disk, you must specify the subdirectory
path. For example, to remove a file named LB3X2.WK1 on our
subdirectory \1232\LB, we would type, at the C prompt:

C>erase c:\1232\LB\LB3X2.WK1 RETURN

Note that you must include the extension .WK1 as a part of
the file name; otherwise, you will get a "file not found"
message. Extensions must be used with DOS commands,
but .WK1 is automatically assigned when using 1-2-3
commands.
        If we wanted to erase a number of files from a disk, we
could use the Erase ? command. For example, if we wanted to
erase all the Chapter 3 files on our diskette in Drive A, we
would type, at the DOS prompt on a PC,

A>erase a:LB3X????.WK1 RETURN

On our XT, we would type, at the C prompt,

C>erase c:\1232\LB\LB3X????.WK1 RETURN

The Erase commands are dangerous, because once you erase
something it is gone, and it is fairly easy to make a mistake if you are not careful. Also, note that if you use the
Erase command and do not specify a file name, then *.* will
be assumed and all files on the disk erased. Further, you
should use the * and ? characters in an Erase command with
caution, because it is fairly easy to end up erasing something you did not mean to erase. We suggest that you get a
listing of the files you plan to erase before doing so using
the Directory command:

```
dir c:\1232\LB\LB3X????.WK1 RETURN
```

Then look at the files and make sure you want to erase all
of them. This has saved us many times from accidentally
erasing files we wanted to keep.

Changing the Name of a File

Suppose you want to change a file's name from Johndoe.WK1 to
Janedoe.WK1. You could use the Rename command to do this.
If the file is on a floppy in Drive A, then from the A
prompt type:


```
A>rename a:Johndoe.WK1 a:Janedoe.WK1 RETURN
```


If you are using a hard disk, you will have to specify the
file directory and subdirectory path. You can also use the
* and ? designators to rename groups of files.

Copying Files

You will occasionally want to copy files from one diskette
onto another diskette. You may want to copy just one file,
a number of files, or all the files. Also, if you are using
an XT or AT, you can create a subdirectory and copy that
portion of the hard disk (with one or more files) onto a
floppy. In this section, we discuss several alternative
copying procedures.

Using 1-2-3 to Copy a Single File from One Floppy to Another

Suppose you somehow erased File LB3X2 from your storage
diskette and had no backup copy, but one of your classmates
did have the file on her diskette. On an XT, you could copy
the file from her diskette as follows:

1. Access 1-2-3 and get a blank worksheet on your screen.

2. Put her diskette into Drive A.

3. If the current file directory was not Directory A, you would need to type /FD a:RETURN to change the current directory to Directory A. Then, type this command:

    /FR LB3X2 RETURN

    This would retrieve File LB3X2 from your classmate's diskette and put it in RAM memory (and on the screen).

4. Take out your friend's diskette and put yours into Drive A.

5. Save the file on your diskette by typing this command:

    /FS RETURN

On a PC, you would do the following:

1. Repeat Steps 1, 2, and 3.

2. Insert your diskette into Drive B.

3. Save the file on your diskette by typing these commands:

    /FS
    b:LB3X2 RETURN

If you are using an AT having two disk drives, use the same Steps 1 and 2 as for copying on a PC. Step 3 would be:

    /FS

Press the ESC key two times to get rid of the current directory. Then type:

b:LB3X2 RETURN

Most infrequent computer users can use the above procedure to copy single files and not bother reading further in this section. However, if you will be using the computer fairly often, it will benefit you to learn the following copying procedures, as they are often more efficient.

Using DOS to Copy a Single File from One Floppy to Another

Assume again that you want to copy your friend's file LB3X2 onto your storage diskette. Turn the computer on, and get a DOS prompt (A> if you are using a PC or C> on an XT or AT). Put your friend's diskette into Drive A, and close the door. If the A prompt is not up, change to Drive A by typing, at the C prompt,

C>a:RETURN

When you copy files, the commands always give the source of the file first, then the target for the file:

Copy file from: Copy to:

If you are using a PC or an AT with two floppy drives, insert the target diskette into Drive B. Then, at the A prompt, type:

A>copy a:LB3X2.WK1 b:RETURN

Be sure to have a blank space after the word "copy", another blank after .WK1, and no other blanks. If you are using an XT, the following message will appear:

        Insert diskette for Drive B: and strike
        any key when ready.

If you are using an XT, take your friend's diskette out and put yours in; then press any key, and her file will be copied onto your diskette.
      Note that, to use the DOS file copy command, you must specify the extension. Otherwise, you will get an error message telling you that the file was not found.

Using DOS to Copy a File from a Floppy Diskette to a Hard Disk, or Vice Versa (Read only if you are using an XT or AT.)

Assume that you want to copy the file LB3X2.WK1 from a floppy diskette into a subdirectory named \1232\LB on your hard disk. Insert the diskette into Drive A. From the DOS prompt (which could be A> or C>), type the following:

        Copy a:LB3X2.WK1 c:\1232\LB RETURN

The file will be copied into subdirectory \1232\LB on your hard disk.
      You can use similar commands to reverse the procedure and copy from the hard disk to a floppy. Note that 1-2-3 does not require the current directory to be specified, so if the current directory is \1232\LB, then you need to type only

        copy a:LB3X2.WK1 c:RETURN

(To determine what the current directory is, you would type
 dir , and the current directory and its files would be listed.)

402

Using *.* to Copy All Files from a Disk

You can also use DOS to copy <u>groups of files</u> from one disk to another. First, suppose you want to copy all the files on your friend's floppy diskette onto your storage diskette. You could use the "star-dot-star" copy command. Put the diskette to be copied from into Drive A and, if you are using a PC or an AT, put the diskette to be copied to into Drive B. Then, at the DOS prompt (which could be A>, B>, or C>), type:

copy a:*.* b:RETURN

Put a blank space after "copy" and another after the second * but no other blanks. The first * tells DOS that you want to copy all files, regardless of file name, with a given extension; the second * tells DOS that you also want to copy all extensions. Thus, you want to copy all files on the diskette.

If you have only one floppy drive, you will then get a series of prompts telling you first to insert the diskette for Drive A and then to insert the diskette for Drive B, as DOS copies the files one at a time. If the diskette has 10 files, you will thus have to switch diskettes 10 times, but the copying procedure will still move along fairly rapidly. The copying procedure is much faster on a PC with two drives; no switching is required, as the source diskette stays in Drive A and the storage diskette in Drive B. However, as we discuss in the next section, there is an even faster way to copy all files from one floppy to another: the Diskcopy command.

With an XT or AT, if you use the *.* copy command to go from a floppy to a fixed disk directory, or vice versa, the procedure will be quite fast, and no diskette switching will be required. For example, suppose you want to copy all the files on fixed subdirectory \1232\LB onto a floppy. Put the target floppy into drive A and then type, at the C>,

Copy c:\1232\LB*.* a:RETURN

The files will then be copied onto the floppy diskette in Drive A.

Using ? to Copy a Group of Files with a Common Characteristic

Suppose you want to copy only the files from Chapter 3 of this book to another diskette. You could either copy the files one by one or use *.*. However, the first way is slow, and the second copies more files than just the Chapter 3 files that you want. However, there is a DOS command that lets you copy all files with a given characteristic, such as the 3 in Chapter 3 files. This command is like *.* except that, rather than using *, which tells DOS to copy anything, you can be more specific.

First, recall that file names can be up to eight characters long plus a three-character extension (which with 1-2-3, Release 2, is always .WK1). Now consider the diskette for this book. It contains 35 files, 9 of which go with Chapter 3. All 35 files begin with LB, then they give the chapter number, then an X (for "exhibit"), and then the exhibit number. We can use the DOS Copy command, set up as follows, to copy the Chapter 3 files from one floppy to another:

copy a:LB3X????.* b:RETURN

This tells DOS that you want to copy all of those files from the diskette in Drive A whose file name begins with LB3X to the diskette in Drive B. The four question marks are needed to fill out the eight characters in the file name, and the .* says you will accept any extension. (You could have used WK1 rather than *.)

Another way to do this copy command is as follows:

copy a:LB3X*.* b:RETURN

You may use a * whenever you will accept any characters as the <u>remaining</u> characters in the file name, as in this case. However, had the common term (LB3X) been at the end of the file name, you would have had to write ????LB3X.*; you could not write *LB3X.*.

Note again that this will be a relatively slow, file-by-file process if you are going from one floppy to another. However, if you are going from a floppy to a hard disk, or vice versa, the copying would be fast. With our system, we have the LB files stored in Drive C in a subdirectory called \1232\LB. To copy the Chapter 3 files to a floppy, we would change the current directory to the \1232\LB subdirectory and then type this at the C prompt:

C>copy LB3X????.* a:RETURN

To take the Chapter 3 files from a floppy to our hard disk, we would type:

copy a:LB3X????.* c:\1232\LB RETURN

Using Diskcopy

If you use copy *.*, you will copy all files from the source diskette to the target diskette, and any files originally on the target diskette will still be there when you finish. (Note, though, that files with the same name will be re-placed; in other words, if LB3X2 were on both the source and target diskettes, the version on the source would replace that on the target.) However, you can use a different DOS command, Diskcopy, to make an exact copy of the source diskette. Diskcopy will remove all files on the target and replace them with the files (and blank space) on the source.

With a PC, you would type, at the A prompt:

diskcopy a: b:RETURN

You would get a message telling you to place the source diskette in Drive A and the target diskette in Drive B and then to press any key. The diskette will automatically be formatted during the diskcopy, so you do not have to worry about using a formatted diskette.

To use Diskcopy to copy a file on a floppy diskette onto another diskette using an XT, which has the DOS commands on the hard disk (as we do), you must first make the root directory the current directory. From 1-2-3, type /S , which takes you to DOS. Then, at the C>, type cd\ RETURN , which makes the root directory the current directory. Then type, at C>:

diskcopy a: b:RETURN

The source material will be copied into RAM memory, and you will receive a message to replace the source diskette with the target diskette to complete the copy. On our XT, it takes two passes to complete the copy--that is, first one, then the other, half of the source diskette is copied.
Note that the Diskcopy command works only with floppy diskettes--it cannot be used to copy to or from a hard disk. (The hard disk contains 10 or more megabytes, and such a large disk obviously could not be copied to a 360K floppy.) Besides, the Diskcopy command is not necessary, because the *.* command is extremely efficient when going from a hard disk to a floppy, or vice versa. However, the target diskette must be formatted before you use *.*.

Some Additional Points about Copying Files

1. In all the procedures discussed in this section except Diskcopy, any files that are on the target diskette when the copying begins, will still be there when copying has been completed. However, Diskcopy erases the original files on the target diskette.

2. If you copy a file with a given name from a source diskette to a target diskette that already has a file with that same name, the old file on the target diskette will be replaced with the new file on the source diskette.

3. If the total number of bytes to be copied exceeds the capacity of the target diskette (generally 360K), you will get an error message telling you that the copy cannot be completed. You must copy fewer files than you had planned onto that diskette and use additional diskettes for storage.

Appendix A Exercises

Note: The following exercises are meant to test your understanding of the concepts covered in Appendix A.

1. Which of the following names are "legal" Lotus file names?

   NUL
   GULF
   WKSHT.EFB
   TEXTBOOKS

2. Why is it best not to add your own extension at the end of a Lotus file name?

3. Suppose you are working on a PC. You have a diskette for which you would like to find out what files are on it. The DOS prompt on the screen is A>. What DOS commands would you have to type in order to get a listing of the diskette files from Drive B?

4. On which of the three machines discussed in the Appendix (PC, XT, and AT) would you use subdirectories? Why would you use subdirectories?

   a. What command would you type in to create a subdirectory called \text\cases?

   b. How would you go about deleting a subdirectory called \123\probs? Explain the process and write the commands you would type to do this.

5. Assume you have been working on your XT with Lotus 1-2-3, that is, you are already in 1-2-3, and decide that you need to format a diskette. Assume your current directory is \1232\cases. What commands would you have to type to get out of Lotus 1-2-3, format your diskette, and go back to Lotus 1-2-3?

6. Assume you have just turned on your PC and are in DOS.
    You have a diskette which contains some files that
    begin with the phrase "text" which you no longer need.
    The file names consist of 8 letters and have varying
    extensions. You wish to delete all of these files.
    There are other files on this diskette which you would
    like to keep. What DOS command would you type to
    delete these files on your diskette in Drive B?

7. Assume you have a PC and have 2 diskettes. Diskette #1
    contains 10 files which you would like to copy onto
    Diskette #2 for back-up purposes. The 10 files have no
    similar file names. Assume Diskette #2 is "fresh" out
    of the diskette box, that is, it has not been
    formatted.

    a. What DOS command would you type, assuming you
        wanted to be very efficient and do the copying
        procedure in one step?

    b. What other DOS copy procedure could you have used
        and what DOS commands would you need to type to
        copy the files onto Diskette #2?

    c. Assume Diskette #2 is a formatted diskette with
        several files already on it which you wish to keep.
        In order to copy the 10 files from Diskette #1 to
        Diskette #2, what DOS commands would you need to
        type now? Could you have used the copy procedure
        that was used in 7a? Explain.

8. Practice the commands discussed in this Appendix with a
    diskette with files that you can afford to lose (in
    case you make a mistake). By practicing you should
    feel more at ease with the DOS procedures that have
    been discussed in this appendix.

Appendix B
Command Tree Diagrams

The 1-2-3 system consists of many components, and while it has a beautifully logical structure, it is sometimes difficult "to see the forest for the trees." This appendix is designed to give you an overview of the forest.

As we noted earlier, 1-2-3 is structured like a tree, with a trunk, main branches, and subbranches. The trunk is the main command menu. In this appendix, we provide a series of diagrams that show the primary elements in the main command menu. Each diagram begins with the main command menu, then goes on to show the structure of one of the primary commands.

Worksheet Commands

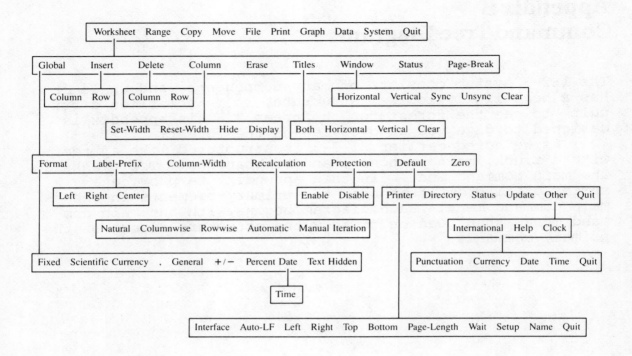

Source: Lotus Development Corporation 1986.   Used with permission.

The worksheet commands are used to adjust settings which affect the entire worksheet. The first entry under Worksheet is Global, whose subparts allow you to do such things as (1) specify the format of values in the worksheet (/WGF), (2) align labels (/WGL), (3) change the default column width (/WGC), (4) set recalculation procedures, (/WGR), (5) protect the worksheet (/WGP), and (6) specify default procedures such as the default directory (/WGDD). Other worksheet commands let you insert rows (/WIR) or delete columns (/WDC), set individual column widths (/WCS), and hide particular columns (/WCH). You can also freeze specified rows and/or columns as titles (/WT) or use the Worksheet Window (/WW) command to split the screen into two sections so that nonadjacent sections of the worksheet can be viewed simultaneously.

410

Range Commands

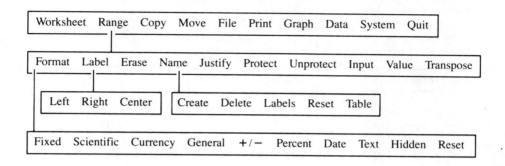

Source: Lotus Development Corporation 1986.   Used with permission.

Range commands are used to perform operations on a single cell or range of cells. Using the Range commands, you can (1) specify how values are to be displayed (/RF), (2) align labels in a range (/RL), (3) erase the contents of a range (/RE), (4) assign a name to the range of cells (/RN), (5) protect or unprotect cells in a range (/RP or /RU), and (6) convert formulas in a range to their values and then copy these values into another location (/RV).

Copy and Move Commands

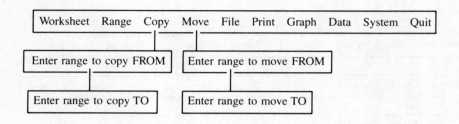

Source: Lotus Development Corporation 1986.   Used with permission.

The Copy command (/C) is used to copy the contents of a cell
or range of cells to another cell or range of cells in the
worksheet.   The Move command (/M) moves the contents of a
cell or range of cells from one section of the worksheet to
another.   When a formula is copied, the cell addresses in
the formula are adjusted if they are relative but remain
unchanged if they are absolute.   When formulas are moved,
they are adjusted so that all relationships within the
worksheet will be maintained.

File Commands

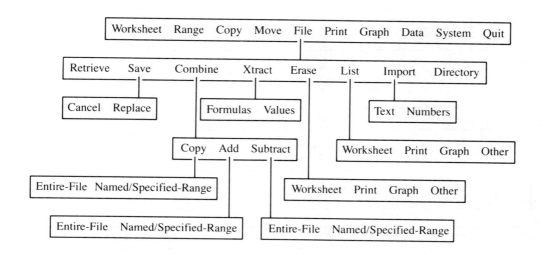

Source: Lotus Development Corporation 1986.   Used with permission.

The File commands are used to retrieve worksheet files, (/FR), to save files (/FS), to combine two files into one file (/FC), to extract a portion of a file as a new file (/FX), to erase files from a diskette (/FE), to obtain a listing of all files stored in the default directory (/FL), and to change the default file directory (/FD).

Print Commands

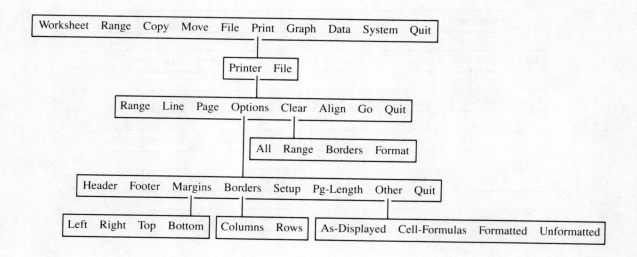

Source: Lotus Development Corporation 1986. Used with permission.

The Print commands are used to print copies of the current worksheet (/PP) or to store the current worksheet in a print file (/PF). A worksheet stored in a print file can be accessed by other programs, such as a word processing package. The Print commands allow you to specify a range to be printed (/PPR) and to set printing options (/PPO) such as headers, footers, margins, type size, and page length. You can also print out formulas rather than the values displayed in cells.

Graph Commands

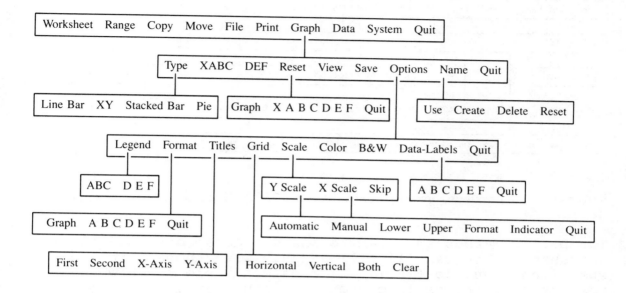

Source: Lotus Development Corporation 1986.   Used with permission.

The Graph commands are used to create and view graphs. You
can specify the type of graph (/GT), the ranges that contain
the data to be graphed, and several graph options (/GO).
You can then view the graph (/GV), name the graph (/GN) so
that it can be recalled for later viewing, and save the
graph as a picture file (/GS) so that it can be printed
using the PrintGraph program.

Data Commands

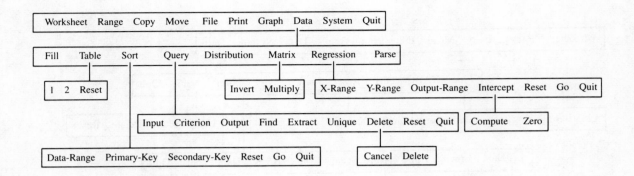

Source: Lotus Development Corporation 1986. Used with permission.

The Data commands are used to analyze data contained in a worksheet. You can (1) fill a range with numbers in a specified sequence (/DF), (2) create a table to show the results of a change in one or two input variables on one or more output variables (/DT), (3) sort the records in a database based on alphabetical or numerical specifications (/DS), (4) select those records with specific characteristics from a database (/DQ), (5) create a frequency distribution of the values in a range, (/DD), (6) perform operations on matrices of data (/DM), and (7) perform linear regression analyses (/DR).

System Command

The System command /S is used to temporarily leave 1-2-3 and
go into DOS. You can return to 1-2-3 by typing the word
exit and then pressing RETURN; you will be returned to the
spreadsheet you were using before issuing the System
command.

Quit Command

The Quit command is used to end a 1-2-3 session. When you
quit the session, you will be returned to the Lotus Access
System Menu.

Index

ABS function key (F4) 7, 92
Abs macro key 224
Absolute cell address 72, 88, 99
Access
 menu 13, 14, 16, 20
 System 13, 20
Accessing 1-2-3
 on a PC 12, 18
 on an XT 19, 22
Address
 absolute 72, 88, 99
 cell 22, 23
 range 52, 23, 24
 relative 72, 88, 99
Advanced macros 221
Aligning
 labels 35, 95
 printer paper 61
Amortization schedule 111
Arguments
 @function 52, 104
Arithmetic formulas 36, 37
Arithmetic operators 36, 37
Arrow keys 32
ASCII codes 202
Assigning file names 58, 386
Asterisks
   (See also Long Number) 54, 58
@functions 51, 104
 arguments 52
 entering arguments 52
 financial 104
 logical 159, 161
 parenthesis in 52
 special 155
 statistical 159
Automatic recalculation 73,
 209, 210
Auxiliary storage unit 4
@AVG function 150, 154

Backslash (\) key 20, 35, 390
BACKSPACE key 40
Backspace macro key 224

Bar graph 125, 129
Basic macros 222
Beep 224
BIG LEFT key 33
Bigleft macro key 224
BIG RIGHT key 33
Bigright macro key 224
Black-Scholes option
   pricing model 371
Bond refunding analysis 362
Borders 68
Braces, in macro 224
Bytes 7

CALC indicator 270
CALC key 7, 73, 270
Calc macro key 224
Cell address 22, 23
 absolute 72, 88, 99
 as argument in functions 151
 in formula 36
 relative 72, 88, 99
 typing 36
Cell contents 23
Cell pointer 23
Cells 22
 anchoring 52
 current 23
 editing 39
 entering data 34
 erasing 42
 formatting 53
 formulas in 36, 37
 protected 211, 241
 removing protection from 212, 241
Central processing unit (CPU) 4
Changing
 column width 49
 file names 399
 label alignment 35, 95
 margins 67
 print settings 67
CIRC indicator 270
Circular reference 208, 270

Clock settings 15
Codes, ASCII 202
Color, in graphs 129
Column width 22, 23
  changing 49
  default 22
Column-wise recalculation 210
Columns
  deleting 57
  freezing 75, 76
  headings 51
  hiding 70
  inserting 55
  letters 22
  redisplaying hidden 70
Combining files 180
Comma (,) format 54, 56
Commands (See also
  specific commands) 24, 31
  Copy 31, 63, 412
  Data 31, 166, 178, 416
  File 31, 179, 413
  Graph 31, 123, 415
  Move 31, 164, 412
  Print 31, 61, 414
  Quit 32, 59, 417
  Range 31, 411
  System 32, 417
  Worksheet 31, 410
Common-size
  balance sheet 249
  income statement 251
Complex equations 204
Compressed print option 201
Computer components 4
Conserving disk space 238
Continuous compounding 116
Control panel 23, 30
Converting formulas
  to values 93
Copy command 31, 63, 412
Copying
  data 63, 88
  files 399
  formulas 63, 88, 93
  labels 94
  range 63, 88
  rules 91

Core (main) memory 4
@COUNT function 150, 155
Creating
  bar graph 125
  database 166
  graph name 133
  graphs from a worksheet 123
  macro 222
  pie chart 125
  range names 222
  subdirectories 393
@CTERM function 110
Currency format 54, 56
Current
  cell 23
  directory 388, 392
  graph 128, 134
Cursor 23

Data (See also
  Formulas; Labels; Numbers)
  copying 63
  entering 34
  hiding 70
  rearranging 164, 238
  types of 35
Data commands 31, 166, 178, 416
  Distribution 179
  Fill 168
  Matrix 179
  Query 179
  Regression 193
  Sort 166
  Table 169, 175, 177
Data Query commands 179
Data Table commands 169, 175, 177
  Data Table 1 169, 177
  Data Table 2 175
Database 166
  entry range 167
  data tables 169
  definition 166
  field names 166
  fields 166
  input range 171
  output range 174
  records 166
  sorting 166

Defaults
  clock 15
  column width 22
  file directory 391
  label prefix 35
  printer settings 67, 138, 201
  PrintGraph settings 136, 137
  recalculation settings 209, 210
  startup directory 393
  status 270, 410
  update 410
DELETE key 40
Delete macro key 224
Deleting (See also Erasing)
  character 40
  columns 57
  file 397
  named graph 133
  rows 57
Directory
  changing 391
  current 388, 392
  file 388
  graph file 138
  organization 389, 390
  pathnames 390, 395
Diskcopy 405
Disk Operating System (DOS)
  11, 19, 388
DOWN key 32
Down macro key 224
Drives 8, 388
Duration 377

EDIT key 4, 7, 40
Edit macro key 224
EDIT mode 27, 40
Editing 39, 40
Editing keys 32-34, 39-42
End macro key 224
END key 33
Enter key 12, 19
Entering
  arguments 36
  @functions 51
  data 34
  formulas 36
  labels 36

macro 223
numbers 36
Erasing (See also Deleting)
  cell contents 42
  entire worksheet 88
  files 397
ERROR mode 27
ESCAPE key 28
Escape macro key 224
Executing macros 226
Exit sub-program 16
Exiting 1-2-3 59, 61
Exiting macro 225
@EXP function 117
Extensions, files 387
  .PIC 135
  .WKI 135
Extracting files 179, 181

Field name 166
Fields 166
File commands 31, 179, 413
  Combine 180
  Directory 388
  Erase 397
  List 150
  Retrieve 60
  Save 58
  Xtract 179, 181
File names 58
Files
  combining 180
  directory 388
  erasing 397
  extension 387
  extracting 179, 181
  graph 135
  listing 150
  names 58
  protection 213
  retrieval 60
  saving 58
FILES mode 27
Financial functions 104
FIND mode 27
Fixed format 53
Fixed storage disk 8
Floppy diskette 8

Fonts 138
Format commands
 Range 54
 Worksheet Global 53
Formats 54-56
Formatting diskettes 58, 395
Formatting spreadsheets 54, 56
Formulas 36, 37
 arithmetic 36
 cell address in 36
 converting to values 93
 in data tables 169, 170
 entering 36, 52
 logical 159
Function keys 4, 7
Functions (See @Functions) 51
Future value 96
 of an annuity 101
@FV function 102

GOTO key 7, 34, 240
GoTo macro key 224
Graph commands 31, 123, 415
 Save 124, 132
 Type 124, 128
 View 124, 129
GRAPH key 7
Graph menu 124
Graph Name commands 132
 Create 133
 Delete 133
 Reset 133
 Use 133
Graph Options commands 127
 B&W 129
 Color 129
 Format 196, 278
 Legend 128
 Scale 140
 Titles 128
Graph settings
 naming 132
 resetting 133
 saving 135
Graph types 124-129, 196
Graphing
 data table 178
 regression lines 196

worksheet data 123
Graphs
 color in 129
 creating 123, 131
 current 128, 134
 displaying 129
 labeling 128
 legends 128
 naming 132
 printing 135
 saving 135
 selecting data for 125
 symbols 196, 278
 titles 128
 X axis 128
 Y axis 128

Hard disk 8
HELP key 7
HELP mode 27
Hiding
 columns 70
 data 56
@HLOOKUP function 156
HOME key 27, 33
Home macro key 224

@IF function 150, 159
IF statements 159
Image-Select command 136
Indicators 27, 227, 270
Input cell 171
Input range 171
Inserting
 character 40, 41
 columns 55
 page break 241
 rows 55
Install sub-program 10, 16
Invoking a macro 226
@IRR function 107
Iterations 210

Justifying ranges 200

Keyboard 4, 6
Key indicators, macro
 (See also Special macro keys) 224

Keys
  ABS 7, 92
  arrow keys 32
  backslash (\) 20, 35, 390
  BACKSPACE 40
  BIG LEFT 33
  BIG RIGHT 33
  CALC 7, 73, 270
  DELETE 40
  DOWN 32
  EDIT 4, 7, 40
  END 33
  ESCAPE 28
  GOTO 7, 34, 240
  GRAPH 7
  HELP 7
  HOME 27, 33
  LEFT 32
  NAME 7
  PAGE DOWN 33
  PAGE UP 33
  QUERY 7
  RETURN 12, 19
  RIGHT 32
  slash (/) 25
  special macro indicators 224
  STEP 227
  TAB 33
  TABLE 7
  UP 32
  WINDOW 7
Kilobytes 7

LABEL mode 27
Labeling
  a graph 128
  a macro 226
Label-prefix characters
  center (^) 35
  default 35
  left (") 35
  in a macro 223
  repeating 35
  right (') 35
Label-Prefix command,
  Worksheet Global 95
Labels 35
  aligning 35, 95

changing column width 49
  entering 35
  entering with macros 223
  long 54
LEFT key 32
Left macro key 224
Legends, graph 128
Line graph 124, 125, 131
Linear regression 191, 276
Listing files in directory 150
Logical functions 159, 161
Logical operators 161
Long
  labels 54
  numbers 54, 58
Lotus 1-2-3 package 10

Macro name 221
Macro syntax 223
Macros 221
Main menu 25, 26
Manual recalculation 73, 210, 243
Margin settings 67
@MAX function 150, 154
Menus
  Access 13, 14, 16, 20
  Data 416
  File 413
  file name 392
  Graph 123, 124
  Main 26, 31
  Print 61
  PrintGraph 136, 137
  submenu 28, 29
  Worksheet 29, 410
MENU mode 27
Menu pointer 15, 21, 28
@MIN function 150, 154
Modes 25, 27, 40
Mode indicators 25, 27
Move command 31, 164, 412
Moving
  around the worksheet 32
  cell pointer 32
  data 164
  range 164
Multiple regression
  analysis 191, 276

NAME key   7
NAME macro key   224
Named graph   132, 133
Named ranges   222
Naming
 files   58
 graphs   132, 133
 macros   225
 ranges   222
Natural recalculation   209
@NPV function   52, 106
Net present value profile   178
Numbers
 entering   36
 formatting   56
 as labels   51
 long   54, 58
 in a range   56
Numeric pad   4
Numeric formats   56

Operating system   11, 19, 388
Operators
 arithmetic   161
 logical   36
Options (stock)   371
Order of operations   36, 37
Output devices   4
Output range   174

Page break (printing)   241
PAGE DOWN key   33
PAGE UP key   33
Parenthesis
 in formula   36, 37
 in @function   52
Passwords   213, 214
Pathnames, directory   390, 395
Payback period   349
PC use   11
Percent format   56, 97
Pgdn macro key   224
Pgup macro key   224
Picture file   135
Pie chart   125, 129
Plus sign (+)   36
@PMT function   110
POINT mode   27

Pointer-movement keys   32, 33
Present value   100
 analysis   307
 of an annuity   102
Primary sort key   167
Print commands (See also
   PrintGraph)   31, 61, 414
 File   62
 Printer   61
 PrintScreen   151
Print File commands   62
Print Printer commands
 Align   61
 Go   61
 Options   67, 68
 Range   61
Printers   4
 dot-matrix   135
 graphics   135
 settings   136
 setup string   202
PrintGraph   10, 16, 135
 aligning paper   138
 entering   136
 hardware settings   138
 printing graphs   135
 returning to Access System   139
 saving graph   132
 selecting graph files   136
 starting   61
PrintGraph commands   16, 136
 Align   138
 Exit   139
 Go   138
 Image-Select   136
 Settings   137
PrintGraph menu   136, 137
PrintGraph settings   136-138
Printing (See also PrintGraph)
 graphs   135
 print range   61
 with PrintGraph   136
Profitability index   344
Protecting   210
 cells   211, 241
 files   213
@PV function   103

QUERY key 6
Query macro key 224
QUIT command 32, 59, 417

Random access memory (RAM) 7
Range 23
  address 23, 24
  copying 64
  defined 23
  hiding 56
  moving 164
  named 222
  naming 222
Range commands 31, 41, 411
  Erase 42
  Format 53, 56
  Justify 254
  Label 95
  Protect 211, 241
  Unprotect 212, 241
  Value 93
Range names
  creating 222
  for macros 222, 225
@RATE function 111
Read only memory (ROM) 7
READY mode 25, 27
Recalculating formulas 209
Recalculation (See also Worksheet
  Global commands) 73, 209
  automatic 73, 210
  manual 73, 210, 243
Records 166
Regression analysis 191, 276
Relative cell address 72, 88, 99
Removing subdirectories 393
Repeating labels 35
Retrieving files 60
RETURN key 12, 19
RIGHT key 32
Right macro key 224
Root directory 390
Row-wise recalculation 210
Rows
  deleting 57
  freezing 74
  inserting 55
  number 23

Saving
  extracted data 180
  files 58
  graph settings 132
  graphs 135
  PrintGraph settings 138
  worksheet 58
Scatter diagrams 125, 129
Scientific format 56
Secondary sort key 167
Sensitivity analysis 68
Setup string 202
Simultaneous equations 204
Slash (/) key 25
Small (compressed)
  print option 201
Solving complex equations 204
Sort keys
  primary 167
  secondary 167
Sort order 167
Sorting database 166
Source drive (Drive A) 8
Special macro keys 224
Splitting screen 76
@SQRT function 52, 150, 155
Stacked bar graph 125, 129
Statistical functions 150, 159
@STD function 52, 150, 154
STEP indicator 227
STEP key 227
STEP mode 227
Stopping a macro 225
Storage disks 11, 18
Subdirectories 389, 393
@SUM function 52
Syntax, macro 223
System command 32, 417

TAB key 33
TABLE key 7
Table macro key 224
Target drive (Drive B) 8
Template model 238, 246
Tilde (~) 223, 224
Titles, Graph 128
Translate sub-program 16
Tree command 395

Underscore character   57
UP key   32
Up macro key   224

VALUE mode   27
Values   36, 38
 converting formulas into   93
 entering   36
 in formula   36
 as labels   51
@VAR function   150
View sub-program   10, 16
Viewing
 formulas   38
 graphs   129
@VLOOKUP function   150, 156

WAIT mode   27
What-if tests
  (See also Data tables)   68
Widening column   49
WINDOW key   7, 77
Window macro key   224
Windows, split   76, 78
Word processing with 1-2-3   197
Worksheet
 cells   22
 changing appearance   53

column   22
erasing   88
formatting   53, 56
moving around in   32
row   23
saving   58
saving graph settings   135
screen   17
status   270
Worksheet commands   29, 31, 410
 Column   49
 Delete   57
 Erase   88
 Insert   55
 Page   241
 Status   270
 Titles   74, 75
 Window   76, 78
Worksheet Global commands
 Column Set-Width   49
 Format   53
 Label-Prefix   95
 Protection   213
 Recalculation   73, 209

XT use   18
XY graph   196